EMPIRES IN COLLISION

EMPIRES IN COLLISION

ANGLO-BURMESE RELATIONS IN THE MID-NINETEENTH CENTURY

OLIVER B. POLLAK

Contributions in Comparative Colonial Studies, Number 1

GREENWOOD PRESS
WESTPORT, CONNECTICUT • LONDON, ENGLAND

0698681

~~112716~~

Library of Congress Cataloging in Publication Data

Pollak, Oliver B
  Empires in collision.

  (Contributions in comparative colonial
studies ; no. 1 ISSN 0163-3813)
  Bibliography: p.
  Includes index.
    1. Burma—History—1824-1948. 2. Burma—
Relations (general) with Great Britain. 3. Great
Britain—Relations (general) with Burma. I. Title.
DS529.7.P64   959.1'03   78-75239
ISBN 0-313-20824-7

Copyright © 1979 by Oliver B. Pollak

All rights reserved. No portion of this book may be
reproduced, by any process or technique, without the
express written consent of the publisher.

Library of Congress Catalog Card Number: 78-75239
ISBN: 0-313-20824-7
ISSN: 0163-3813

First published in 1979

Greenwood Press, Inc.
51 Riverside Avenue, Westport, Connecticut 06880

Printed in the United States of America

10 9 8 7 6 5 4 3 2 1

for
karen

CONTENTS

069868|

112716

ILLUSTRATIONS

SERIES FOREWORD

The Imperial Revolution has been one of the most significant and far reaching in modern history, for it transformed both the nations of the West and those societies upon which their imperialism encroached. In an important sense, the history of the twentieth century must be understood in terms of the multifaceted revolution brought on by the world's experience with imperialism: a revolution in political and economic relations, in social systems, in communications, and perhaps most of all, in knowledge and perception. In the final analysis, the history of imperialism is less economic and political than it is an aspect of intellectual history: of how high-technology societies affected, for good and for ill, societies with less technology, and how their impact changed the perceptions entire cultures have had of each other.

One means of illuminating the interaction between societies is through comparative studies. Certainly the phenomenon so conveniently (and on occasion misleadingly) labeled *imperialism* is best understood in a comparative context, when British imperialism, or French imperialism, or American imperialism is compared with the others. In addition, responses are often, although not invariably, better studied comparatively, as when one examines forms of resistance in African, Asian, or Pacific Island societies together. Few scholars, however, can command the variety of indigenous, as well as European, languages necessary for such comparative study, and there are, therefore, few studies of colonialism and imperialism that are

overtly comparative. All the more reason, then, to plan a series in which
the books collectively provide the kinds of comparative insights most help-
ful to the scholar and student of empires, even if the individual books themselves are not always comparative. This is the intention of the present series.

Oliver Pollak's book *Empires in Collision* provides many useful insights
into how two empires interacted. It is firmly rooted in the sources, Eastern
as well as Western, as all good imperial history must be; it is an excellent
account of a little understood and seldom studied subject. It joins a small
shelf of books by John Cady, J. S. Furnivall, G. E. Harvey, D. G. E. Hall,
Frank and Helen Trager, and Hugh Tinker that are Western in approach;
yet—as with Maung Htin Aung, Ba Maw, and D. P. Singhal—it is conversant
with the Eastern view of the events and problems examined. It is, at the
same time, a monograph, closely researched and argued, with the intention of answering a set of relatively precise questions concerning competition, annexation, and the diverse exercise of power. In this sense it joins
the work of such scholars as Singhal (again), Paul Bennett, or Sao Saimong
Mangrai. I am delighted, therefore, that the first title in this series should
be on this subject and of this nature.

ROBIN W. WINKS

Series Editor

New Haven, Connecticut

January 1979

ACKNOWLEDGMENTS

A number of people and institutions have been associated with this study. Thanks are due to Professor J. S. Galbraith, who taught me to wed imperial and authochthonous history. The primary research was accomplished during 1970. The Southeast Asia staff at the School of Oriental and African Studies, London, assisted with Burmese translation, and Professor Emeritus D. G. E. Hall kindly fielded my sometimes impertinent questions.

The record collections in England are rich. I am indebted to the archivists and librarians at the India Office Library and Records; British Library; Public Record Office; Royal Commonwealth Society; SOAS Library; Sheepscar Library, Leeds; the Scottish Record Office, Edinburgh; as well as the Baptist Missionary Archives, Valley Forge, for personal assistance and permission to quote from their collections.

This study was transformed from note slips to typescript while I taught at the University of Rhodesia in Salisbury, a location sometimes called the "last of the British Raj." I am solicitous of my chairman there, Professor R. S. Roberts, and my colleagues and students for their patience as I explored nineteenth-century Burma while living a ten-minute walk from some of the most exciting imperial and Africanist archives in the world. While I was in Rhodesia, the Senate Research Committee at the University of Rhodesia provided timely financial aid to obtain microfilms. The UCLA Senate Patent Fund served a similar, useful function.

There has been a resurgence of Burmese studies in America and Europe
in the last decade. I am grateful to the Burmese Studies Group of the
Asian Studies Association for the 1977 award of the Burma Studies Prize
and to the insightful criticism of Professor J. F. Cady at the First Burma
Studies Group Conference at Denison University, Granville, Ohio, in
1976. The ultimate publication of this study has been fostered by the
good offices of Professor Robin Winks and the editors of Greenwood
Press and their encouragement of comparative imperial scholarship.

Permission for reproduction of certain illustrations and use of quoted
material is gratefully acknowledged to Revell Publishers, the *Illustrated
London News*, British Library, India Office Library and Records, and the
Earl of Harewood, owner of the Canning Papers. Sections of the early
chapters have appeared in *Albion, Modern Asian Studies, Southeast
Asian Studies,* and the *Journal of Southeast Asian Studies*. I thank the
editors for their use.

Finally, thanks are due to Karen, my wife, who in 1970 endured a
Golders Green bedsitter and pregnancy, yet managed to cook lacquered
duck regularly on a Baby Belling stove and provided understanding and
criticism.

ABBREVIATIONS

BPC	Bengal Political Consultations
BSP	Bengal Secret and Political Consultations
BSPP	Bengal Secret and Political Proceedings
IPF	India Political and Foreign Proceedings
IPP	India Political Proceedings
ISP	India Secret Proceedings
J.B.R.S.	*Journal of the Burma Research Society*

EMPIRES IN COLLISION

INTRODUCTION

During the late eighteenth century the British Indian and Burmese empires encroached on their mutual buffer zone. Contact between the two empires had been intermittent and unfriendly.[1] Burma under the early Konbaung dynasty had expanded by military force at the expense of the Siamese. But the resilience of Siam under the Chakri dynasty after 1782 caused Burma to turn her martial energies westward, toward Arakan, Assam, Manipur, and Cachar. By 1815 the Burmese empire extended over fourteen hundred miles from the Isthmus of Kra to Assam. The Burmese and British Indian empires collided, and so began almost a century of Anglo-Burmese conflict. Britain and Burma had three violent confrontations during the nineteenth century: 1824-26, 1852-53, and 1885-86. The first and second wars resulted in Burma's losing territory, treasure, and manpower. The third war extinguished her sovereignty.

The history of this bitter relationship has been written from a predominantly Eurocentric conqueror's perspective. Historical accounts of travelers, diplomats,[2] and civil servants[3] had the force of myth making. The Burmese were described as xenophobic, arch practitioners of oriental duplicity, and unable to learn from the harsh experience of defeat to accommodate to changed circumstance. The Burmese did not rule their own people well. Conquest and annexation by the British were a blessing in disguise. They brought good government and development.[4] This colonial apologetic has recently been criticized.[5] Burmese scholars have been slow to challenge the Eurocentric school. There is a tendency toward narrative rather than interpretive accounts,[6] though a strident indigenous point of view is slowly being formed that throws the blame for conflict on the British.[7] The indigenous school receives support from economically oriented, Liberal English historians who point to Britain's need for markets and raw materials as the engine of imperial expansion.[8]

The focus of this study, 1837-67 and the Second Anglo-Burmese War, has not received as close historical scrutiny as the first and last wars.[9] This period forms a mid-nineteenth-century centerspan in imperial history and the relations between a modern nation and an administratively and technologically backward state. The causes of the second war have been confused by rhetoric and polemics. Anglophile and Burmanophile historians have been quick to lay the blame for the conflict at the doorstep of the recalcitrant and xenophobic Burmese or to the imperialistic will to power of Governor General Dalhousie, the East India Company, and grasping traders. The recent debate on "the imperialism of free trade" has not added much fresh insight to this unplanned accession to the British Empire. There is sufficient element of credibility and attractiveness in each of these separate assertions to permit continued advocacy. However, truth is not best served by monocausal or ethnocentric explanations, which are based on partial perceptions and incomplete evidence.

Contemporaries tended to ignore the divergent world views and traditions of their opponents. The British did so from a position of power. The Burmese did so at the cost of their freedom. Historians, however, searching out the causes of confrontation cannot ignore the manifestations of religious, cultural, racial, economic, and administrative self-interest. These were the ingredients of tension along the "turbulent frontier" that climaxed in war. The West exported missionaries, agents of militant Christianity. Britain brought to her Indian Empire and portions of Southeast Asia ideas of formal frontiers, "free trade," and the explicit rule of law.

The Burmese concept of frontiers was one of independent kingdoms separated by unfamiliar, barbarian tribes.[10] Frontiers shifted, expanding and contracting, as the kingdoms went on the march. The intervening tribes either moved out of the way, were reduced, or, more rarely, were assimilated.[11] The British introduced permanent frontiers in rivers and watersheds in place of human buffer zones.[12] The British applied their standards of administrative efficiency and government accountability to

Burma. The British held the Burmese King answerable for border tension though it occurred seven hundred miles from his royal court. Provincial Governors were regarded as integral parts of national government rather than the autonomous agents they were. Few British officials appreciated the Burmese monarch's inability to control the periphery of his kingdom.[13]

The Burmese had an exaggerated notion of their power. They meant to treat all foreigners as inferiors. Diplomacy consisted of sending a decennial mission to China. In return the Chinese sent valuable gifts to their vassals. The Governor General in Calcutta was merely the head of a trading company in Bengal, neither of royal blood nor ultimate authority. The Burmese had an abysmal knowledge of geography. Few Burmans had been as far as Calcutta. Burma was the center of the universe, and by it all things were measured.

"Free trade" was completely beyond the ken of the Burmese. Burma exercised a "mercantilist" policy governed by the dictates of national self-interest and self-sufficiency. Wealth was not to leave the country lest the kingdom be impoverished and weakened. The Burmese suspected foreigners with interests in Burmese mineral, forest, and agricultural resources. The King closely guarded his traditional economic monopolies in bullion, precious stones, and rice.[14]

Christians were a distinct minority in Asia. Thus added to their sense of moral superiority was a feeling of insecurity due to their small numbers. Nonetheless the missionaries evangelized. Ironically, in nineteenth-century Burma it was the American Baptist missionaries who had marginal success converting "little tradition" or animist tribes but made virtually no headway against the satisfied and secure adherents to the great Buddhist tradition.

Neither Britain nor Burma created policy in a vacuum. Burma tended to be guided by a warranted suspicion of the white, Christian, English-speaking intruders who sought their own gain at the cost of Burma. Britain, more often than not, was reacting to its local officials and to rumors of Burmese intentions. British officials in London and Calcutta were guided by concern for security and economy. They were not eager imperialists when it came to conquering and annexing portions of Burma. However, they might become captives of local circumstances and their own frontier officials. The man on the spot had a provincial outlook and was spurred on by what he deemed was the "Burmese problem" and its solution. He served as an agent of subimperialism in the name of local vested interests.

Conflict is an important part of this study, as is Burma's response to defeat at Western hands. Defeat in 1853 had creative ramifications felt over the next decade and a half, as it prompted the Burmese monarch to spearhead a modernization program and partial transformation of society. Burma selectively adopted Western ideas, practices, and technology to forestall another clash with the West. A full appreciation of the interaction and reaction process can only be obtained by the study of the pertinent British *and* Burmese institutions and mores that produced conflict and the method by which conflict modified them.

NOTES

1. See D. G. E. Hall, *Early English Intercourse with Burma, 1587-1743* (London: Longmans, 1928); "The Tragedy of Negrais," *J.B.R.S.* 21 (1931): 59-133; and *Europe and Burma* (London: Oxford University Press, 1945).

2. Michael Symes, *An Account of an Embassy to the Kingdom of Ava* (London: Bulmer, 1800); Hiram Cox, *Journal of a Residence in the Burmhan Empire* (London: Warren, 1821); John Crawfurd, *Journal of an Embassy from the Governor General of India to the Court of Ava* (London: Goulburn, 1829); Henry Yule, *A Narrative of the Mission sent by the Governor General of India to the Court of Ava in 1855* (Kuala Lumpur: Oxford University Press, 1969 [orig. publ. 1858]). See also D. G. E. Hall, "British Writers of Burmese History from Dalrymple to Bayfield," in D. G. E. Hall, ed., *Historians of South-East Asia* (London: Oxford University Press, 1961), pp. 255-66, and Hugh Tinker, "Arthur Phayre and Henry Yule: Two Soldier-Administrator Historians," in Hall, ed., *Historians of South-East Asia,* pp. 267-78.

3. Arthur P. Phayre, *History of Burma* (London: Susil Gupta, 1969 [orig. publ. 1883]); and Geoffrey E. Harvey, *History of Burma* (London: Cass, 1966 [orig. publ. 1925]).

4. D. G. E. Hall, *Burma* (London: Hutchinson University Library, 1960 [orig. publ. 1950]), pp. 65-6; "Anglo-Burmese Conflicts in the 19th Century: A Reassessment of their Causes," *Asia* 6 (Autumn 1966): 33-52; Geoffrey E. Harvey's chapters on Burma in H. H. Dodwell, ed., *The Cambridge History of the British Empire,* 8 vols. (Cambridge: Cambridge University Press, 1929), 4; John Sydenham Furnivall, *Colonial Policy and Practice* (New York: New York University Press, 1956 [orig. publ. 1948]),

pp. 23 and 70; *An Introduction to the Political Economy of Burma*, 2d ed. (Rangoon: People's Literature Committee, 1957 [orig. publ. 1931]), p. 1; and Paul Knaplund, *The British Empire, 1815-1939* (London: Hamish Hamilton, 1942), p. 147.

5. See Michael Adas, "Imperialist Rhetoric and Modern Historiography: The Case of Lower Burma Before and After the Conquest," *Journal of Southeast Asian Studies* 3 (1972): 175-92; Emanuel Sarkisyanz, "On the Changing Anglo-Saxon Image of Burma," *Asian Studies* 4 (1966): 226-35, and *Peacocks, Pagodas and Professor Hall* (Athens: Ohio University Center for International Studies, 1972).

6. U Tin (of Sagaing), *Kòn-baung-zet Maha-ya-zawin-daw-gyi* [Great royal chronicle of the Kon-baung dynasty], 3 vols. (Mandalay: Hanthawaddy Pitakat Press, 1922-3). See also U Tet Htoot, "The Nature of the Burmese Chronicles," in Hall, ed., *Historians of South-East Asia*, pp. 50-62; Maung Htin Aung, *Burmese History Before 1287* (Oxford: Asoka Society, 1970); Pe Maung Htin and Gordon H. Luce, *The Glass Palace Chronicle of the Kings of Burma* (Rangoon: Rangoon University Press, 1960 [orig. publ. 1923]); and U Hla Pe, "Burmese Chronicles," typescript (London: 1964?).

7. Maung Htin Aung, *A History of Burma* (New York: Columbia University Press, 1967), and *The Stricken Peacock: Anglo-Burmese Relations, 1752-1948* (The Hague: Martinus Nijhoff, 1965).

8. Dorothy Woodman, *The Making of Burma* (London: Cresset Press, 1962).

9. For an overall view of the three wars see Anil Chandra Banerjee, *Annexation of Burma* (Calcutta: Mukherjee, 1944). For the first war see his *The Eastern Frontier of British India, 1784-1826* (Calcutta: Mukerjee, 1964 [orig. publ. Calcutta, 1943]) and Laurence Kitzan, "Lord Amherst and the Declaration of War on Burma, 1824," *Journal of Asian History* 9 (1975): 101-27. For the third war see D. P. Singhal, *The Annexation of Upper Burma* (Singapore: Eastern Universities Press, 1960); A. T. Q. Stewart, *The Pagoda War* (London: Faber and Faber, 1972); and Charles Lee Keeton, *King Thibaw and the Ecological Rape of Burma* (Delhi: Manohar Book Service, 1974).

10. G. Gordon to Government of India, 30 January 1841, IPP/52.

11. Edmund R. Leach, "The Frontiers of Burma," *Comparative Studies in Society and History* 3 (1960): 49-68.

12. Edmund Blundell to Government of India, 19 June 1840, in *Selected Correspondence of Letters Issued from and Received in the Office of the Commissioner* (Rangoon: Government Printers, 1929), pp. 189-90.

13. Minute by George Eden, Earl of Auckland, 30 July 1840, Auckland
Papers, British Library, Add. Mss. 37700; and Barbara J. Stewart, "Administrative Beginnings in British Burma, 1826-1843" (Ph.D. diss., University
of London, 1931), p. 309.

14. Siamese monarchs practiced similar monopolistic rights. See Neon
Snidvongs, "The Development of Siamese Relations with Britain and France
in the Reign of Maha Mongkut, 1851-1868" (Ph.D. diss., University of
London, 1960), p. 22.

1
THE POLITICS OF DYNASTICISM

STRUCTURE OF BURMESE RULE

The Burmese kingdom was unstable. Instability has been frequently explained in terms of national character.[1] Burma was called the Ireland of the Orient, whose citizens were equally vivacious and ungovernable.[2] Government was one of the five evils of Burmese folklore along with fire, water, robbers, and enemies.[3] Burmese society was egalitarian: "a community of equals. . .that had probably never been known elsewhere."[4] There was no caste or hereditary aristocracy, which tended to promote stability. Only the monkhood constituted a permanent institutional, though otherworldly, elite. Burmese kingship was modeled on a fusion of Hindu and Buddhist ideas of the universal or semi-divine monarch. Kingship was theoretically elective and contractual. If the contract was violated it could be broken. This promoted unstructured and unrestrained individualism and led to despotism, unrest, and revolution.[5] These explanations are idealizations and stereotypes that stem from British preconceptions seen through Indian-tinted spectacles.

Only by comparison to caste-ridden India was Burma casteless. Burmese society was highly structured, ranging from slave to king in about seven gradations.[6] There were economic divisions between landowner, landless, and debtor. The repeated scenes of political chaos in Burma emerged from the structure of kingship and from geopolitical factors. At the center there was a constant struggle for the throne. On the periphery there were frequent battles for tribal and provincial autonomy.

The capital of Burma, located in the Burmese heartland, was the political, racial, and religio-cultural center of the country. The palace where the King resided was the center of the universe, the Mount Meru of Buddhist cosmology. Command of the palace and the throne was synonymous with being "rightful" King.[7] The King was the earthly defender of the faith and the focal point of national politics, power, and wealth. Around him revolved several family factions attempting to influence the monarch, obtain access to the perquisites of power, and perhaps direct the destiny of the nation. The King had an immense claim to power, and this invited abuse. He had a fragile hold on the throne, and this invited pretenders. In this paradox lay the root of instability.

Burmese Buddhism was an amalgam of ancient Hindu beliefs, Theravada Buddhism, nat worship (a form of animism), and astrology. Burmese Buddhism was otherworldly and taught the impermanence and depravity of all earthly things.[8] Humility and the abnegation of self were the ideals to be striven for. Structurally and ideologically religion fostered instability. The King, in theory, was absolute. He might be considered a reincarnation of the Buddha. Past goodness had raised him to his present station in life. Ritual, ceremony, language, and accoutrements elevated the King above mortal man. The language of everyday use was forbidden in the palace precincts. A King did not "die" like ordinary folk; he "ascended to the palace of the nats." Commoners had to prostrate themselves when a member of the royal family went by. "No Chinese emperor ever regarded himself as all-sovereign more unqualifiedly than did the Burmese Kings." From rising to retiring, his day was forecast by court astrologers.[9]

The "ideals of kingship" were theoretical checks on the monarch. The King was to love and extol the three gems: the Buddha, *Sangha* (monkhood), and *Tripitika* (scriptures). There were several virtues. The King should love wise men and monks as though they were his own children. Honesty, trustworthiness, and bravery were extolled. He should know the capacity of his ministers, who could serve him by feat of wisdom or feat of arms. He should reward the deserving. All this would increase the King's *karma*.[10] Pretenders to the throne invariably claimed superior *karma*. If a King was "bad," guiding the country to ruin, the usurper made a case that he was called to act—better still, was forced to act—in the interests of an unhappy people. How far the ideals of kingship and the fear

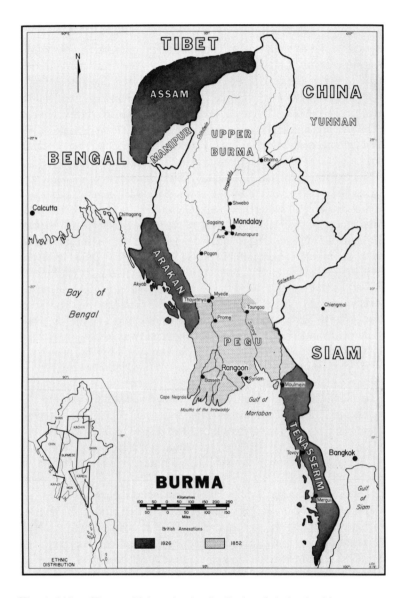

Historical Map of Burma with inset showing distribution of ethnic minorities.

of rebellion by virtue of moral superiority served as a check on the King's actions is a moot question.[11]

Successful revolt was further sanctioned by the suspension of punishment for offenses committed during the unrest. The *Dhammathat* provided that after a revolution or change of rulers certain suits could not be prosecuted. Among them were murder, assault with wounding, theft, adultery, and obscene language. Moreover, the royal family was immune from most of the civil and criminal laws to which the commoners were liable.[12] What was a heinous crime for a commoner was legitimate for a Prince becoming King.

The universal problem of monarchy is determination of succession. The special problems of the Burmese were biological, genetic, and psychological. Peaceful succession in nineteenth-century Burma was virtually nonexistent. The accessions of 1819, 1837, 1846, 1856, and 1878 were all violent. The intervening periods were peppered with unsuccessful coups and palace murders, most notably in 1845, 1850, 1851, 1866, 1870, and 1879. Theoretically, the succession of the dynasty ruling Burma from 1752 to 1885, variously called the Konbaung, Alompra, or Alaungpaya dynasty, passed from the King to his brothers before his sons. This "rule" was constantly disturbed by polygamy and ambitions. The six Kings ruling Burma from 1781 to 1885 had among them two hundred wives.[13] The function of polygamy was to weld territorial and familial alliances and to increase prestige. The result was family conflict in determining seniority among the scores of offspring.

Despite high infant mortality many children survived to maturity.[14] During late adolescence important princes received palaces of their own away from the central palace complex. The princes' palaces were on a smaller scale, as though waiting in the wings to replace the present monarch. They had their own "households," ministers, and soldiery. The princes collected wives, who in turn had sons. These sons and grandsons felt power within reach. As they aged it seemed to slip away.

The King could choose his successor, an act often fatal to the nominee. The temptation was to oust one's brother in favor of one's sons. The eldest or most powerful son tended to become *Einshemin*. The King's brother and sons looked upon themselves as possible heirs and upon their opposite numbers as competitors to be liquidated. The palace was filled with intrigue. Proximity to the throne created a temptation to revolt. In a society that emphasized impermanence and ready religious validation, temptation frequently led to action. A usurper with a small force could capture the palace and proclaim himself King. Possession of the throne and the symbolic trappings sufficed for de facto legitimacy. However, when pretenders failed and were caught, they, their families, and generally their entire households were executed. Institutionalized violent succession may have been a necessary or vital element of leadership selection. Bloodshed validated the right to the throne, as well as removing a generation of competitors.

Several of the Burmese monarchs exhibited bizarre or aberrant psychological attitudes. This may have been genetic in origin, fostered by the practice of kings' marrying their half-sisters.[15] It may also have been a consequence of continual tension at the political center. Kings, as they aged, often feared to leave the security of the palace precincts, which alone were guarded by his trusted soldiers. The psychological effect of family strife, "perhaps most disastrous of all, doomed persons of Royal blood to live in such anxiety that neuroses were everpresent and psychoses common, so that many kings were emotionally unstable and unfit to govern."[16]

Central power and patronage were the monopoly of the King. He could administer personally or he could share power with sons, wives, and ministers.[17] The King was assisted by four *Wungyis* who sat in the *Hluttaw*, or national council. Theoretically the King needed the approval of the *Hluttaw* before making important decisions. In practice this procedure of consultation was often ignored. Several *Wundauks* assisted the *Wungyis*. The King's personal household advisors were called *Atwinwuns*. Affairs of state were managed by these ministers in as many as fourteen departments.[18] Central government was rich in ceremony and ritual and lacking in efficiency and peripheral control.

Instability at the center was duplicated in the provinces and among the encircling ethnic minorities.[19] Topography and ethnic demographic distribution militated against efficient central control. Mountain ranges and rivers running north to south inhibited communications and gave the advantage to outlying regions. The King's power emanated from the center and filtered down to the village level via province, district, township, and circle administration. The royal family often had affinal links with provinces and districts. Burmese local officials recruited from a hereditary gentry class, and ethnic minority leaders would send their daughters to court as a sign of fealty. The King could marry or assign her to one of his sons.

The King appointed his kinsmen and his wives' families to lucrative posts throughout the kingdom. They were generally created *myosas* and received the taxes on the King's provincial properties, often without any administrative or compensatory responsibilities. Appointment to the far reaches of Burma could be a sign of trust or exile. Because of the great distances and poor communications, accountability was low. Royally appointed local officials had the power of life and death without appeal. They collected taxes and customs duties and managed relations with the *kulas*, or foreigners. Having no official salary, they took their income from revenues collected.

Provincial politics were the realm of the *Myothugyi*, headmen recruited from the local hereditary elite. They were responsible for the police system and were the maids of all work.[20] *Myothugyis* were distinctly parochial in outlook, often disagreeing and refusing to obey the edicts of the center. Conflict over payment of taxes, the provision of corvée labor and military conscripts, corruption, and the existence of local tyrannies were common. The center had marginal control over the *Myothugyi*.[21]

The Kings of Burma knew their own weakness and glossed over it. Standard instructions to provincial commanders were to "make important difficulties to become trivial and the trivial to disappear."[22] The center aspired to rule the periphery through salutary neglect and local acquiescence. But when seriously challenged the center was obligated to demonstrate real power, and troops would be sent to quell breakaway provinces.

Control problems were compounded where ethnic differences existed. The Burmese are a distinct racial and linguistic group. They constitute a majority only in the heartland, the fertile valley of the Irrawaddy River. Outside the heartland Burmese existed in scattered pockets of settlement. Ringing the heartland were the Chins, Shans, Kachins, Karens, and Mons, who treasured their autonomy and were uneasily incorporated into the kingdom by conquest.[23] The Burmese considered themselves superior to all these groups. They had a haughty disdain for the southerners.[24] The Karens were "the wild cattle of the hills," and the Chins were "the wild or stinking Chins."[25] The minorities were not treated as citizens and could not become *ahmudan* or *atha.* The Karens and Chins paid annual family taxes and gave heavy unpaid labor digging canals and building walls.[26] The Shans were the most numerous and sophisticated of the minorities. They emulated the Burmese, paid tribute, and gave assistance in time of war.[27]

Tribal control was disrupted by inter- and intratribal wars. Allegiance was in a constant state of flux as minority subgroups would vacillate between homage to Burmese, Chinese, Siamese, and later British overlords. Alien forces attacking the Burmese heartland had first to pass through tribal areas. The attackers often received assistance from the minorities. Shans and Karens aided the Siamese. In 1824 and 1852 the Mons assisted the British. If Burma repulsed her enemies, she took revenge on the offending minorities. The desire for autonomy was chronic. The greater the distance from the heartland, the more difficult it was for the center to enforce its commands.

The structure of kingship created a governmental system heavily dependent on the ability of the monarch. Polygamy and easy recourse to rebellion militated against the stability of the crown. Control of the kingdom was also unstable as ethnic diversity and difficult communications led to frequent challenges to decentralized control.

BURMA DURING THE REIGNS OF KING THARRAWADDY AND PAGAN MIN

When King Bagyidaw ascended the throne in 1819, the Burmese kingdom was at its height. He inherited the throne through his deceased father, who had been *Einshemin*.[28] Within a decade the empire was severely reduced in size. The cause of this turn of fortune can be found in the failure of the confrontation policy of his advisers, General Maha Bandula,[29] Queen Mai Nu,[30] and her brother, the Salin Myosa.[31] Burma's westward expansive policy presented the British Indian frontier with sporadic murder, robbery, kidnapping, disruption of trade, and clashes with British border forces. The East India Company in Calcutta was patient and forbearing. Britain was reluctant to take up arms, as victory over Burma offered few financial or territorial rewards. But the Company was not solely governed by profit-and-loss columns; the question of security also loomed large. When the Burmese threat came too close to Calcutta and the East India Company was free from other entanglements, the Company reacted defensively. The First Anglo-Burmese War was the most arduous and drawn out of the three nineteenth-century engagements. The British applied a two-front strategy and experimented with steam-powered gunboats. Superior discipline and technology, coupled with the death of General Maha Bandula while defending a stockade in

April 1825, slowly turned the Burmese offensive into a defense of the homeland.[32] Following defeat in the lower provinces the Burmese court sought peace. The war was concluded by the Treaty of Yandabo, which ceded Arakan and Tenasserim to the British, removed the Burmese threat to Cachar and Manipur, established a British Resident at the Burmese capital, and provided that the Burmese pay the British a war indemnity. Pegu Province was held as security to insure payment of the indemnity. A reciprocal commercial treaty was later concluded.

Bagyidaw, despite losing two-fifths of his kingdom, retained his throne. Mai Nu and her brother continued their ascendancy at court. While Bagyidaw always seemed to have been controlled by his advisers, in the early 1830s a new dimension was added. In 1831 Bagyidaw became uncommunicative and had frequent fits. A Regency was formed, consisting of the Queen's brother and three of the King's five brothers: princes Tharrawaddy (a full brother), and the half-brothers Thibawmin and Kowounmin. Despite the Regency containing three of Bagyidaw's kinsmen, power clearly resided with the non-kinsmen: the Queen, and the Salin Myosa, who continued a firm hold on crown patronage. They showed little regard for the King's brothers or the King's son, Nyaung Yin Mintha, borne by Bagyidaw's deceased chief Queen. Nyaung Yin Mintha, also known as Setkya Min, the equivalent of a Chakravartin monarch, was the heir apparent. Mai Nu had one daughter whom she hoped to wed to Setkya Min. The marriage plan disturbed some kinsmen, who feared the succession would pass out of the royal family.

Of the kinsmen only Prince Tharrawaddy openly opposed the Queen and her brother. He probably led the peace faction in 1826.[33] During the Regency he kept to himself and maintained a large household reported to contain "the most turbulent and saucy set of fellows in Ava."[34] Of his twenty sons only seven survived childhood, and they reached maturity in the 1830s. The Salin Myosa suspected the kinsmen and watched them closely. Some of the kinsmen were hoarding arms. On 21 February 1837 the Salin Myosa employed this as a pretext to order the arrest of the influential Pagan Princess, a full sister of Bagyidaw and Tharrawaddy, and her chief household officer. Both fled to Tharrawaddy's palace. Tharrawaddy told his sister to give herself up.[35] Tharrawaddy, at this early stage, harbored no designs on the throne. Nonetheless, he took defensive action and prepared his household lest he be caught by surprise like his sister. It would be a simple move to make his defensive posture a bid for the throne. On 24 February Tharrawaddy fled the city after defeating one of the King's regiments. When departing Tharrawaddy swore at a pagoda, by all that was holy, that he had no intention to rebel and did not aspire to the throne. He regarded Bagyidaw as his father and could not harm him.[36]

Despite Tharrawaddy's protestations of innocence he rapidly took the path of traditional revolt. The Prince withdrew to Shwebo, which was to the northwest of Ava and was the seat of the Alaungpaya dynasty. There he collected followers from among the disaffected classes. Tharrawaddy, a reluctant pretender, was swept up by his children and turbulent followers who wanted decisive action. Tharrawaddy's eldest daughter, one of Burma's greatest astrologers, declared that the revolt's success was ordained in the stars. She was later to be Mindon's chief Queen. Tharrawaddy set about organizing his followers and demoralizing the royal forces by spreading rumors of Chin and Kachin support.

The British Resident, Colonel Henry Burney, played an ambiguous role in the overthrow of Bagyidaw.[37] The British Indian government waited for four years after signing the Treaty of Yandabo before they sent a Resident to the Burmese court. On the establishment of the Residency in 1830 Burney had been instructed to steer clear of court politics.[38] But Burney was not a man to remain aloof. Despite repeated instructions to maintain strict neutrality Burney formed plans to increase British influence.[39] During the 1837 revolt Burney eagerly assumed the roles of mediator and messenger. He claimed that the Burmese requested his aid, while the *Chronicle* states he volunteered.[40] Burney declared he would do all in his power to keep the peace. In the early stages of revolt Burney made no headway toward conciliation at court. He proposed marriage alliances, but the Salin Myosa opposed them at every turn as detracting from his power. Burney was admitted to see Bagyidaw on 4 March and noted that he was completely under his brother-in-law's power.[41] The royal forces, commanded by a former member of the now-defunct Regency, were dispirited. By mid-March the royal cause appeared lost. The Salin Myosa called on Burney as the last hope of counsel and assistance. He asked Burney to visit Tharrawaddy, which he did on 24 March. Burney again tried the marriage ploy to link the two factions, but Tharrawaddy rejected the idea. Burney talked of the power of the royal troops. The Prince laughed, adding that he had contacts in the capital and well knew the sorry state of the royal forces. Burney's several audiences with the Prince convinced him that there was no chance of reconciliation. Burney dropped the role of mediator and attempted to minimize bloodshed and save the capital from plunder. He got Tharrawaddy to agree not to harm his enemies if the city gates were opened. Burney made Tharrawaddy repeat this "promise" several times. Nonetheless, Burney did not trust Tharrawaddy and offered Bagyidaw asylum in British territory.[42]

Tharrawaddy's forces were closing in on the capital. The Mekkara Prince, a brother of Bagyidaw's and Tharrawaddy's father, and some Buddhist priests visited Tharrawaddy in his camp. Tharrawaddy made additional demands. He wanted the Queen separated from the King and thirteen ministers handed over to Tharrawaddy's son. The list was headed by the Salin Myosa and included Prince Bowun, Myawadi Wungyi, Wundauk Maung Khan Ye, young Princess Myalatwun, six other subordinate ministers, and seven generals faithful to Bagyidaw and the non-kinsmen faction.[43] The royal position was so weak that Tharrawaddy's demands were acceded to, and the officials involved handed themselves over on 7 April 1837. They were immediately thrown into jail. On 9 April Burney called on Tharrawaddy to remind him of his pledge. Burney's usefulness to Tharrawaddy had ended, and the pledge was a dead letter. So began the decline of the Residency, which had been established by the Treaty of Yandabo.

Tharrawaddy's first task was to secure the throne. Late in April 1837 Tharrawaddy ordered the execution of Bagyidaw's three ministers responsible for the raids on the Pagan Princess. Shortly thereafter, Tharrawaddy announced that Bagyidaw had resigned the throne to himself, the younger brother. As he ascended the throne he declared: "My brother's reign was a bad one, and I only desire to replace everything in the excellent condition in which it was in the reigns of my grandfather and ancestor Alompra."[44] Tharrawaddy's first impulse was to look to traditional standards. The corruption of the later years of Bagyidaw's reign caused much litigation. Mai Nu's appointees were accused of taking undue profits in reaching their judicial decisions. Tharrawaddy proclaimed that the *Dhammathat* and custom should henceforth be the judicial guides. Rapacious judges were to be removed.[45] The revenue system was slightly modified so as to conform more closely with Alompra's.[46] Tharrawaddy moved the palace and the capital to Amarapura, the birthplace of his father, and declared that the people would not be taxed for its reconstruction.[47]

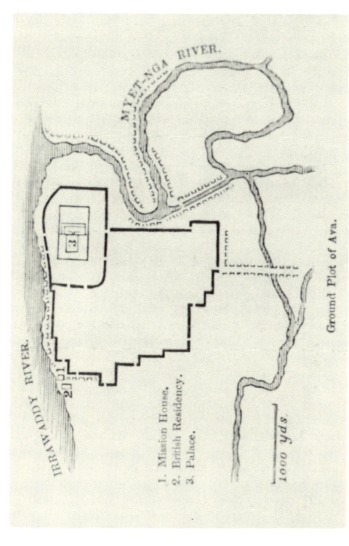

Map of Residency location in Ava, 1836. From Howard Malcom, *Travels in South-eastern Asia* (Boston: Gould, Kendall, and Lincoln, 1839).

Within a few months Tharrawaddy had taken charge of patronage and
supplanted Bagyidaw's and the Salin Myosa's supporters throughout the
kingdom. Incumbents either fled to British territory in Arakan or Tenasserim or went up to the capital in disgrace and an uncertain fate. The
royal proclamation claiming the throne also declared Tharrawaddy's
son, Thiat Ten Gyeh, who had served as military commander during the
revolt, as head of the *Hluttaw*, and he was created Prince of Prome. The
remaining sons were raised in status and given the lands and fiefs of the
ousted faction. Members of the old court and Bagyidaw's line slowly disappeared. Valid cause or pretext were sufficient grounds for execution.
Bagyidaw was spared either out of brotherly love, or in recognition that
the execution of the ex-King would be a bad example, or because Bagyidaw was politically impotent. He died a natural death in 1846, preceding
Tharrawaddy to the grave by one month. In June 1837 one of Bagyidaw's
most able and faithful military officers was executed.[48] In April 1838
the Setkya Min was executed on trumped-up charges of conspiracy and
raising troops. The charges were laid by the princes of Prome and Pakhan.
Setkya Min was executed along with his immediate household.[49] Fabricated charges were later used to eliminate Mai Nu and the ex-Salin Myosa
on the heels of a Shan-Burman rising in late 1840. They, as well as thirty
or forty former followers, were executed. Many people in Burmese and
British territory did not believe that Setkya Min had been executed. This
proved a political liability. Over the next two decades several risings with
millennian overtones would claim the leadership of or support for the
Chakravartin monarch.[50]

Tharrawaddy applied a variation of traditional practices toward the
British. He felt they had no place in Burma. If they did remain it would
not be by treaty rights but by the magnanimity of the Burmese monarch.
Britain should be treated like other tribal minorities and pushed out to
the periphery. To rid the capital of the Resident, Tharrawaddy took
counsel from expatriate Britishers. He learned quickly that Britain and
the East India Company had little interest in Burma. Short of direct
confrontation, nothing would make the Company enforce their Yandabo
treaty rights. Tharrawaddy then set about rejecting the treaty without
actually breaking it. In the weeks following the revolt Tharrawaddy turned
his fury on Burney, the treaty, and English customs. In an interview with
Burney over the Yandabo treaty Tharrawaddy declared, "Do not refer to
any acts of the late government. I have nothing to say to any treaties

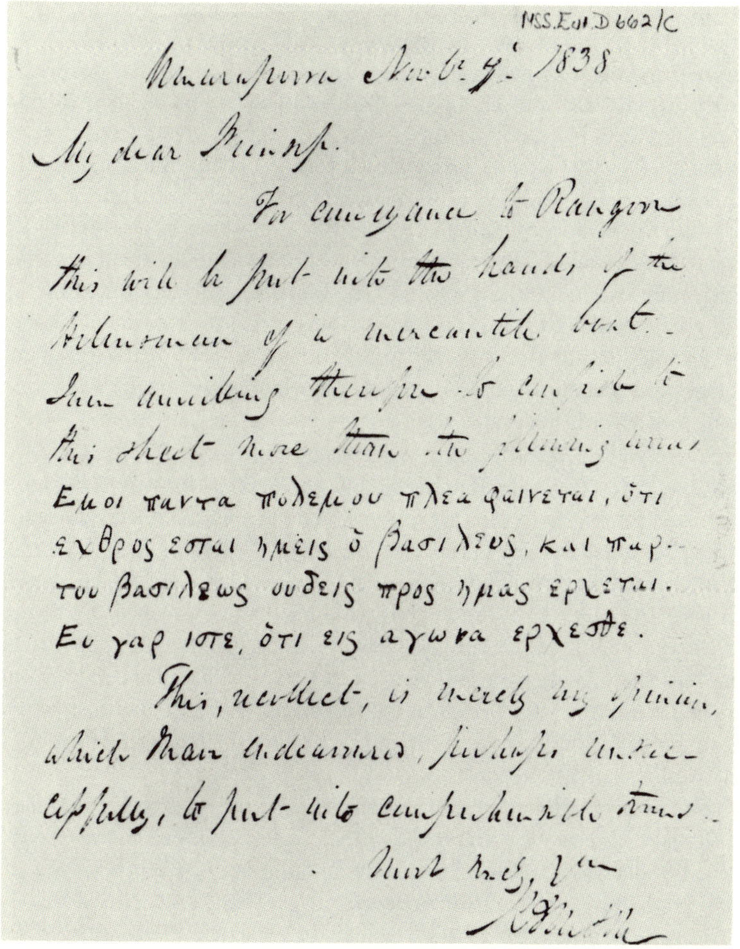

MSS.Eur.D 662/C

Ummerapoora Nov. 7th 1838

My dear Prinsep.

For conveyance to Rangoon this will be put into the hands of the Helmsman of a mercantile boat. I am unwilling therefore to confide to this sheet more than the following lines.

Εμοι παντα πολεμου πλεα φαινεται, ότι εχθρος εσται ημεις ό βασιλευς, και παρ του βασιλεως ουδεις προς ημας ερχεται. Ευ γαρ ιστε, ότι εις αγωνα ερχεσθε.

This, recollect, is merely my opinion, which I have endeavoured, perhaps unsuccessfully, to put into comprehensible terms.

Most truly, Yrs

R Benson

Letter from R. Benson to H. T. Prinsep, 7 November 1838, employing Greek in absence of cipher. Prinsep Papers, D/662/C, reproduced by courtesy of the Director of the India Office Library and Records, London.

0698681

which they may have entered into." It was not Burmese practice to
necessarily honor treaties of previous monarchs.[51]

Tharrawaddy mocked the King of England and the Governor General,
who were subservient to a parliament of five hundred men. Tharrawaddy
proclaimed, "I am a king and have nothing but the gods above me and
am not responsible like the Kings of England."[52] Burney, in ill health,
resolved to withdraw the Residency in early May. On 17 June 1837
Burney and his staff pulled up stakes. Three American Baptist missionaries, Eugenio Kincaid, Thomas Simons, and Webb, who had shortly before been forbidden to disseminate religious tracts, accompanied the
British party downriver to Rangoon. Governor General Auckland in
Calcutta censured Burney for his involvement in the revolt and for with-
drawing the Residency. Colonel Richard Benson was sent as a replacement. The transfer of the capital from Ava to Amarapura meant that the
Residency also had to be relocated. The Burmese provided some low-
lying swamp ground for this purpose. It was called the "Residency on a
sand bank." As the river rose the foundations crumbled. Benson declared
following a gruelling four-and-one-half-hour interview with Burmese
ministers that his treatment was "such as no English gentleman or more
exclusively as no British subject ought to be exposed to."[53] Benson's
health was deteriorating. By Greek cipher he wrote, "*We would like to
go home*, for owing to the frequent menace to which they were subject
all our servants consider themselves in danger."[54] To save face, Governor
General Auckland declared for economy's sake "that we would be better
without than with a resident, and it would be bad to wage war for so un-
profitable a point of honour."[55] Benson withdrew in March 1838, leaving
the Residency in charge of his assistant, Captain William McLeod,[56] who
advised sending British troops to the capital to "dissipate the ideas of Tharrawaddy being able to cope with us."[57] In mid-1839 McLeod withdrew
the Residency to Rangoon.

The rough treatment given the Resident and the reports of the King
sending his three sons with armies to the south raised the specter of war.[58]
British India was deeply and tragically committed in Afghanistan and
could not allow her resources to be spread too thin. It was feared that
a war with Burma might escalate to include Nepal and then China. Moreover, the Company was trying to raise a loan in a bad money market. A
war with Burma would further depress shares.[59] The Secret Committee in
London instructed that "all means short of a sacrifice of national honour,

are to be adopted" to avoid war with the Burmese. Withdrawal to Rangoon was sanctioned.[60]

To gloss their weak position, Calcutta said most liberally that "a nation has a right to its own usages. . . .We can do nothing by beating the Burmese a second time."[61] Auckland hoped that in time Tharrawaddy and his ministers would cease "to cling to the old usage of force and insult, and that their haughty acrimony would be tempered."[62] Burma was "quite beyond the proper sphere of our Indian power and influence in the east" and "nearly out of the pale of our essential Indian relations."[63] Calcutta was not averse to relations falling into a "condition of declared non-intercourse."[64] Not even the prospect of French activities in the shape of the adventuresome Comte de Marquis de Maisonfort in Burma could divert Auckland. The French were no better treated than the English.[65]

When the British Resident withdrew from Rangoon on 6 January 1840 the Governor General breathed a sigh of relief.[66] Tharrawaddy breathed more easily as well. He had succeeded in filibustering the British diplomatic agent out of his kingdom without actually breaking the treaty. A British merchant in Rangoon was appointed postmaster-cum-newswriter. He had no official status. For over a decade he would report fact and rumor, sometimes not distinguishing between them.

As a Buddhist monarch Tharrawaddy's activities often had religious dimensions. He built pagodas and monasteries and erected fresh images to Buddha. Canals and dams were repaired to care for the needs of his people. The greatest religio-political act was the King's progress down the Irrawaddy River to visit and worship at the Shwe Dagon Pagoda in Rangoon in late 1841. Preparations for the journey started in late 1840. Contributions of men, rice, and gold leaf to re-gild pagodas came in from all over the kingdom.[67] Tharrawaddy was accompanied by his sons, wives, ministers, ex-king Bagyidaw, and upward of fifteen thousand troops. Some rumors put the troop strength as high as one hundred thousand. It was the first visit of a Burmese monarch to Rangoon in many years and was an exercise in demonstrating the grandeur of his reign to his people and perhaps the British as well.

During the early 1840s the character of Tharrawaddy's rule slowly changed. His perception and psychological well-being deteriorated. The rapid increase in the number of his wives from sixteen as a Prince to almost one hundred as King may have exacerbated his problems. Several wives were expelled from the palace for "taking a gallant."[68] Tharra-

Sketch of King's ship, 1836. This should be compared to the illustration in the *Illustrated London News* of 27 March and 26 June 1852, which purports to depict the identical or similar vessel seized by the *Hermes*. It is shown to have three masts and at least five cannons on its port side.

waddy's mature sons began to harbor their own designs on the throne. By 1840 they were contending for the post of heir. Territorial cession to the British and the termination of further expansion meant that the princes now had to seek their fortunes at the center rather than on the periphery. They had to compete for the throne rather than territory.

The sons vied for their father's attention. The Prince of Prome had a good claim for his active role in the 1837 revolt. But for this very reason he may have been suspected as being too eager. Likewise his younger brother, Prince Pakhan, was similarly suspect. The brothers were mistakenly referred to as "illegitimate" sons by British observers, as they were born to the third Queen. All sons were legitimate whether borne by chief Queen, lesser Queen, or concubine. The closer the mother to the central palace, the closer the son to the source of power. Sons of high queens were more equal than sons of lesser queens, but no sons were illegitimate. Pagan stayed in the background, taking little interest or action in national affairs. Perhaps he was emulating his father's position from 1826 to 1837. Pagan had the best dynastic claim to the throne as son of the chief Queen. Moreover, he did not appear as a threat to the existing King. When Tharrawaddy was officially crowned in July 1840 Pagan received titles tantamount to *Einshemin.* Once appointed, the princes of Prome and Pakhan and other younger brothers would be excluded from positions of power unless they acted.[69] By late 1842 succession conflict was being waged openly. Four parties were prepared to seize the throne if the King had an "accident." The Prince of Prome had influential support. The Prince of Pakhan had some army backing. The Pagan Prince was backed by those who wanted the line through the first son. Tarop Min, a son by a concubine, also had pretensions. Prome and Pakhan were jealous of Pagan and deprived him of his arms.[70]

Amid princely strife it was also becoming evident that the administration was not running well. Three high-ranking cavalry officers were called before the *Hluttaw* in September 1844 for taking bribes and mistreating troops. Against the King's wishes they were acquitted. The King dismissed two of his *Wungyis,* both kinsmen, including the intellectual Mekkara Wungyi.[71] Princes Pagan and Mindon were elevated in their place. The Prince of Prome, head of the *Hluttaw,* was slowly falling out of Tharawaddy's favor. Shortly thereafter a provincial official, Maung Dang Wun, was executed for failing to turn over captured weapons to central authorities. A formidable revolt by about seven hundred men, headed by the executed official's kinsmen, including his uncle and two sons, broke out during March and continued through April 1845. The leader of the revolt, the Bagyi Wun, was a cousin of Tharrawaddy's and had been instrumental in Tharrawaddy's behalf in the 1837 revolt. He had been commander of Ava when Tharrawaddy shifted his capital.[72] One of his daughters was also a minor Queen of Tharrawaddy's.[73] Though a short-lived revolt and handily put down, it indicates the problems Tharrawaddy was having maintaining control. Weakness in the *Hluttaw* and the provinces presaged the first revolt of the sons. Reports trickled down the Irrawaddy that Tharrawaddy was suffering from a brain malady.[74] Unrest increased as the King's grip on affairs weakened and the different interests prepared to battle for position.

The Prince of Prome was making secret loyalty pacts with various ministers in the event of the King's death. Tharrawaddy seized Prome's armory as a precaution. Several ministers and their families were executed for suspected collaboration. The Pagan Prince was elevated to head of the *Hluttaw* in Prome's place.[75] In late August 1845 Tharrawaddy interrogated the Yindaw Atwinwun. Finding him implicated in the Prince of Prome's plans, the King speared him to death from the throne. The King then dispatched troops to arrest the Prince of Prome. Prome resisted arrest, seventy men were killed, and he escaped. Tharrawaddy then purged other high-ranking military officials.[76] The Pagan Prince was made commander of the forces. No better means could have been devised to insure Prome's capture. Pagan had a vested interest in his half-brother's demise. By the second week in September the Prince of Prome had been captured and paraded in the capital in rags and suffering from fever.

Tharrawaddy's erratic behavior played into Pagan's hands. After one of Tharrawaddy's violent fits Pagan ordered that his father be disarmed and placed under restraint. As commander in chief and head of the *Hluttaw* Pagan was the most powerful man in the kingdom. He reinstated the Mekkara Prince, father of his chief wife and therefore his father-in-law and uncle, to the *Hluttaw*.[77] Pagan ruled as Prince Regent and applied himself personally in the bloodletting and the countrywide administrative shakeup necessary to secure his hold on power. Pagan wanted to wrest patronage from those connected by blood or marriage to Tharrawaddy. Tharrawaddy's most powerful wife and leading Burmese poetess, the Queen of the Western Palace, was dispossessed of her wealth and put out of the palace. Those who held appointments by her influence suffered. Pagan raised the King's suspicions against her by showing him depositions of cross-examinations which linked her to the Prince of Prome.[78] The

Western Palace Queen, the Prince of Prome, his two sons, and various other family and household members were executed.[79] Several of the officials who were dismissed and survived the purges later formed the nucleus for Mindon's revolt in 1852.

Pagan's position was now relatively secure. In November 1845 he moved to a larger palace and started to redistribute the spoils of patronage. He kept close surveillance on affairs. Prince Mindon was made head of the *Hluttaw*. Pagan continued to weed out possible opponents. Early in 1846 several officials were executed, purportedly for conspiring to place Bagyidaw back on the throne.[80] Initially the British were pleased about the rise of Pagan. He seemed a refreshing change from his father. He called the European merchants to the *Hluttaw* and assured them they were in no danger. Pagan Min's appointment of Wundauk Maung Shway Meng as Governor of Rangoon was particularly gratifying. He had held the post previously and then fallen out of favor with Tharrawaddy. One of his first acts was to reduce port duties.[81]

Tharrawaddy died in November 1846, as the *Chronicle* records, "with pain due to constricted wind in the body."[82] There is little question that he was also mentally unbalanced. The Book of Burmese Royal Administration records: "Being himself a rebel against his brother, whenever he was suspicious of plots he executed men and women and whole families. At first his madness was known only at high levels and the Crown Prince Pagan was given special powers but it became common knowledge."[83] On the death of his father, Pagan took the title of King and ascended the throne in 1846 at the age of thirty-five. The transition was smooth, for in fact it had really taken place the previous year. Unrest had been limited to the confines of the royal family. Most of Tharrawaddy's widows remarried lesser officials.

Pagan Min's reign was remarkably different from his Regency. After uncontested control was established he appears to have relied on his advisers to carry out the affairs of state. Pagan Min directed energy to religion. The pages of the *Chronicle* are dominated by merit-worthy acts such as the abolition of animal slaughter for certain periods, the freeing of criminals to become pagoda slaves, freeing of caged animals, searches for the highly treasured white elephant, great charities, and ceremonies involving thousands of the faithful.[84] Pagan Min's voluntary withdrawal from control had wide-ranging ramifications as the perquisites of power fell to more grasping individuals. National administration was controlled by Atwinwun Maung Bwa, foster brother of Pagan Min. He encouraged the King to good

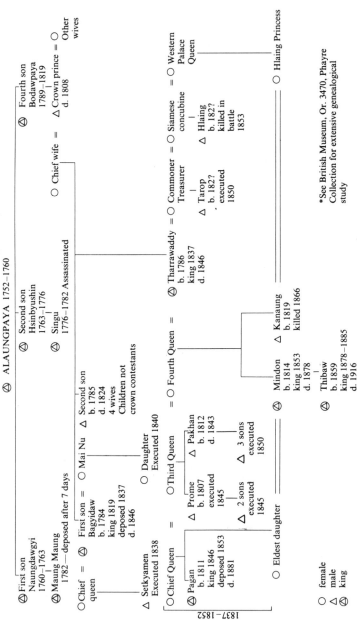

KONBAUNG DYNASTY (special emphasis on 1837–1852)*

Ⓐ ALAUNGPAYA 1752–1760

Ⓐ First son
Naungdawgyi
1760–1763

Ⓐ Second son
Hsinbyushin
1763–1776

Ⓐ Singu
1776–1782 Assassinated

Ⓐ Fourth son
Bodawpaya
1789–1819

Ⓐ Maung Maung
1782—deposed after 7 days

○ Chief wife =

△ Crown prince =
d. 1808

○ Other
wives

○ Chief =
queen

Ⓐ First son =
Bagyidaw
b. 1784
king 1819
deposed 1837
d. 1846

○ Mai Nu

△ Second son
b. 1785
d. 1824
4 wives
Children not
crown contestants

△ Setkyamen
Executed 1838

○ Daughter
Executed 1840

= ○ Fourth Queen =

Ⓐ Tharrawaddy =
b. 1786
king 1837
d. 1846

○ Commoner =
Treasurer

○ Siamese
concubine

= ○ Western
Palace
Queen

△ Tarop
b. 182?
executed
1850

△ Hlaing
b. 182?
killed in
battle
1853

○ Chief Queen =

○ Third Queen

△ Prome
b. 1807
executed
1845

△ Pakhan
b. 1812
d. 1843

△ Kanaung
b. 1819
killed 1866

○ Hlaing Princess

Ⓐ Pagan
b. 1811
king 1846
deposed 1853
d. 1881

△ 2 sons
executed
1845

△ 3 sons
executed
1850

Ⓐ Mindon
b. 1814
king 1853
d. 1878

○ Eldest daughter

Ⓐ Thibaw
b. 1859
king 1878–1885
d. 1916

1837–1852

○ female
△ male
Ⓐ king

*See British Museum, Or. 3470, Phayre
Collection for extensive genealogical
study

works and gradually took command of government business. Two *Myowuns*, Pathi Mg Saing Sahit and Mg Pain, were indicted for killing six thousand people, confiscating property, and promoting favorites. British observers soon noted a change in the government's attitude toward foreigners. The major British merchants in the capital, Hugh Spiers and Thomas Spears, were charged with the export of silver. They were beaten, confined for eight days without investigation, and fined Rs. 5,000. The court clamped down on illicit exports. Rangoon officials opened mail packets and reinstated higher port charges and more stringent rules on shipping. The movement of Burmese women was restricted.[85] The turnover in Rangoon Governors was rapid, and their varying policies brought them into conflict with a small but vocal European merchant and missionary population. To this group it appeared that the sole guiding principle in Burmese administration was to reward as many followers as possible with lucrative posts. Rangoon was an eyesore to profit-hungry freetraders and militant proselytizing Christians. Pagan Min was called the "cockfighting king," and several excesses, including gambling, drinking, bloodsports, and womanizing, were unwarrantedly attributed to him.

Pagan Min still had living siblings. Family strife had not yet exhausted itself. Pagan Min deprived Tarop Min of his fief and placed him under military arrest for sheltering some of the Prince of Prome's followers. In May 1850 Tarop escaped and during June attempted to raise a rebellion. He was recaptured and along with eighty-three kinsmen and followers was executed.[86] One final coup attempt was launched just prior to the war with the British. Although the Pakhan Prince had died of cholera in 1843 he was survived by three mature sons. In mid-1851 they plotted to depose Pagan Min. The conspiracy was suppressed, and thirty or forty people were executed.[87]

A final indicator of instability within the kingdom was ethnic unrest. During the 1840s several Shan and Karen chieftaincies attempted to break their allegiance with Burma and opt for British, Chinese, or Siamese suzerainty. In 1849 Burma had to resist Shan pretensions of expanding the area under Shan control at the expense of the Burmese.

Familial instability in the shape of continuous strife among several claimants for the throne and increasing monarchical debility in the form of deteriorating psychological well-being and the will to rule created and reinforced structural instability among the geopolitical components of the kingdom. Fairly rapid changes in monarchs and more frequent faction fights undermined control both at the center and on the periphery. During the decade following the First Anglo-Burmese War the Burmese court accommodated to the presence of the British Resident. Bagyidaw created Burney "the Wungyi of the English" and called him "my great, victorious, and noble son." The Burmese used the Resident to further Burmese ends and ignored many of the residents' requests.[88] Tharrawaddy succeeded in forcing the Resident out to the periphery and finally out of the kingdom. In so doing he may have furthered national pride by removing the offending symbol of humiliation, but Burma also lost a contact with the outside world and the possibility of a temporizing influence of direct contact between decision-making centers in the event of a diplomatic crisis. It necessarily placed the focus of Burmese-British contact on the periphery, on the frontier, an area that both Burmese and British found difficult to control. While Tharrawaddy's action did not necessarily make a future war inevitable, it would be more difficult to avoid. When in 1851 Burmese-European clashes on the periphery prodded British India to reassert claims for respect, security, free trade, and the honoring of the Yandabo treaty, the old Burmese order faced two crises. Monarchy and central control were in decline, and no avenues of communication existed between Burmese and British decision-making centers. The conflict of the Second Anglo-Burmese War was presaged in the *Chronicle* by two omens:

> The Royal Stearsman reported that the Royal Boat roared
> [omen of war] for one nay [about twenty-five minutes] on
> the 12th day after the full moon of Tazaunmoung in 1213 B.E.
> On the same day from the southwest corner under the ceiling
> of the Golden Palace a light appeared towards the north for
> about one nay. On the same night light appeared from the south-
> west to northeast strong enough to cast a shadow. [Unusual
> meteorological phenomenon showing movement from direction
> of India and Rangoon towards Burma.] [89]

NOTES

1. Emanuel Sarkĭsyanz, "On the Changing Anglo-Saxon Image of Burma," *Asian Studies* 4 (1966): 226-35.

2. John Ebenezer Marks, *Forty Years in Burma* (New York: E. P. Dutton, 1917), p. 123.

3. Kyin Swi, "The Judicial System of the Kingdom of Burma" (Ph.D. diss., University of London, 1965), p. 1. On the distinction be-

tween benign local and evil national rulers see Manning Nash, *The Golden Road to Modernity* (London: John Wiley, 1965), p. 75; and Ma Mya Sein, *Administration of Burma* (Rangoon: Zabu Meitswe Pitaka Press, 1938), p. 73.

4. Everett E. Hagen, *The Economic Development of Burma* (Washington, D.C.: National Planning Association, 1956), p. 57; and Harold Fielding-Hall, *The Soul of a People* (London: Richard Bentley, 1899), p. 54.

5. Maung Htin Aung, *The Stricken Peacock: Anglo-Burmese Relations, 1742-1948* (The Hague: Martinus Nijhoff, 1965), p. 2; *Burmese Monk's Tales* (New York: Columbia University Press, 1966), p. 5; John Talboys Wheeler, "Memorandum on Political Status of Ava," 21 January 1871, IPP/760, p. 10; John F. Cady, *A History of Modern Burma* (Ithaca: Cornell University Press, 1958), p. 5; D. Mackenzie Brown, *The White Umbrella* (Berkeley and Los Angeles: University of California Press, 1953); Bhasker Anand Saletor, *Ancient Indian Political Thought and Institutions* (London: Asia Publishing House, 1962), pp. 322-7; Ma Thaung, "Burmese Kingship in Theory and Practice During the Reign of Mindon," *J.B.R.S.* 42 (1959): 171-85; and Yi Yi, "Life at the Burmese Court under the Konbaung Kings," ibid., 44 (1962): 85-129.

6. Ma Mya Sein, *Administration,* p. 45; Kyin Swi, "Judicial System," p. 80; and James George Scott [Shway Yoe], *The Burman, His Life and Notions* (New York: Norton, 1963 [orig. publ. 1882]), p. 406.

7. Charles Duroiselle, *Guide to the Mandalay Palace,* 2d ed. (Calcutta: Government of India Publications, 1931), p. 36; Robert Heine-Geldern, "Conceptions of State and Kingship in Southeast Asia," *Far Eastern Quarterly* 11 (1942): 15-30; and Yi Yi, "The Thrones of the Burmese Kings," *J.B.R.S.* 43 (1960): 97-123.

8. For inheritance procedures see Maung Maung, *Law and Custom in Burma and the Burmese Family* (The Hague: Martinus Nijhoff, 1963), p. 48.

9. Hagen, *Economic Development,* p. 12; C. J. F. S. Forbes, *British Burma and Its Peoples* (London: John Murray, 1878), p. 226; and "A Note by Major Phayre on the importation of court astrologers, who were Brahmins, from Benares," in Henry Yule, *A Narrative of the Mission sent by the Governor General of India to the Court of Ava in 1855* (Kuala Lumpur: Oxford University Press, 1969 [orig. publ. 1858]), p. 87.

10. U Tin (of Sagaing), *Kòn-baung-zet Maha-ya-zawin-daw-gyi* [Great royal chronicle of the Kòn-baung dynasty], 3 vols. (Mandalay: Hanthawaddy Pitakat Press, 1922-3) 3: 52.

11. Wheeler, "Memorandum," 21 January 1871, IPP/760, pp. 26-7.

12. David Richardson, *The Damathat or the Laws of Menoo* (Moulmein: American Baptist Mission Press, 1847), p. 43.

13. R. C. Temple, "The Order of Succession in the Alompra Dynasty of Burma," *Indian Antiquary* 21 (1892): 287-93; and Phayre Collection, British Library, Oriental Mss. 3470.

14. Burma has the world's second-highest infant mortality rate. Nash, *Golden Road*, p. 257.

15. E. C. V. Foucar in his romanticized histories, *They Reigned in Mandalay* (London: Dobson, 1946) and *Mandalay the Golden* (London: Dobson, 1963), states that the Alompra line had sloped foreheads and "kinks in their heads."

16. Hagen, *Economic Development*, p. 16.

17. Women's role in Burmese society exceeds child rearing and homemaking and in daily life was remarkably coordinate with men. They were equal except in religion, a woman having to be reborn a man before aspiring to Buddhahood. The queens Mai Nu and Supayalat exercised substantial control over their husbands, kings Bagyidaw (1819-37) and Thibaw (1878-85). See Nash, *Golden Road*, p. 52; Maung Maung, *Law and Custom*, pp. 45-53; and Mi Mi Khaing, *Burmese Family* (London: Longmans, 1946).

18. Ma Mya Sein, *Administration*, p. 27; and William Louis Barretto, *King Mindon* (Rangoon: Burma Union Press, 1935), pp. 24-6.

19. Burma approaches the "great tradition—little tradition" model of low-technology, traditional decentralized agricultural societies. See Robert Redfield, *The Little Community* (Chicago: University of Chicago Press, 1956).

20. Ma Mya Sein, *Administration*, p. 73. *Myothugyis* are often compared to justices of the peace in Tudor England. Tudor comparisons are common among Burmans educated in the English tradition. Bodawpaya's antimonastic activities are likened to those of Henry VIII.

21. Ibid., pp. 73, 182, and 205; Kyin Swi, "Judicial System," p. 70. For a list of chief officers in the Burmese province of Tavoy see Maingy to Fullerton, 22 October 1825, in *Selected Correspondence of Letters issued from and received in the Office of the Commissioner* (Rangoon: Government Printers, 1929), p. 33.

22. J. S. Furnivall, Ms. notes on Burmese regalia, in Cady, *History*, p. 26.

23. Peter Kunstadter, ed., *Southeast Asian Tribes, Minorities, and Nations* (Princeton: Princeton University Press, 1967); Frank M. Lebar, Gerald C. Hickey, and John K. Musgrave, *Ethnic Groups of Mainland Southeast Asia* (New Haven: Human Relations Area Files Press, 1964); Nigel J. Brailey, "A Re-Investigation of the Gwe of Eighteenth Century Burma," *Journal of*

Southeast Asian Studies 1 (1970): 33-47; and Victor B. Lieberman, "Ethnic Politics in Eighteenth-Century Burma," *Modern Asian Studies* 12 (1978): 455-82.

24. Maung Htin Aung, *Epistles Written on the Eve of the Anglo-Burmese War, 1824* (The Hague: Martinus Nijhoff, 1967), pp. 4-6.

25. Harry I. Marshall, *The Karens of Burma* (London: Longmans, 1945); F. K. Lehman, *The Structure of Chin Society* (Urbana: University of Illinois Press, 1963), pp. 29 and 82; and H. N. C. Stevenson, *The Economics of the Central Chin Tribes* (London: Gregg, 1969 [orig. publ. 1943]).

26. Marshall, *The Karens,* p. 30; and Janell Ann Nilsson, "The Administration of British Burma, 1852-1885" (Ph.D. diss., University of London, 1970), p. 34.

27. Maurice Collis, *Courts of the Shan Princes* (London: China Society, 1939); Ney Elias, *Introductory Sketch of the History of the Shans in Upper Burma and Western Yunnan* (Calcutta: Foreign Department Press, 1876); Sao Saimong Mangrai, *The Shan States and British Annexation* (Ithaca: Cornell University, Department of Asian Studies, 1965); Leslie Milne, *The Shans at Home* (London: Murray, 1911?); W. W. Cochrane, *The Shans* (Rangoon: Government Printers, 1915); and Edmund R. Leach, *Political Systems of Highland Burma* (London: Athlone Press, 1954).

28. Bagyidaw was the eldest son of the chief wife. His father had twenty-two wives. Bagyidaw had two full brothers and thirteen half-brothers. Only one half-brother was his elder (by three years). Several of the family members were imprisoned in 1819 when Bagyidaw ascended the throne.

29. Geoffrey E. Harvey, *History of Burma* (London: Cass, 1967 [orig. publ. 1925]), p. 301, describes him as "an imperialist of the most aggressive type."

30. For an unsympathetic treatment see Walter Sadgun Desai, "The Rebellion of Prince Tharrawaddy and the Deposition of Bagyidaw as King of Burma, 1837," *J. B. R. S.* 25 (1935): 109-20. For a more sympathetic account see R. R. Langham Carter, "Queen Me Nu and Her Family at Palangon," ibid., 19 (1929): 31-5.

31. For a description of the Salin Myosa see Kyin Swi, "Judicial System," p. 195; and Henry Gouger, *Personal Narrative of Two Years Imprisonment in Burmah, 1824-26* (London: Murray, 1860), p. 45.

32. C. M. Enriquez, "Bandula—A Burmese Soldier," *J.B.R.S.* 11 (1921): 158-62.

33. See G. T. Bayfield, "Historical Review of the Political Relations between the British Government in India. . . ," in R. Boileau Pemberton, *Report on the Eastern Frontier of British India* (Gauhati, Assam: Department of Historical and Antiquarian Studies, 1966 [orig. publ. 1835]), p. llxxii.

34. D. G. E. Hall, "Burney's Comments on the Court of Ava, 1832," *Bulletin of the School of Oriental and African Studies* 20 (1957): 308.

35. Henry Burney to Government of India, 3 March 1837, IPP/194/35, in Desai, *History of the British Residency in Burma, 1826-1840* (Rangoon: University of Rangoon, 1939), p. 235; *Maulmain Chronicle,* 15 April 1837; and *Konbaungzet,* 2: 496-7.

36. Burney to Government of India, 3 March 1837, Par. 4-7 and 10-11, IPP/194/35, in Desai, *Residency,* pp. 253-8; and *Konbaungzet,* 2: 501.

37. British Resident Col. Henry Burney's despatches to Calcutta are reprinted *in extenso* in Desai, *Residency.* He absolved himself of the charge of meddling in "The Burmese Revolution," *Colonial Magazine and Commercial Maritime Journal* 7 (1842): 71-80 and 176-84. See also D. G. E. Hall, *Henry Burney: A Political Biography* (London: Oxford University Press, 1974).

38. Instructions to Burney, 31 December 1829, BSPP/351, in Desai, *Residency,* p. 61.

39. Burney's Observations of 24 June 1830, Par. 141-2, BSPP/358; Burney to Government of India, 9 March 1831, BSPP/360; and Governor General's Secretary to Burney, 18 April 1831, BSPP/361, in Desai, *Residency,* pp. 90-1 and 190-2.

40. Burney, "Burmese Revolution"; and *Konbaungzet,* 2: 524.

41. Burney to Government of India, 3 March 1837, Par. 16, IPP/194/35, in Desai, *Residency,* p. 261.

42. Burney to Government of India, 24 May 1837, Par. 8-19, IPP/194/41, in ibid., 265-74.

43. Burney, "Burmese Revolution," p. 80.

44. Burney to Government of India, 12 July 1837, Par. 20, ISP/8, in Desai, *Residency,* p. 299.

45. *Maulmain Chronicle,* 2 December 1837.

46. Ibid., 24 June 1837; and Bayfield Journal, Par. 214, ISP/10, in Desai, *Residency,* p. 340.

47. *Maulmain Chronicle,* 9 December 1837; and C. M. Enriquez, "Capitals of the Alaung-paya Dynasty," *J.B.R.S.* 5 (1915): 117-28.

48. Burney to Government of India, 12 July 1837, Par. 9, ISP/8, in Desai, *Residency,* p. 284.

49. G. T. Bayfield Journal, in Bayfield to Government of India, 30 April 1838, Par. 196-9, ISP/10, in Desai, *Residency,* p. 335.

50. John Brown to Edmund Blundell, 31 May 1840, ISP/40; Brown to John R. Colvin, 10 December 1847, ISP/145; and Emanuel Sarkisyanz, "Messianic Folk-Buddhism as Ideology of Peasant Revolts in Nine-

teenth and Early Twentieth Century Burma," *Review of Religious Research* 10 (1968): 32-8.

51. Burney to Government of India, 24 May 1837, Par. 38, IPP/194/41, in Desai, *Residency*, pp. 286-7.

52. George Eden, Earl of Auckland to Henry Fane, most private, 25 August 1837, citing letter from Burney dated 12 July 1837, Auckland Papers, British Library, Add. Mss. 37691.

53. Richard Benson's Journal, 30 November 1837, Par. 1051, ISP/15, in Desai, *Residency,* p. 384.

54. Benson to Henry T. Prinsep, 16 November 1837, Prinsep Collection, India Office Library and Records, D662. (Underlined portions translated from Greek.)

55. Auckland to John C. Hobhouse, private, 9 December 1838, Broughton Papers, Add. Mss. 36473.

56. Prinsep to Benson, demi-official, n.d., Prinsep Collection, D662/C.

57. William C. McLeod to ?, extracts in Auckland to Hobhouse, private, 17 June 1838, Broughton Papers, Add. Mss. 36473.

58. McLeod to Prinsep, 2 May 1839, Prinsep Collection, D662/C; and *Maulmain Chronicle,* 22 May and 10 July 1839.

59. Auckland to Archibald Robertson, 16 June, Auckland to James C. Melville, 18 June, and Auckland to Naval Commander in Chief, 29 July 1839, Auckland Papers, Add. Mss. 37696.

60. Secret Committee to Governor General of India in Council, 11 October 1839, Ellenborough Papers, Public Record Office, 30/12/33, pt. 2/1, and Auckland to Hobhouse, 20 April 1840, Auckland Papers, Add. Mss. 37698.

61. Colvin to Robertson, private, 24 November 1838, Auckland Papers, Add. Mss. 37694.

62. Minute by Governor General, 13 June 1839, in ibid., 37695.

63. Colvin to Bayfield, private, 27 November, and Colvin to Blundell, private, 27 November 1837, in ibid., 37692.

64. Instructions to McLeod, 2 May 1839, and reference to Governor General's Minute of 15 January 1839, ISP/20, in Desai, *Residency,* p. 412.

65. McLeod to Benson, 10 December 1839, Prinsep Collection, D662/C; and *Maulmain Chronicle,* 18 and 26 December 1839.

66. Minute by Governor General, 30 July 1840, Auckland Papers, Add. Mss. 37700.

67. Gordon to Thomas Herbert Maddock, 5 July 1843, ISP/63: and Governor of Khumbot to Political Agent at Manipur, received 30 December 1841, IPF/196/33.

68. *Maulmain Chronicle,* 28 April 1841; May Flower Crisp to Maddock,

18 March 1841, ISP/57; and Yule, *Narrative of a Mission*, p. 228.

69. Brown to H. V. Bayley, 12 August 1840, ISP/43.

70. McLeod to Blundell, 6 September 1842, ISP/86; and George Broadfoot to Thomas R. Davidson, 23 July 1843, ISP/98.

71. Rangoon observers thought his dismissal stemmed from his occidental leanings. He received letters from an American scientific society and translated Burmese treatises into English. Brown to Government of India, 23 November 1844, ISP/113.

72. William Spiers to Frederick Currie, 12 April 1845, ISP/116; and Desai, *Residency*, pp. 275 and 329, on his military role in 1837.

73. She slipped out of the palace and saved herself. Statement by Gua Shway, annexed to Henry M. Durand to Currie, 28 April 1845, IPF/197/18; and see R. R. Langham Carter, "U Htaung Bo's Rebellion," *J.B.R.S.* 26 (1936): 33-4.

74. W. Spiers to Currie, 4 August 1845, IPF/197/25. Spiers, a Royal Navy Lieutenant on half pay, replaced his deceased cousin John Brown as postmaster.

75. W. Spiers to Currie, 25 August 1845, ISP/119.

76. Report by Captain Spiers, 7 September 1845, ibid. Spiers also offers the unlikely story that Tharrawaddy, tired of ruling, offered the throne back to Bagyidaw. See *Konbaungzet*, 3: 46-9.

77. W. Spiers to Currie, 16 September 1845, ISP/119.

78. W. Spiers to McLeod, 26 September, and Spiers to Currie, 30 September 1845, ISP/119; and *Konbaungzet*, 3: 47. Her daughter, the Hlaing Princess, was spared and became the chief wife of Prince Kanaung. Like her mother she was a writer of romantic poetry. Tragedy stalked her: her children and her husband were assassinated in the abortive coup of 1866.

79. W. Spiers to McLeod, 14 October 1845, ISP/119.

80. W. Spiers to Currie, 18 November 1845, ibid; *Konbaungzet*, 3: 49; and McCullock to G. A. Bushby, 7 November 1845, ISP/122.

81. W. Spiers to Durand, 25 October 1845, and Spiers to Currie, 9 December 1845, ISP/122. Spiers to Currie, 12 January and 23 March 1846, ISP/123.

82. *Konbaungzet*, 3: 50; and John Brown to Bushby, 16 November 1846, IPF/197/53.

83. U Tin (of Pagan), *Myanma Min Okchopon Sadan* [Administration of Burma under the Burmese kings], 5 vols. (Rangoon: Government Printers, 1931-33), 2: 25 and 75.

84. Niharranjan Ray, *An Introduction to the Study of Theravada Buddhism in Burma* (Calcutta: University of Calcutta Press, 1946),

pp. 243-4; W. Spiers to Currie, 10 October 1845, ISP/119; and John Brown to Bushby, 15 September 1846, ISP/126. In spite of his good works Pagan Min is held in low esteem by Burmans and fails to find a place in *Encyclopedia Birmanica*.

85. *Konbaungzet*, 3: 86-9; and Hugh Brown to P. Melville, 28 September 1849, IPF/198/57.

86. *Konbaungzet,* 3: 79-80.

87. Ibid., pp. 86-7; Charles M. Crisp to Grey, 1 July, Crisp to Archibald Bogle, 7 July 1851, IPF/199/41; and Crisp to Grey, 4 August 1851, IPF/199/43. The remaining three brothers, Mindon, Kanaung, and Hlaing, will be accounted for in Chapter 6.

88. Burney's Journal, 24 June and 15 December 1830, BSP 358 and 360, in Desai, *Residency,* pp. 86 and 172.

89. *Konbaungzet,* 3: 89.

2
THE TURBULENT
FRONTIER (1840-51)

The years between the withdrawal of the British Residency and the outbreak of the Second Anglo-Burmese War have been neglected by historians who assumed that since diplomatic contact between the centers had been broken all contact withered. However, this was hardly the case. The existence of a common frontier, mobile populations in search of material gain, and a European community in Rangoon constituted the basic elements of a "turbulent frontier."[1] This turbulence engaged Britons in a continuous debate among themselves. British policy creation, implementation, and enforcement occurred in widely spaced geographic locales and at different levels in the chain of command. The Secret Committee and the Court of Directors of the East India Company were situated in London, as was the Cabinet Minister with ultimate responsibility for Indian affairs, the President of the Board of Control. Calcutta was the seat of the Governor General and his Council. Moulmein was the British administrative center of Tenasserim. Free trade and the role of government in commerce led to a series of clashes between government interests and the public or mercantile interests. If Burmese topography hindered communications between the center and the periphery, messages in the British Empire before the introduction of the telegraph were limited to the speed of sail, steam, and camels over several thousand miles of oceanic and Middle East highways. In the mid-nineteenth century it might take as long as six months to receive a reply to an "urgent" question. Personalities in power, national ethos, and distance governed the intensity of expression of the various interests.

Britain's policy in Southeast Asia was cautious and guided by the principles of economy and security. Southeast Asian politics were confusing, fraught with traditional antipathies and ambitions. A persistent nineteenth-century East India Company policy in Southeast Asia was "minimal involvement." The Court of Directors in 1846 wanted nothing to do with Siam and referred the question of opening commercial relations with that country to the Foreign Office. In 1867 the Secretary of State for India was pleased to relinquish control of Singapore to the Colonial Office. William Pitt, Earl of Amherst, voiced a perennial concern when he noted that "even treaties [were] open to serious objections lest we have to resent a breech of treaty in the future" and incur China, the suzerain through a tributary system of most mainland polities, as a foe.[2]

Britain reacted rather than initiated. Policy was ad hoc. Britain reacted to Burmese expansion and went to war in 1824. London and Calcutta were guided by treaties that had been concluded with foreign nations to gain special privileges. But even the enforcement of these treaties was guided by the factor of economy. When it appeared the enforcement of the Treaty of Yandabo would be costly, the British Resident was withdrawn from Burma.

Despite a reluctant posture the British Indian Empire expanded into Burma and wider Southeast Asia. Britain had few aims at the outset of the first war except perhaps "to obtain an advantageous adjustment of the eastern boundary, and to preclude the recurrence of similar insults and aggressions in the future."[3] British forces were denied quick victory by Burmese troops, unfamiliar terrain, and monsoons. As costs soared policy was reformulated to include territorial expansion. By August 1825 the Secret Committee in London, on the advice of naval and local authorities, had decided to annex "a small part of Arakan and establish a naval station" there, thus securing a strategic position on the east coast and depriving France of it.[4] By the end of the war Britain had decided to annex the whole of Arakan. Tenasserim, comprising the eastern coast, was retained with intentions of giving it to Siam or selling it back to Burma. Pegu was temporarily held in lieu of the war indemnity payments. The Treaty of Yandabo provided for Rs. 10,000,000 in reparations. Upon payment of Rs. 2,500,000 the British army would

retire from Rangoon. There are several indications that the East India
Company may have wanted to annex Pegu as well, or create an independent Mon state there, rather than holding it for ransom, but for the fact
that the Treaty of Yandabo was signed before definite plans materialized.[5]
London and Calcutta initially viewed the annexed provinces as political
and economic white elephants.[6] They were sparsely populated and economically underdeveloped, and their future as part of the British Indian
Empire was in doubt. Should they be developed or retroceded? By late
1830 strategy outweighed economy in Arakan, where British influence
was to be maintained at all cost.[7] Arakan, impregnable from the interior,
commanded valuable control over the Bay of Bengal. Thereafter, Governor
General Lord William Cavendish Bentinck applied himself personally to
making Arakan economically useful and viable, as well as strategic. In-
tensive rice cultivation was the path to prosperity.

Tenasserim was not so easily turned to profit. Geographically isolated,
850 miles by sea from Calcutta, it did not have the obvious strategic
importance of Arakan, and its hinterland bordered on little-known and
unsettled peoples. It was unclear what to do with Tenasserim, and the
decision was delayed. Not clear, that is, except to one man, Edward Law,
Earl of Ellenborough, sometime President of the Board of Control (1828-
30, 1834-35, 1841, and 1858) and the only President to exert what little
muscle London had over dependencies eleven thousand miles away. Ellenborough's aim was to bring India as close to England and ministerial control as possible.[8] He advocated less involvement in the marching areas
between India, Burma, and China and wanted Tenasserim disgorged. Ellenborough directed Bentinck

> to take any favorable opportunity of opening a negotiation
> with the King of Ava for the retrocession of. . .provinces to the
> south of the Salween. . .ceded to us by the Treaty of Yandabo. . .
> calculated to bring us into an intimacy of relations with both
> states which can lead to no benefit.

Britain must not be drawn by her geographic position into a new system
of political relations. Tenasserim should be sold or exchanged for some
piece of strategic property, like the island of Negrais. In his eagerness
to be rid of Tenasserim, Ellenborough proposed giving it a false value
by demonstrating that Britain really meant to keep it. This actually

seemed to undermine Ellenborough's own position, not necessarily in
relation to Burma or Siam, but between the metropole and the men on
the spot. In 1829 he advised local officials on defense, "You will have
seen the prudence of appearing to prize what you wish to part with."
However, military entrenchment made local officials prize Tenasserim
more and not wish to part with it.[9]

Resident Burney was unsuccessful in obtaining any concession from
Burma in exchange for Tenasserim. Burma knew the East India Company
was losing money in administering the province and waited for better
terms. In March 1833, when Ellenborough was out of office, the Court
of Directors broke off negotiations and authorized the government of
India to retain the province permanently and to tolerate the recurring
losses.[10]

When Ellenborough returned to the Board of Control in 1841 he still
thought Tenasserim a dead loss. Tharrawaddy's recent visit to Rangoon
and the subsequent rumors of war spurred Ellenborough to broach once
more the subject of retrocession. He referred Governor General Auckland to his earlier despatches. But Ellenborough was caught up short by
the man he respected most in all the world, the Iron Duke, who wrote:
"I earnestly recommend to you not to hint the notion, which was a favour-
ite one of yours heretofore, that is, the retrocession of the Tenasserim
Provinces. Any power in Europe or America would consider the possession
of these provinces a colonial fortune."[11] Auckland looked at Ellenborough's 1828 and 1829 despatches and replied, "I should be sorry if you
retained the thoughts of its [Tenasserim] abandonment. It is growing in
importance, slowly perhaps, but certainly."[12] That was the end of Ellenborough's attempt to rearrange the eastern frontier.

Tenasserim was British for good or ill, and they seem to have made the
worst of a bad job. Early insecurity of tenure demoralized local officials
and "produced a feeling of indifference."[13] Tenasserim soon had a reputation as a bad appointment. Assignment to Burma could be laid to two
causes: either a man was being punished, or he had enemies in high places.
A late nineteenth-century civil servant wrote, "Men were sent to Burma for
their sins or for a term of years."[14] Burma became associated with low pay
and slow promotions. These generally unattractive conditions were blamed
for the poor quality of recruits and the frequent scandals, including embez-
zlement, private trading, and rape. It seemed that the moment a man was
promoted he requested a transfer.[15]

While the views of London and Calcutta were governed by notions of economy and strategy, local opinion was concerned with more immediate matters. Merchants saw Burma as a potentially lucrative free-trade area. Administrators looked on the Burmese across the border as savages who disturbed local tranquility and demanded to be taught a lesson. The missionaries saw fresh fields for conversion. Local relations during the 1840s focused on several problems: the actions of local British officials, which often produced new conflicts; low-level friction along the frontier; teak-hungry merchants complaining about Burmese restraints on trade; and antipathetic culture contact in Rangoon.

After the Residency's withdrawal, frontier contact with Burma was in the hands of the Tenasserim Commissioner. Calcutta found it as difficult to control its frontier agents as it did its diplomatic agents at the Burmese court. Tenasserim officials with wide experience in British India were, however, better able to keep the peace than eastern-coast (Singapore and Bay of Bengal) career men, who often intensified conflict. It is significant that of the five Tenasserim commissioners, 1834-52, the three with India-wide and Great Game (Northwest-Frontier, Russia watchers) experience are cited in the *Dictionary of National Biography,* while the two locally recruited officials, alarmists to a man, are not mentioned. To the well-placed professionals Henry M. Durand and John R. Colvin, who had been secretaries to Governor Generals Ellenborough and Auckland, Burma was seen as a temporary assignment and not part of the Great Game. The old Burma hands, however, had vested interests, were parochial in outlook, and unwilling to subordinate their hostility toward Burma to larger Indian issues. They tried to formulate policy independently of Calcutta. A Moulmein military officer summed up the problem: "To us, it is a near and an only object of interest, and of thought; to you, a *remote* one among many other important objects demanding your attention."[16]

When McLeod withdrew the Residency from Rangoon in 1840, he proposed two future lines of policy: continued contact with the Burmese court through the reestablishment of the Residency, or the termination of political contact with consequent uncertainty bordering on hostility.[17] The Government of India accepted neither of these proposals. They wanted little or nothing to do with Burma and reasoned that forbearance would result in tranquility, not hostility. But forbearance was not always applied by local officials. Tenasserim Commissioner Edmund A. Blundell was an eastern-coast career man. He craved an independent power base and frequently disregarded Calcutta's instructions. In 1838 Blundell wanted to align Siam and her tributaries in the northern Shan States with the British by presenting a treasured white elephant to the King of Siam. This he hoped would excite jealousy between Burma and Siam, and the latter would assist Britain in case of war. Blundell frequently asked Calcutta for preemptive permission to disperse imagined Burmese enemy forces.[18] On several occasions Blundell may have been attempting to start a war.

The Salween River marked the boundary between Burma and Tenasserim. There were islands in the Salween whose ownership was disputed. In March 1840 Blundell claimed several islands, about thirty to thirty-five miles from Moulmein, as British. His intention was to raise more revenues and to eliminate dacoit "havens." He invoked an order of sovereignty he purported to have seen several years earlier. The Burmese retaliated by setting up landmarks. Blundell removed the landmarks. Auckland was furious with Blundell, whose "trifling acts of indiscretion" could lead the British Indian Empire to war.[19] Regardless of the British claim "the time assuredly was not propitious for disturbing the actual state of possession and even had circumstances" been right, Calcutta should have been referred to first. Blundell was directed to use "prudence and circumspection. . .to allay the irritation he had. . .excited." Blundell frequently took action and spent money without authorization, for which he was admonished several times.[20]

Blundell sent a continuous stream of inflammatory reports to Calcutta. These reports were received with more than a grain of salt. The following reply was characteristic: the Governor General "would willingly hope that these reports, like the many which have preceded, will like subsequent accounts, be proved to have been exaggerated."[21] Blundell was repeatedly ordered to stop sending missives of complaint and requests for extradition to the Burmese authorities, as these letters were calculated to aggravate rather than ameliorate relations.[22] Auckland, who was luckless in choosing his agents in Afghanistan, had almost as dismal an experience in Burma. He left a personal assessment of Blundell:

> I have but little confidence in Mr. Blundell's discretion. . .
> and should be disposed to give him reinforcement and
> equipment but not power to act without reference except

in extreme cases. He seems to be too impatient for war, and would take no measure of reason or other considerations so that he can but have war.[23]

King Tharrawaddy's 1841 visit to Rangoon inflamed Moulmein opinion. Officials found it hard to accept that the visit had no aggressive aims. Reports from Rangoon and Amarapura fanned suspicions. Cipher messages reported that seventy thousand men were being mustered to regain the lost provinces. Even alarmist Blundell found this hard to believe, though he felt that such a large force under the command of Tharrawaddy's sons would inevitably encroach on British territory and cause disturbances. Blundell repeated his interminable requests for power to take preventive and preemptive action if the Burmese were hostile.[24] Governor General Auckland absorbed the Moulmein reports. First he felt that the King would "at least like to bluster and feel his ground."[25] Auckland was then swept up by the alarmist military commander at Moulmein who thought war was "inevitable." Auckland did not think that war could be avoided.[26] While he had wanted to leave the Burmese to their own customs, he could not understand Tharrawaddy, whose "intentions are not the same for twenty-four consecutive hours."[27] Auckland sanctioned the use of troops where Burmese intentions were hostile without a shadow of a doubt. Temporary reinforcements were sent, and Auckland wrote the local commander, "I would have you. . .bear in mind that the large force sent is for the purpose of *protection, and rather to maintain peace than to make war.*"[28] The Burmese took no offensive action in the four months the King was at Rangoon. Slowly Blundell concluded that the King was there to try British patience and to cause "expense and annoyance."[29] If this was Tharrawaddy's aim, he succeeded.

The Anglo-Burmese frontier was over one thousand miles long. But conflict only arose in the vicinity of Moulmein and Rangoon. It seemed to Calcutta that Burma had a window for war in the south and one for peace in the northeast. Local British agents on the northeast frontier exchanged friendly visits and cooperated with Burmese officials in quelling tribal incursions and exchanging troop-movement information. Disturbances, if any, were caused by hill tribes, who recognized neither British nor Burmese suzerainty. It was through this frontier that Tharrawaddy sent messengers to get medical supplies from the British.[30]

Burma's most prized natural resource was teak timber. It was in demand by the British navy and by merchantmen. Moulmein and Rangoon teak merchants constituted a strong interest, closely connected to the large Calcutta commercial houses, with some influence in government circles.[31] As early as 1837 greed and unscrupulous practices had brought "sad havoc" in the form of neglected forests.[32] Teak was felled and from May to July floated down the Salween River to the sea. At narrow confluences the river current washed logs up on the Burmese shore. The British merchants had to pay salvage to retrieve the logs. As early as 1834 a chain had been strung across the river, about seventy-five to eighty miles upriver from Moulmein, to prevent timber drifting to the Burmese side.[33] The chain or rope was attached to the Burmese shore. In 1842 the Burmese objected to this practice and cut the rope. Blundell insisted that it be reattached and rattled his saber. Calcutta was unsure as to the legality of attaching a chain to the Burmese bank.[34] Blundell argued that the chain had been attached for eight years without Burmese objection and that upward of Rs. 200,000 were involved for the timber people. The merchants petitioned Blundell for stern measures. Blundell did the merchants' bidding and sent a guard under McLeod to ensure that the Burmese did not cut the rope.[35] McLeod had Blundell's authority to retaliate if the Burmese used violence. McLeod obeyed, though he felt the territory involved was "indubitably. . .Burmese [and the chain] was vulnerable and impolitic" and the merchants' claim to "innocent and temporary use of the river to promote interests of the province were irrelevant." Blundell would have liked to have burned down Martaban town, as had been done in 1829, as an object lesson.[36]

Lord Ellenborough replaced Auckland as Governor General in 1842. Auckland had given his subordinates their heads. When they went beyond judicious bounds their knuckles were lightly rapped. Lord Ellenborough, however, felt keenly that government and taxpayers should not take a loss in administering a forlorn possession so that a few well-placed speculators and adventurers could make profits. Ellenborough was determined to rout out officials who disobeyed orders, caused frontier friction, and participated in trade in contravention of the 1833 Company charter.[37] Ellenborough carefully handpicked his frontier agents. Blundell was forced to take the leave due him despite protestations, acrimonious correspondence, and his "mortification." Ellenborough wanted a military man at Moul-

mein and assured Blundell this was meant as no reflection on him.[38]
The man for the job was Major George Broadfoot, the hero of Jellahabad,
a military man to the core. Like Ellenborough, Broadfoot advocated efficient, disinterested government and acted as a troubleshooter. Broadfoot had been stationed in Moulmein in the late 1830s, when he had
called the civilian officials "a set of jobbing intriguers."[39] On taking the
appointment he wrote:

> I look with much anxiety to taking it up. My experience
> there leads me to think there is much reform needed.
>
> Lord Ellenborough has been kind to me beyond measure—
> my only fear is that one [of] these days he will find he
> has overrated me.[40]

When Ellenborough learned from Broadfoot the full gravity of Blundell's
actions concerning the chain, he removed Blundell with a vengeance, can-
celling his appointment as Governor of the Straits Settlements. Ellenborough had been kept in the dark on issues that might have led to war.
Britain was in the wrong, and it all arose "out of encouragement given to
low mercantile speculation by a commissioner in the hands of merchants
and their press."[41] Ellenborough hoped the stern action against Blundell
would serve as an example to other would-be transgressors. Ellenborough's
relations with London were the roughest of any Governor General, and he
thought that his suppression of Blundell would give him "*the coup de
grace*. . .with the court."[42]

Broadfoot brought to Tenasserim a genius for understanding the Burmese and alienating the merchants. Calcutta gave vague and contradictory
instructions. He was to have as little intercourse with the Burmese authorities as possible. Limited hostility and turning the other cheek were
preferable to a collision. But if an amicable settlement appeared possible
he should proceed accordingly.[43] Broadfoot reasoned that "much of our
embarrassment with the Burmese [was due] to our not having sufficiently remembered that Ava is recognized by Treaty as an independent power,
treating with India as an equal and not as a subordinate with a paramount
state." The Burmese resented being treated as inferiors. Tharrawaddy was
an intelligent, determined, patriotic barbarian.[44] Broadfoot correctly predicted that "while the present king live[s] we can rely on hostility," but
war may be avoided; "after that it is doubtful."[45]

The vagaries of Burmese and English translation caused misunderstanding. Britain had considered war over the breach of the Yandabo treaty. The English version allowed for a Resident, but the Burmese version merely permitted "an officer" with some armed men from each power to live and build a house at the capital of the other.[46] Government translators purposely mistranslated documents to place the Burmese officials in an unfavorable light, and Broadfoot discharged translator Cotton, who had been a translator at the Ava Residency as early as 1830, for such an offense.[47]

Broadfoot saw no reason to place all the blame on Burma for the turbulent frontier; "on the contrary, the Burmese side was more thriving and industrious with an active though rude police." There were probably more robbers on the British side. British problems were caused by an ineffective policy and a ramshackle flotilla unable to prevent crime and inadequate to suppress it. Blundell had broken up the flotilla shortly before being relieved in what must have been a combination of spite and false economy.[48]

The great cause of misunderstanding and frontier conflict was the local British community itself. Moulmein had a reputation as an assembly point for motley groups from all parts of Asia. Broadfoot found that merchants never went into the interior. They sat in Moulmein counting profits. The cheaper the method for obtaining the teak the better.[49] "The forest and timber departments [were]. . .sinks of abuse. . .and scandalous waste."[50] Sharp practices in private enterprise and government abounded, impeding good relations and hindering local administration. Some British merchants had arrangements with Martaban officials to obtain stolen teak from competitors. British officers dealt in private trade in direct violation of the East India Company charter of 1833. Merchants and officials would plot against the rights of the Burmese. Broadfoot was shocked at the peculation of his assistants J. A. Corbin, J. de la Condamine, and the almost illiterate W. N. Butcher. The local press, the *Maulmain Chronicle*, thrived on rumor and scandal, pitting Britisher against Burman, merchant against bureaucracy. Broadfoot mused that "it is unfortunate not to have officers of judgment and standing up the Salween."[51]

Broadfoot thought the timber chain was cut by thieves or even the timbermen themselves.[52] By the time Broadfoot arrived in Moulmein the chain question, in which the British were admittedly in the wrong, had been joined by a substantiated case of Burmese theft of British timber. In addition the Burmese claimed a 10 percent "duty" for its return. Though no friend of the timber merchants, Broadfoot reveled in being the injured party and would not brook the Burmese impositions. He issued a notification declaring it a crime for a British subject to pay the duty.[53] There was a skirmish in which British forces burned a village. Broadfoot sent his assistant David Richardson to the Martaban Myowun to declare that Martaban officials had exceeded their authority in charging duty.[54] The Myowun was "particularly averse to referring the question to Ava." After negotiations certain recalcitrant headmen were removed, and "salvage fees" replaced "duty."[55] Calcutta's congratulations for smoothing relations were quickly forthcoming.[56]

Broadfoot wanted to eliminate frontier confusion. The Salween was "an unfortunate boundary," as nomadic tribes respecting no international law inhabited both sides and their allegiance was to Burma and not Moulmein. Broadfoot hoped that claims to contested islands could be cleared up by a joint Burmese-British survey commission. Calcutta approved of the plan in principle but did not authorize it. There was "no objection to inviting the Court of Ava to send a person to make a settlement provided no one be sent to Ava for the purpose."[57]

Broadfoot fulfilled Ellenborough's expectations and then was transferred to the northwest frontier. He was succeeded by Henry Marion Durand, who was even more an Ellenborough man than Broadfoot, having served as the Governor General's private secretary.[58] When the Court of Directors removed Ellenborough, the outgoing maverick Governor General prophesied that there would be little or no change in policy under his successor, Sir Henry Hardinge, his close friend of thirty years. Nonetheless, with Ellenborough now in London his remaining appointees became the focus of a continuing anti-Ellenborough campaign.

Teak continued to be a fertile source of contention both within the British community and with the Burmese. Durand wrote, "Maulmain is a very troublesome place, the European part of the community incite[s] the mixed population to discontent whenever they have the opportunity," always with the view of bettering the European position. Broadfoot had been unsuccessful in stemming timber abuses. When Durand arrived he found the "most gross neglect and the most barefaced violation of the Forest Rules." The result was widespread deforestation among the most easily accessible teak stands.[59] In attempting to enforce the strict letter of the teak timber regulations Durand built his own political coffin.

Durand uncovered a flagrant case of merchants misrepresenting facts. He concluded that the Burmese had a strong legal claim to salvage. Two British officers aided a merchant to take timber wrongfully from the Burmese side.[60] Captain White was soon to leave the East India Company service and become an independent timber merchant in his own right. The other officer, Butcher, from his "letters" appears a barely literate, aggressive frontiersman. Moulmein merchants, Calcutta mercantile houses, and old political enemies combined to make Durand's commissionership a continuous struggle. He ultimately was removed from the post of Commissioner. During the timber transit season of 1847 the border flared up once more over timber. By this time Durand had been replaced by Commissioner Colvin, who prohibited the importation of logs in anything but rough state with clearly branded ownership markings.[61] Ownership of hewed logs could not be determined. Merchants continuously attempted to evade the timber regulations.

At mid-century two new developments occurred in the teak trade. By 1850 local teak forests had been exhausted, and timbermen were forced to go deeper into Siam and Burma.[62] Merchants attempted to get foreign teak to sea without paying British duties. The most ingenious plan was ex-Captain White's. White argued that a vessel leaving Martaban going to sea through the southern channel of the Salween River was not subject to British port regulations. Moulmein officials were horrified when the Advocate General in Calcutta decided that commercial and innocent traffic was not subject to Moulmein port regulations if it did not stop at the port and if the channel was natural.[63]

Dacoity, or brigandage, was a continuous problem. Many pointed an accusing finger at Burmese authorities across the river for harboring vandals. During the commissionerships of Broadfoot, Durand, and Colvin the problem was minimal. Broadfoot understood the Burmese official who wrote, "If you make an affair of what is not worthy of it, I have many of such little affairs."[64] Locally recruited commissioners Blundell and Archibald Bogle were not as adaptable and viewed Burma as a haven for robbers and stolen property. It is to Bogle's credit that he was aware and critical of the forward nature of his subordinates and the shoddy acts they perpetrated, which alienated Burmese officials. Nonetheless, Blundell and Bogle thought the solution was extradition and retributory raids rather than a more efficient police force. Local officials and subordinates had to be watched closely lest they create new problems.[65]

In March 1851 Moulmein opinion was raised to a fever pitch against the Burmese because of a particularly audacious robbery committed against a Mohammedan merchant, Aga Baker. A five-man committee of local merchants, which included May Flower Crisp, called a public meeting and unanimously resolved to press for energetic action, troop reinforcements, and cordoning off Martaban. Crisp had arrived on the eastern coast during the First Anglo-Burmese war. They accused the Martaban officials of sheltering criminals. Commissioner Bogle wrote the Burmese for information. Martaban replied, "If robberies on east side—blame it on the west and vice versa."[66] Bogle supported the merchants' resolutions and sought permission to "pursue them [the culprits] as pirates and enemies of all nations, where ever they may be."[67] To Bogle it was "as clear as [the] sun at noon day that the dacoity by which the inhabitants of Maulmain and its vicinity are harrassed and injured are concocted and set afoot on the Burmese side and that the perpetrators are harboured and protected by the authorities there."[68]

Calcutta, however, failed to see the sun in the sky and thought that Bogle had gone well beyond his evidence.[69] Bogle countered, pointing to the anarchy that reigned on the Burmese side: "It is well known that Burmese officials have no political authority and that they always try to evade the exercise of a discretionary power where there is any responsibility, unless indeed benefit to themselves is obvious and immediate." Bogle would have his argument or burst. He forwarded to Calcutta a 113-paragraph summation of numerous Burmese-inspired dacoity in the years 1846-51. Bogle concluded: "I close this prolix review in the certainty that I have now adduced sufficient proof of the nefarious conduct of the Burmese up to a recent period, and of the very ample grounds which exist for any opinions I have recorded unfavorable to them."[70]

Calcutta, though not convinced by Bogle of Burmese complicity, did think "that sufficient had been shown to justify a remonstrance with the Burmese government against the general conduct of the subordinate officers stationed at Martaban."[71] To Bogle's chagrin, British intervention in Burma would hinge on Rangoon's rather than Moulmein's problems.

Rangoon was the focal point of Anglo-Burmese aspirations and antagonism. Before the first war Rangoon was the major Burmese coastal town, with a population of about ten thousand, and after the war it stabilized at around nine thousand. By the late 1830s Moulmein surpassed Rangoon as a trading center and had a population of about twenty-nine thousand.[72]

Despite decline Rangoon was still the major Burmese seaport and contact point with the outside world. British, American, and Chinese vessels stopped regularly to obtain teakwood, catechu (for tanning and dyeing), sticklac (insect-derived shellac), beeswax, elephants' teeth, raw cotton, orpiment (yellow arsenic), gold, silver, rubies, and horses. Rangoon was one of the most "profitable" appointments the Burmese monarch could bestow. Ministers were not paid salaries, and they were expected to make their living from local revenues. Rangoon was also a difficult town to administer. Important people were posted there, separated from the court; they lost influence and were replaced. The Governor of Rangoon and the southern province of Hanthawaddy were changed no less than six times during the 1840s. In addition to Burmese the Rangoon community contained a significant number of Karens, Taliens, and a handful of Indian and European traders. Because of its distance from the Burmese center greater powers were accorded the Governor. Complaints of extortion and oppression were common, and there was little recourse to higher authority.[73]

The Europeans at Rangoon were not all the outcasts of Europe, but they were without the restraints of European society, and they frequently compromised their sense of equity for the sake of greater profits. They were accorded little respect by the Burmese administration. The merchant-post-master-newswriter appointed in 1840 was acutely aware of his position: "Burmese authorities do not recognize me as an officer of the British Government, and as it were by sufferance alone permit me to receive and despatch letters."[74] The merchants trafficked in piece goods, local products, and teak, which fostered a thriving shipbuilding industry. The most lucrative trade was the illicit export of bullion.[75]

Throughout the 1840s the European community in Rangoon worked to bring Rangoon into the orbit of the British Indian Empire. The most common cry was "Send a gunboat, show the flag," followed by requests for the enforcement of the Yandabo treaty, the establishment of a consul, and annexation. The merchants claimed that the Burmese were arbitrary and that monopolistic practices were pernicious to free trade. If trade were free it would be more profitable. Calcutta applied a stringent policy of economy, restraint, and noninterference toward Rangoon. It was preferable to have no communication than to hazard a representative at the Burmese court.[76] To a complaint of a Rangoon merchant shortly after the Residency was withdrawn from Rangoon, Calcutta replied with what was to be firm policy until 1850:

"Rangoon, The Principal Port of the Birman Empire," *Illustrated London News*, 6 December 1845.

A private trader who thus ventures into an unfriendly port,
for his own profit, does so at his own risk, and cannot claim
the intervention of his Government as a matter of right. His
Honor in Council therefore sees no necessity for. . .making the
present complaint the subject of discussion with the viceroy
or any other official personage at Rangoon.[77]

Burma's restrictive or "mercantilistic" trade policy was sanctioned by
a commercial treaty with the British and had deep roots in the tradition-
bound idea of national self-sufficiency. John Crawfurd had gone to Ava
in 1826 to negotiate a commercial treaty. After much haggling Crawfurd
conceded the Burmese right to prohibit the export of bullion. Ships
were searched, mail packets opened, and ships' captains and merchants
jailed if bullion was found. Burmese authorities often received their
information on illicit exports from competing English merchants. A
certain McCalder and, until his death in the early 1840s, a man called
Staig, were the *bêtes noires* of the English merchant community in Rangoon as the two Englishmen acted as commercial spies for the Burmese.
Law enforcement was difficult as the merchants were tricky. With the
removal of the pro-British Governor in late 1847 amid controversy
over enforcement of the bullion-export prohibition the Burmese redoubled
their efforts to stem the flow. The movement of Burmese women, especially those married to Europeans, was restricted.[78] Merchants' complaints
intensified. Commissioner Colvin wrote in reply:

> The situation of British traders in the Burmese territory is,
> undoubtedly, harassing and precarious, but they have engaged,
> or persevered, in their speculations, after intercourse be-
> tween their own and the Burmese Government by means of
> political or other official agents, has virtually, for a long
> period altogether ceased; and no protection could be given
> to them in their dealings regarding the export of silver.

Calcutta was pleased to hear that local officials were exercising restraint.[79]
     The most vociferous special pleader was merchant-captain May Flower
Crisp. When Tharrawaddy visited Rangoon in 1841 his building program
created an insatiable need for teak, to the detriment of the local traders.
Using the royal prerogative the King monopolized the market. Crisp complained that this was an infraction of the Treaty of Yandabo and the com-

mercial treaty. However, there was nothing in the treaty or convention that prohibited traditional royal monopolies.[80] Calcutta replied: "With respect to the injury sustained by members from the establishment of a timber monopoly at Rangoon the Governor General in Council is not of the opinion that under existing circumstances that measure will demand any special notice from the British Government."

The monopoly was lifted in early 1844 on the order of the Prince of Prome and the Mekkara Prince, who declared no further deductions for royal benefit were to be taken from timber sold and bought in Rangoon.[81] Article 2 of the 1826 commercial convention provided a duty on ships whose main decks were over a certain width. Crisp, an experienced ship designer and self-proclaimed naval expert and publicist, circumvented this duty by a strange design of narrow deck and wide hull. Crisp was arrested and deported several times by the Burmese for exporting bullion, being rowdy, insulting local Rangoon officials, and slandering the Burmese monarch in a letter to the editor in the *Calcutta Star*, 23 December 1842. Broadfoot, from across the bay, noted his punishment was less than for a similar offense committed in Europe.[82] Crisp continued his diatribe for free trade ad nauseam from Moulmein.

The merchants were irrepressible. The more Calcutta replied that their complaints "call[ed] for no interference on the part of this government" the more the merchants pressed their requests. In 1845 they petitioned the Calcutta Chamber of Commerce, requesting a Consul. Government quickly vetoed this idea and severely rebuked the merchants when this notion was again broached later.[83] The merchants were at their wits' end. They had bided their time in hopes of change, but the only thing that changed was the Rangoon Governor, who, the merchants claimed, became more oppressive. H. Brown, postmaster and merchant, tried special pleading to the Scots in Calcutta, especially the newly appointed Governor General, Lord Dalhousie:

> If trade with this country is considered of any importance
> [for] it imports a large quantity of British goods especially
> and worthy of the attention and consideration of his Lord-
> ship the right honorable Governor General in Council I would
> most humbly and respectfully suggest that some protection
> be given to the British merchants if they cannot be granted
> the trade must in great measure cease, and were it to do so I
> believe that it would be most seriously felt in Calcutta and
> especially by those houses of business connected with mer-
> chants in Glasgow.[84]

Shortly thereafter Brown decided to resign. The Rs. 150 per month as
newswriter were insufficient enticement to remain. Calcutta then considered canceling the position. However, the Calcutta postmaster reported the mail volume large enough to warrant its continuance. In
1848 Calcutta sent 2,134 and received 658 letters from Rangoon.[85]
The job went to Hugh Spiers, who died the following year, in July 1850.
Charles M. Crisp, son of the irascible May Flower Crisp, volunteered his
services. The appointment was confirmed in September 1850.[86]

On the evening of 28 December 1850 Rangoon was devastated by fire,
which destroyed three-fourths of the city. Some fifteen hundred to two
thousand buildings burned, including brick and government buildings,
and eight ships were destroyed. The fire destroyed possessions and put
many out of work. One British official linked the increased brigandage
around Moulmein, instanced by the Aga Baker case, to the Rangoon
fire. The robbers were desperate people out of work. The rebuilding of
the devastated city demanded increased revenues. The Governor of Rangoon, an ex-customs collector, revived the ancient tide tax for shoreline
used to repair large boats.[87] The Rangoon merchants appealed to Moulmein, claiming this threatened to further disrupt an already injured trade.
Commissioner Bogle requested British intervention in their behalf.

> It is essential to the prosperity of the Tenasserim Provinces
> and particularly of the town of Maulmain that the long
> established intercourse with Rangoon should be maintained
> and extended. . . .It is not necessary that I should allude to
> the measures which might be adopted. . . [to give the British
> merchants in Rangoon the rights which they are] entitled to
> in most other parts of the world.[88]

Despite the fact that the injured party, Captain Potter, claimed to have
friends on the Calcutta Chamber of Commerce close to the Governor
General, the President in Council declared that he "sees no occasion for
the interference of the British Government in the matter."[89]

Within a few months of rejecting Potter's and Bogle's requests the
Government of India took serious notice of two confrontations between
merchant-captains and Rangoon officials. They were only distinguished
from earlier conflicts by the magnitude of the alleged crime and the de-
fendants' use of Palmerstonian rhetoric. The first case involved ship

captain Robert Sheppard, a "quiet, steady, and highly respectable person."[90] He entered Burmese waters in the *Monarch* downstream from Rangoon on 2 June 1851, employing a pilot to guide him past the shoals. The next day the ship struck a shoal, and "the pilot through fear or shame jumped overboard." When Sheppard finally arrived in Rangoon, a Chittagonian, purporting to be the pilot's brother, told the Rangoon officials that Sheppard had thrown the pilot overboard. Sheppard was arrested. Although Sheppard, the ship's crew, and officers testified that the charges were false, Sheppard was fined Rs. 325. Moreover, Sheppard denied the Burmese right to try such cases: "Had your petitioner been guilty of the crime alleged, he would be amenable to the laws of his country and not to the Burmese, particularly as the pilot was a British subject, a native of Chittagong, and lately resident in Maulmain." Sheppard alleged a loss of Rs. 1,000 after bribes and lost business.[91] His agents, Creaton and Company, raised the claim to Rs. 5,000 and then to Rs. 10,000.[92]

The second complaint was that of Captain Harold Lewis of the barque *Champion,* a man of questionable reputation. Lewis arrived in Rangoon on 11 August 1851, and shortly thereafter his crew deserted and demanded their discharge wages. Rangoon merchants advised Lewis that it was easier to pay than resist on a point of law. A charge of murder was then laid against Lewis for the death of a seaman while at sea. The trial lasted several weeks. Lewis wrote the Rangoon Governor that he was going to complain to Calcutta. He denied the crime and also the Burmese right to try an English subject and claimed protection under Article 9 of the Treaty of Yanda bo: "I am an Englishman commanding a British vessel, and on board of that vessel one of the crew (a *British subject*) dies at sea; I am reported to have killed him. I can therefore *only* be tried by a *British* Court."[93]

This was a misapplication of the 1826 treaty, though in accord with the current, blustery English spirit. This enraged the Governor, and Lewis was imprisoned and placed in stocks. Lewis was later acquitted and deported after being "squeezed" for Rs. 200. Sheppard and Lewis complained to the government of India in the spirit of *Civis Romanus Sum* after Lord Palmerston's famous speech in defense of the rights of the Gibraltar-born (and therefore a British citizen) Portuguese Jew, Don Pacifico, who laid a claim of £80,000 damages against the Greek government. Palmerston sent a fleet in 1850 to reinforce this claim. Sheppard and Lewis demanded compensation. All Europeans in Rangoon hoped that a remonstrance would be forthcoming, followed by war.

The final expansionary agents on the frontier were the missionaries. Catholic missionaries had been in almost continuous residence around the Burmese capital for over one hundred years. The Catholics stayed clear of court politics and subordinated their evangelizing to education and natural history.[94] In 1813 Felix Carey of the American Baptist Missionary Society arrived in Burma. The Baptists' greatest success was in the conversion of the Karens, whose own cosmology seemed to anticipate a white deliverer with a holy book, and as an oppressed minority group looked for a countervailing force against the dominant Burmese Buddhists. The Baptists failed among the Burmese Buddhists. They quit Burma proper in 1837 at the height of Tharrawaddy's anti-treaty campaign and dispersed to Tenasserim and Arakan or returned to America. The American Baptists were at low ebb during the 1840s. The death of Tharrawaddy was welcomed by the expelled missionaries and spurred them on to try anew in Burma.[95]

Adonirum Judson and Eugenio Kincaid carried the thrust of the revitalized good word. Neither was a stranger to Burma. Judson first arrived in Burma in 1813 in the train of Felix Carey. He spent two years in the Ava prisoner-of-war camp during the first war. Resident Richard Benson wrote of him: "This gentleman avows himself predisposed for war as the best, if not the only means of eventually introducing the humanising influences of the Christian religion."[96] In January 1847 Judson and his third wife arrived in Rangoon. His first impressions were favorable. Judson had known the Governor for twenty years and was received on friendly terms.[97] The Governor would not permit proselytizing but hoped the missionaries would open a church and minister to the spiritual needs of the local European community. Judson interpreted this as a reflection of tolerance.[98] However, Judson quickly developed the familiar, jaundiced view of Burmese officialdom. He wrote home that Rangoon was "discouraging. . . . The present administration of government, though rather more friendly to foreigners, is more rigidly intolerant than that of the late King Tharrawaddy."[99] The Vice-Governor was "the most ferocious, blood-thirsty monster I have ever known in Burma. It is said that his house and court yard resound, day and night with the screams of people under torture." "Jesus Christ's religion," as the Burmese called Christianity, was a prohibited import. Burmans attending services might be arrested.[100]

In September 1847 a new Governor arrived. He, too, was a firm proponent of the old religion and reflected the anti-European policy current

at Amarapura. Judson moved to Moulmein and planned a trip to
Amarapura to plead for religious toleration.[101] Judson died in 1850, and
the task of establishing the mission in Rangoon and planning the trip to
Amarapura was passed to Eugenio Kincaid. Kincaid had left Ava hur-
riedly in 1837 and harbored the idea that "the soon[er] war begins, the
sooner Burmah will be saved."[102] Kincaid returned to Rangoon in early
March 1851 and observed that the city was a burned-out hulk and that
"several foreigners have been imprisoned during the last six months on
the most frivolous pretences, and money extorted from them."[103] Despite
this, Kincaid and his brother-in-law, Dr. J. Dawson, opened a hospital and
treated patients. Kincaid was permitted to preach, though local authorities
discouraged Burmans from attending.[104] Plans were proceeding for a trip
to the capital. The Governor's anti-European stance was tempered by
court orders issued in early May granting the missionaries special protection and ordering that the Karen converts not be molested.[105] The
Burmese Governor used missionary Kincaid as a mediator, translator,
and adviser in the trial of Lewis. In early November 1851 Kincaid fell
out with the Governor over the conversion question. "There is one thing
[the Governor] did not like about our religion," wrote Kincaid. "It
aimed to destroy any other and this was uncharitable. . . [and] its
great object."[106] When a shipment of printed conversion tracts arrived
they were closely counted and bonded at the customs house. Kincaid
was allowed to take away the bound volumes but not the tracts. Kincaid was furious and swore that he would call on world opinion to bring
wisdom to "this little, dark, ignorant spot called Burmah."[107]

For more than ten years Calcutta had managed to keep alarmist local
officials and truculent merchants at bay. Burma had been virtually ignored by Calcutta and was almost unheard of in London. While the
forces for conciliation between Britain and Burma were nil, peace was
maintained by the aloofness of power and the weakness of all parties
directly involved. However, by mid-1851 several interests were conspiring
simultaneously but separately to capture the notice of the Government
of India and revise Calcutta's Burma policy. Toward the close of the
1840s Calcutta may have already been reevaluating her eastern-frontier
policy. The Medical Department recommended occupying some Burmese
islands as sanitariums.[108] Interest was slowly reviving in Calcutta in the
overland trade with China. McLeod's request to go to the Shan States
in 1842 had been refused. After an eleven-year lull Dalhousie in 1850

sanctioned Rs. 5,000 for an unofficial expedition to Burmese tributary Shan States to investigate caravans coming to Moulmein.[109] Despite these minor hints of Calcutta's changing attitude the impetus for a change in British India's Burma policy was clearly generated on the frontier. Officials aroused by increased border unrest, teak merchants seeking new fields in Moulmein, militant missionaries, and desperate, profit-hungry traders in Rangoon were yearning to expand British control and therefore the pale of their own operations. Imperial expansion would mean law and order on the frontier, control of British merchants who had evaded legitimate British imposts, free scope for proselytizing, and the expansion of the free-trade and natural resources market.

NOTES

1. See John S. Galbraith, "The 'Turbulent Frontier' as a Factor in British Expansion," *Comparative Studies in Society and History* 2 (1960): 150-68.
2. Barbara J. Stewart, "Administrative Beginnings in British Burma, 1826-1843" (Ph.D. diss., University of London, 1931), p. 121.
3. Proclamation by the Right Honorable Governor General in Council, 5 March 1824, in Geoffrey E. Harvey, "Burmese and English Despatches on the Eve of the First Anglo-Burmese War, 1824-26," *J.B.R.S.* 17 (1923): 109-28; and Laurence Kitzan, "Lord Amherst and the Declaration of War on Burma, 1824," *Journal of Asian History* 9 (1975): 101-27.
4. Secret Committee to Governor General in Council, 3 August 1825, Home Miscellaneous Series/680, in Stewart, "Administrative Beginnings," p. 30; and Gerald S. Graham, *Great Britain in the Indian Ocean* (Oxford: Clarendon Press, 1967), p. 359.
5. Prinsep to G. Hillier, 17 July 1838, Prinsep Collection, D662/D; Crawfurd to Commander in Chief, 12 May 1826, in Anil C. Banerjee, *The Eastern Frontier of British India, 1784-1826* (Calcutta: Mukherjee, 1964 [orig. publ. 1943)], p. 463; and Colesworthy Grant, *Rough Pencillings of a Rough Trip to Rangoon in 1846* (Calcutta: Thacker, 1853).
6. George D. Bearce, *British Attitudes Towards India, 1784-1858* (London: Oxford University Press, 1961), p. 50.
7. Minute by Bentinck, 30 December 1830, in Stewart, "Administrative Beginnings," p. 148.
8. Albert H. Imlah, *Lord Ellenborough* (Cambridge: Harvard University Press, 1939), p. 23.
9. India Board to Governor General in Council, Draft of Secret Despatch, 23 December 1828 and 1 October 1829, Secret Letters Re-

ceived from Bengal and India, L/P & S/5/7.

10. Banerjee, *Eastern Frontier*, p. 475; and Walter S. Desai, *History of the British Residency in Burma, 1826-1840* (Rangoon: University of Rangoon, 1939), p. 141.

11. Ellenborough to Auckland, private and confidential, 19 September 1841, in Algernon Law, ed., *India under Ellenborough* (London: Murray, 1926), p. 15; and Duke of Wellington to Ellenborough, 29 December 1841, in Lord Colchester, *History of the Indian Administration of Lord Ellenborough* (London: Bentley, 1874), p. 200.

12. Auckland to Ellenborough, private, 20 November 1841, Auckland Papers, Add. Mss. 37706.

13. Maingy Report, 12 October 1825, and A. D. Maingy to George Swinton, 18 October 1827, in *Selected Correspondence of Letters issued from and Received in the Office of the Commissioner, Tenasserim Division* (Rangoon: Government Printers, 1929), pp. 4 and 67.

14. Herbert T. White, *A Civil Servant in Burma* (London: Edward Arnold, 1913), p. 7. In 1892, when offered the Chief Commissionership of British Burma, an official said "Thank you, but no thank you." H. M. Durand to Lord Lansdowne, 3 May 1892, Durand Collection, India Office Archives, D727/4. See also Ralph Braibanti, ed., *Asian Bureaucratic Systems Emergent from the British Imperial Tradition* (Durham, N.C.: Duke University Press, 1966), pp. 67-8.

15. Janell A. Nilsson, "The Administration of British Burma, 1852-1885" (Ph.D. diss., University of London, 1970), pp. 222-4; and Broadfoot to Cullin, 24 November 1839, Broadfoot Papers, Add. Mss. 40127.

16. Hillier to Prinsep, 14 September 1838, Prinsep Collection, D662/D.

17. McLeod to Maddock, 21 March 1840, ISP/35; and McLeod Journal, Par. 1379-1431, 1-7 January 1840, ISP/34.

18. Blundell to Prinsep, before December 1838 and 25 December 1838, Prinsep Collection, D662/D.

19. Blundell to Secretary of Government of India, 21 March 1840 ISP/40; and Auckland to Robertson, private, 1 May 1840, Auckland Papers, Add. Mss. 37699.

20. Henry W. Torrens to Blundell, 4 May 1840, ISP/40 and IPP/195/50.

21. Torrens to Blundell, 12 October 1840, ISP/45.

22. Maddock to Blundell, 6 December 1841, ISP/47.

23. Auckland to Prinsep, private, 29 January 1839, Auckland Papers, Add. Mss. 37695. See also Auckland to Robertson, private, 8 March 1840, Auckland Papers, Add. Mss. 37698, for comments on Bogle.

24. John Brown to H. V. Bailey, 11 September 1841, ISP/63; Blundell to Maddock, 13 July 1841, ISP/60, and 21 September 1841, ISP/63.

25. Auckland to George Lyall, private, 20 August 1841, Lyall Collec-

tion, India Office Library and Records, D552.

26. Halstead to ?, 24 September 1841, ISP/63; Auckland to William
G. K. Elphinstone, private, 3 October 1841; and Auckland to Commander
in Chief, private, 10 October 1841, Auckland Papers, Add. Mss. 37706.

27. Auckland to Ellenborough, 22 December 1841, Auckland Papers,
Add. Mss. 37707. A similar comment was made of Auckland's successor,
Lord Ellenborough: "As to the Governor General there is no depending
upon him for being for two councils together in the same mind relative
to the same subject." He was unmanageable, and "a soldier as a soldier is
the thing he worships." Julia Cameron to Broadfoot, 11 September 1843,
Broadfoot Papers, Add. Mss. 40127.

28. Maddock to Tenasserim Commissioner, 8 November 1841, ISP/65;
and Auckland to Logan, 7 December 1841, Auckland Papers, Add. Mss.
37703 (original emphasis).

29. Blundell to Maddock, 27 October 1841, ISP/65.

30. Colvin to Robertson, 30 July 1839, Auckland Papers, Add. Mss.
37696; Gordon to Bushby, 29 October 1842, IPP/196/22; Gordon to Maddock, 28 October 1841, ISP/45; McCullock to Bushby, 7 April 1846, ISP/
123; Gordon to Bushby, 18 March 1843, IPP/196/29; and Gordon to Davidson, 14 December 1843, IPF/196/42.

31. Auckland to Minto (Admiralty), 20 March 1841, Auckland Papers,
Add. Mss. 37703.

32. Pauline Nostitz, *Travels of Dr. and Mrs. Helfer in Syria, Mesopotamia, Burma and Other Lands*, 2 vols. (London: Bentley, 1878), 2: 92.

33. Stewart, "Administrative Beginnings," p. 323.

34. Blundell to Maddock, 8 March and Maddock to Blundell, 5 April
1842, ISP/78.

35. Blundell to Bushby, 30 January and 13 February 1843, and Merchants' Petition, ISP/94.

36. Blundell to McLeod, 11 February, McLeod to Blundell, 25 February,
and Blundell to Bushby, 8 April 1843, ISP/94; and Desai, *Residency*,
pp. 37-41.

37. Memo by Lord Ellenborough on Indian Foreign Policy, 27 April
1842, Ellenborough Papers, Public Record Office, 30/12/31/10.

38. Ellenborough to Blundell, 10 October 1842, Ellenborough Papers,
PRO 30/12/110; and IPP/196/26.

39. Broadfoot to Col. [Cullin?], 25 November 1839, Broadfoot Papers,
Add. Mss. 40127.

40. Broadfoot to Lock, 20 December 1842; and Broadfoot to Jessie,
21 January 1843, Broadfoot Papers, Add. Mss. 40127.

41. Ellenborough to Fitzgerald, 17 April 1843, Ellenborough Papers,

PRO 30/12/77; and Ellenborough to Duke of Wellington, 22 April 1843 in Law, ed., *India under Ellenborough*, p. 362.

42. Ellenborough to Duke of Wellington, 9 June 1843, Ellenborough Papers, PRO 30/12/28/12.

43. Davidson to Broadfoot, 7 and 24 April 1843, ISP/94.

44. Broadfoot to Davidson, 6 April 1843, ISP/94; and Broadfoot to Ellenborough, 19 July 1843, Ellenborough Papers, PRO 30/12/73.

45. Broadfoot to Davidson, 19 May 1843, ISP/96; and Broadfoot to Ellenborough, 23 July 1843, Ellenborough Papers, PRO 30/12/73.

46. Broadfoot to Davidson, 10 August 1843, ISP/98; and Desai, *Residency*, pp. 463-7, for side-by-side Burmese and English versions.

47. Broadfoot to Davidson, 19 May 1843, ISP/96.

48. Broadfoot to Davidson, 10 August 1843, ISP/98; Broadfoot to W. Smith, 10 May 1843, ISP/95; and Broadfoot to Richardson, 20 June 1843, ISP/98.

49. *Selected Correspondence*, p. 127; and Notification by Broadfoot, 9 June 1843, in *Maulmain Chronicle*, 3 June 1843.

50. Broadfoot to Ellenborough (draft), 17 March 1844, Broadfoot Papers, Add. Mss. 40127.

51. Broadfoot to J. Thomason, 31 August 1843, ISP/101.

52. Notes on the Salween Frontier by Broadfoot, ISP/94.

53. Burmese deposition, 1 June, and Broadfoot to McLeod, 6 June 1843, ISP/98; and *Maulmain Chronicle*, 7 June 1843 (notification dated 3 June 1843).

54. Broadfoot to Ellenborough, 23 July 1843, Ellenborough Papers, PRO 30/12/73.

55. McLeod to Broadfoot, 8 July 1843; and Richardson letters and notes on interviews with Tseekay of Martaban, 3 June to 23 July 1843, ISP/98.

56. Thomason to Broadfoot, 2 August 1843, Ellenborough Papers, PRO 30/12/110; and Thomason to Broadfoot, 5 August 1843, ISP/98.

57. Notes on the Salween Frontier by Broadfoot, ISP/94; Broadfoot to Davidson, 10 August, Thomason to Broadfoot, 19 August, and Edwards to Broadfoot, 14 October 1843, ISP/98; and Ellenborough Papers, PRO 30/12/110.

58. H. M. Durand, *The Life of Major-General Sir Henry Marion Durand*, 2 vols. (London: W. H. Allen, 1883); "Tenasserim Teak Timber Traffic," *Calcutta Review* 21 (1853): 98-169; and "The Tenasserim Provinces— Their Statistics and Government," *Calcutta Review* 8 (1847): 72-145.

59. Durand to Ellenborough, 31 January 1845 and 17 June 1846, Ellenborough Papers, PRO 30/12/21/6.

60. Durand to McLeod, 30 April 1846, ISP/135.
61. Notification of 8 July 1847, ISP/138.
62. Edward O'Riley to Bogle, 15 February 1850, IPF/199/6; and H. H. Dodwell, ed., *The Cambridge History of the British Empire*, 8 vols. (Cambridge: Cambridge University Press, 1929), 4: 567.
63. C. R. M. Jackson (Advocate General) to A. R. Young, 5 August 1851, IPF/199/41.
64. Military Commander of Sittang and Martaban to the Myowun of Maulmain, translated by de la Condamine, IPF/199/31.
65. *Selected Correspondence*, pp. 154-67, 176, 188-9, and 208-9; and Durand to F. J. Halliday, 17 November 1846, IPF/199/46.
66. Report of Public Meeting at Maulmain Exchange Room, 7 March 1851; and Bogle to Henry Hopkinson, 7 March 1851; and Maha Min Hla Htai Kya, Great Tseekay of Martaban City to Maulmain Tseekay, March 1851, IPF/199/34.
67. Bogle to Halliday, 22 March 1851, IPF/199/34.
68. Bogle to Halliday, 21 May 1851, IPF/199/42.
69. Halliday to Bogle, 9 June 1851, IPF/199/43.
70. Bogle to Halliday, 21 July 1851, ibid.; and 18 August 1851, IPF/199/46.
71. Halliday to Henry Elliot, 10 October 1851, forwarding Bogle's summation of 18 August 1851, IPF/199/46.
72. Bertie Reginald Pearn, *A History of Rangoon* (Rangoon: American Baptist Mission Press, 1939), pp. 72 and 131; and *Asiatic Journal* 36 (November 1841): 275.
73. John Brown to Maddock, 14 November 1842, IPF/197/35.
74. Brown to Broadfoot, 5 July 1843, ISP/98.
75. Colvin to Elliot, 29 February 1848, ISP/146.
76. R. S. Edwards to Broadfoot, 13 October 1843, ISP/101.
77. Bushby to Blundell, 22 June 1842, ISP/80.
78. Hugh Brown to Colvin, 10 and 13 December 1847, and Colvin to Bushby, 20 December 1847, ISP/145; and Colvin to Elliot, 20 March 1848, ISP/146.
79. Colvin to Elliot, 29 February 1848; and Elliot to Colvin, 7 April 1848, ibid.
80. Crisp to Maddock, 9 November 1841, ISP/66; and McLeod to Blundell, 1 February 1842, ISP/75.
81. Maddock to Blundell, 20 December 1841, ISP/67; and Ministers of Ava to Governor of Rangoon, 20 January 1844, ISP/104 (signed Prince of Prome and Mekkara Prince).
82. Memo on Crisp case, June 1844, IPF/196/56.

83. Currie to Tenasserim Commissioner, 20 July 1844, IPF/196/56; Petition to the Calcutta Chamber of Commerce, 16 July 1845; and Bushby to M. F. Crisp, 14 February 1846, IPF/197/32; and Crisp to Bushby, 28 January 1848, and Elliot to Crisp, ISP/145.

84. Hugh Brown to Melville, 14 March 1848, ISP/146.

85. Hugh Brown to Taylor, 27 August 1849, IPF/198/57; Grey to Under Secretary to Government of Bengal, 28 July 1849, IPF/198/51; and Taylor to Grant, 10 August 1849, ISP/159.

86. Grey to C. M. Crisp, 6 September 1850, IPF/199/13.

87. C. M. Crisp to Grey, 30 December 1850, IPF/199/57; Hopkinson to Bogle, 21 March 1851, IPF/199/34; and Crisp to Grey, 22 January 1851, IPF/199/29.

88. Bogle to Halliday, 10 February 1851, IPF/199/31.

89. C. M. Crisp to Bogle, 27 January 1851; and Halliday to Bogle, 14 March 1851, IPF/199/31.

90. Bogle to Halliday, 15 July 1851, IPF/199/45.

91. Robert Sheppard to Bogle, 27 June 1851, IPF/199/45.

92. Messrs. Creaton and Co. (agents for ship *Monarch*), to Bogle, 4 August 1851, IPF/199/45.

93. Lewis to Governor of Rangoon, 15 September 1851, IPF/199/46.

94. Henry Burney, "Memoir of Giuseppe d'Amato," *Journal of the Royal Asiatic Society, Bengal Branch* 1 (1832): 349-53; Paul Ambrose Bigandet, *An Outline of the History of the Catholic Mission from the year 1720 to 1887* (Rangoon: Hanthawaddy Press, 1887); and several articles during the 1960s by Vivian Ba in the *Guardian* and *J.B.R.S.* (see Bibliography).

95. Adonirum Judson to Colvin, 8 February 1847, ISP/133.

96. Benson to Government of India, 18 July 1838, ISP/11, in Desai, *Residency*, p. 351.

97. Francis Wayland, *A Memoir of the Life and Labors of the Rev. Adonirum Judson, D.D.,* 2 vols. (Boston: Phillips, Sampson and Co., 1854), 2: 276.

98. Judson to Colvin, 8 February 1847, ISP/133.

99. Judson to Corresponding Secretary, 28 March 1847, *Baptist Missionary Magazine* 27 (1847): 337.

100. Judson to Corresponding Secretary, 20 May 1847, ibid., p. 422.

101. Judson to Corresponding Secretary, 19 September 1847, ibid., 28 (1848); and Mrs. MacLeod Wylie, *The Gospel in Burmah* (New York: Sheldon and Co., 1860), p. 159.

102. Alfred S. Patton, *The Hero Missionary or a History of the Labors of Rev. Eugenio Kincaid* (New York: Dayton, 1858), p. 81.

103. Kincaid to Corresponding Secretary, 10 March 1851, Kincaid Papers, American Baptist Foreign Missionary Society, Valley Forge, Pa. (microfilm).

104. Kincaid to Corresponding Secretary, May-July 1851, *Baptist Missionary Magazine* 31 (1851); and Kincaid Papers.

105. Kincaid to Corresponding Secretary, 8 July, 11 August, 8 October, and 13 November 1851, Kincaid Papers.

106. Kincaid to Corresponding Secretary, 8 October 1851, ibid.

107. Kincaid to Corresponding Secretary, 13 November 1851, ibid.

108. James Ronald Martin, *Memoir on the Political, Naval, Military and Commercial Advantages to the Re-Occupation of Negrais Island* (Calcutta: N. p., 1843); and "Martin on the Re-Occupation of Negrais," *Calcutta Review* 11 (1849): 257-81.

109. Maddock to Bushby, 29 November 1842, ISP/87; and Minute by Dalhousie, 16 May 1850, IPF/198/65.

3

THE ORIGINS OF THE SECOND ANGLO-BURMESE WAR

Previous accounts of the outbreak of the Second Anglo-Burmese War are prone to polemics, cultural bias, and an emphasis on monocausality. Asian historians find Europeans culpable. Governor General Dalhousie "was an imperialist of the deepest dye, who longed to extend his Indian empire at the cost of the Burmese."[1] The East India Company coveted Burma, as it had an unquenchable "thirst for conquest."[2] Anglophile historians blame the Burmese. Dalhousie's official biographer declared that the "court of Ava drove [Dalhousie] into war."[3] The doyen of British Southeast Asian scholars remarked that the war was "inevitable" because of the "intransigence and xenophobia which radiated from the court of Ava."[4] Historians with an economic bent generally "believe there was a desire for war on the part of the British trading community in Burma. . .as it would permanently safeguard commercial interests in the country."[5] However, these historians split on the legitimacy of the merchants' claims, between the assertion that they were justified "grievances"[6] and the claim that the "whole ugly truth" was that the merchants' complaints were totally fraudulent.[7] In a different vein, the war was another example of "the imperialism of free trade."[8] The previous chapter, however, established that the origins of conflict must be sought in long-term causes (perennial local grievances) and short-term causes (Sheppard and Lewis and Bogle complaints). This chapter deals with "immediate" causes. To ignore this developmental build-up, as have the authors cited above, is to misunderstand the British remonstrance and the uses to which local interests employed it.

Bogle's prolix review and the complaints of Sheppard and Lewis arrived in Calcutta while the Governor General, Lord Dalhousie, was in Durbar (Council) with the Sikh chieftains at Pinjore. Concurrently there was an ongoing debate over administrative primacy between the Governor General and the President in Council. Two members of Council wrote minutes denying Dalhousie's authority over them when he was away from Calcutta. They asserted that the President in Council had coordinate authority with the Governor General in all things when the Governor General was absent from the seat of government, Calcutta, or Simla. This was not a new issue. It was the very problem that led to Ellenborough's demise as Governor General and his hatred for Maddock, a member of Council. In respect to the business allotted to the President in Council, he had authority exclusive of that of the Governor General. The Governor General was absent, and the Burmese problem seems to have been a test of these ideas.[9]

Dalhousie had received despatches on the Aga Baker case in August 1851, but it appears that his private secretary did not think them important enough to show the Governor General. This oversight was unusual, as Dalhousie prided himself on personally going through all despatches.[10] Calcutta had been preparing the Burmese case since at least early September. Events of March 1851 and the following six months were discussed in Council in early October. They rejected intervention in the case of Aga Baker and Bogle's accumulation of ten years' circumstantial evidence. What they wanted was a pretext upon which to place Anglo-Burmese relations once more on a formal basis and to demonstrate Council's independence of the absent Governor General. The Indian government did not feel justified in acting on past grievances that had remained officially unnoticed. The degree of commercial lobbying culminating in the new policy is unclear. Frederick Halliday, Dalhousie's choice as Home Secretary to the Government of India, was important in policy formation and had commercial ties. Ellenborough had marked him as a meddler and would have removed him, as he had Blundell, but for Ellenborough's own removal by the Board of Directors.[11] The desired pretext was the combined Sheppard-Lewis case. Calcutta argued that the treaties of 1826 were still valid; the "mere omission to exercise right implies no denial of its existence or of the validity of the document by which it is secure. . . . It must be considered binding still." It was high time "to protect from oppression and injury British subjects engaged in the lawful prosecution of trade in a Burmese port."[12] The early and all-important decisions over changing Burmese policy were out of Dalhousie's hands. Dalhousie received word of the Sheppard and Lewis cases *after* the President in Council had already determined a tentative course of action. The despatch was mailed to Dalhousie on 10 October 1851, and it was several more days before he received it. Moreover, the President in Council's chosen instrument of British power, Commodore Lambert of the Royal Navy, was also independent of the Government of India. The Commodore was directly responsible to the Admiralty in London. As with the problem of coordinate authority within Council, the Royal Navy's relationship with the Government of India had always been unclear, since the East India Company maintained its own navy.

Commodore George Robert Lambert was born in 1795. He entered the navy in 1809. His family was steeped in the tradition of military service. In 1850 he was placed in charge of the Eastern Seas. A usually calm, judicious man, he steered clear of politics and devoted himself to military efficiency. Honor, excitement, and power served as the navy's creed. A recent naval historian has captured the navy's mid-nineteenth-century mission:

> The Navy was on call to promote and protect British interests in those parts of the world where respect for a British citizen and his property was not automatic, where conceptions of justice differed from those of Western Europe, or were not enforced with sufficient regularity and thoroughness.[13]

A young naval officer wrote in 1851 when rumor reached him of a fray in Burma: "At Madras we inquired anxiously about the Burmese war and we were relieved to hear that it was still going briskly, so our hopes were high for seeing some service when we sailed for Rangoon."[14] Lambert had spent much of 1851 on the Acheh Coast of Sumatra, where he had been asked to intervene in local matters. He refused to establish orderly trade by force, observing, "There is much fraud practiced by the purchasers as well as the vendors: neither have laws or government to guide them in their transactions."[15] Lambert had orders on leaving Acheh to touch at Penang, Calcutta, and Bombay en route to the Persian Gulf. He arrived at Calcutta on 4 October 1851 and tendered his respects to the Governor General by letter without mentioning Burma.[16] A week later he again wrote Dalhousie, relating that when at Penang, he had heard of British subjects being abused in Rangoon by Burmese authorities. Since arriving in Calcutta he had received more information from Captain Lewis, which confirmed what he had heard earlier. Lambert was in a hurry. He wanted to go to the Persian Gulf but did not want to miss the opportunity of action in Rangoon. He wanted to serve two masters well. Lambert offered to visit Rangoon before heading for the Persian Gulf.[17] The same day, Halliday, a close confidant of Dalhousie's, wrote privately, recommending the enforcement of the Treaty of Yandabo. Halliday and Lambert had conferred and agreed that the Commodore's services were required for a redress of grievances.[18] When Dalhousie received Lambert's 11 October offer of assistance, he had not yet received the consultation of Council of 10 October. Personal letters were quicker than official mail, as the latter would first have to be processed by his secretary.[19] When he finally received the official documents he wrote a lengthy minute concurring with the President in Council on the need for a reasoned remonstrance. Redress should be sought from the Governor of Rangoon, and if this was unfruitful, a letter should be sent to the King of Burma asking for the Governor's dismissal. The following day Dalhousie added that to mix in Bogle's case would weaken the strong points of Sheppard and Lewis.[20]

Lambert's record of moderation in Acheh recommended him to Dalhousie. Dalhousie hoped that discretion would continue to be his guide. Dalhousie's letters continuously implored Lambert to refrain from premature or rash acts that would precipitate hostilities.[21] Nonetheless, Lambert's actions in Rangoon earned him the undying title, the "Combustible Commodore." Following his incandescence in November 1851 and January 1852 he became once more the calm, considered officer who won respect by merit from Dalhousie, the army, and private citizens and on occasion was accused of being overcautious.[22] The cause of his "combustion" must be sought in the inflammable agents with whom he came in contact: namely Captain Lewis, his official advisers, and the local Rangoon community. Even before Lambert left Calcutta he had preconceived ideas. He fully believed Lewis had been grievously wronged. He felt that the Rangoon Governor was a worthless character, little better than a savage. There was also a need for hasty action. Lambert had by now set aside his orders to the Persian Gulf. However, if the Burmese question was not settled shortly, an entire year would elapse, due to the monsoon, before it could again be taken up.[23]

Lambert left Calcutta on 18 November 1851 with instructions to investigate. The Government of India assigned him two assistants with previous Burmese experience, Captain Thomas Latter and R. S. Edwards. Latter had served in Burma and had written a Burmese grammar. Contemporary comments damn Latter. How he was chosen as Lambert's assistant can only be explained by the fact that he alone volunteered and that he seemed qualified. A Bengal army officer, he was the all-too-familiar alarmist, prone to exaggerate, act rashly, and believe the worst of the Burmese. He was erratic and unbalanced. Latter, as translator, did his utmost to prejudice and poison relations and provoke war. Latter thought the Burmese all trickery, and "falsehood [was] looked upon as the highest art of diplomacy."[24] After war commenced Latter hired a notorious European as his assistant and set him up as a robber-chief. Dalhousie contemplated transferring Latter from Burma for his irregular activities and false intelligence, but Latter's mysterious murder removed the necessity. R. S. Edwards, a Madrasi, was an assistant clerk in the Foreign Secretary's office and had been Resident Burney's interpreter. It was reported that he "would give any opinion he thinks will be most acceptable and is a dangerous adviser."[25]

Rumor of the squadron's sighting circulated in Rangoon on the afternoon of 23 November. Kincaid "thought the news too good to be true." When he actually saw the ships he was in ecstasy and wrote: "The emotions of joy & gratitude diffused can only be understood by those who have seen & *felt* the deeds of insane & brutal tyranny—the navy guard spoke to us of *peace & security* . . . God's own hope, he will hear our prayers for deliverance."[26] Kincaid hoped to use Lambert's visit to create an irreversible imbroglio between Britain and Burma. Since Kincaid had fallen out with the Governor over the distribution of religious conversion tracts, the Governor had turned to Charles M. Crisp for advice. The senior Crisp arrived shortly in Rangoon from Moulmein and placed his local knowledge at the disposal of Commodore Lambert while simultaneously selling muskets to the Burmese Governor. When the squadron was sighted on Monday, 25 November, the Governor sent Crisp to meet the squadron downstream and to inquire as to its intentions. Lambert sent Crisp back to the Governor to set a day and hour to receive communications. The squadron arrived in Rangoon harbor on Tuesday, 26 November.

Missionary Kincaid and the merchants greeted the squadron as the savior on the day of deliverance. Commodore Lambert invited Kincaid to come on board. Kincaid told Lambert that the Governor was refurbishing his cannon and threatened to set the city afire and behead any person who went to the wharf to greet the squadron. Kincaid had a two-hour interview with Lambert as head of a delegation of merchants. Kincaid related how the European and merchant community of Rangoon did not appeal to Calcutta for fear of Burmese reprisal. Lambert asked that these complaints be put in writing. Shortly after the interview Kincaid exclaimed triumphantly that they had moved

> the noble, kind hearted commodore. Our several statements
> turned the whole current of affairs. The Commodore came to
> demand redress for outrages committed on Captains Lewis and
> Sheppard; but he now found that hundreds of British subjects
> had suffered as great, and many of them greater injuries, and
> that several had died under torture.[27]

Crisp also visited the ship on its arrival Tuesday and reported that the Governor appointed Thursday at 11 A.M. to receive communications at the customs house. Latter noted that Tuesday and Wednesday were otherwise without visitors, as "the Governor had threatened to cut off the heads and break the legs of all the foreigners, British or others, who went down to the wharf to welcome the frigate."

Wednesday, nonetheless, was an important day for decision making. Within twenty-four hours of arriving in Rangoon Lambert cast a die that would either lead directly to war or to the Burmese accommodating British demands. Latter called on Rangoon's English residents. He met Crisp going to the frigate with a request from the Governor to move the squadron a few yards lower among the merchant ships. Lambert asked Edwards the propriety of this.

> Mr. Edwards replied, that nothing of the kind was the case,
> and that it was only their usual way in trying to commence a
> quantity of petty annoyances, such as were employed in cases
> of former Residents and Agents. The Commodore consequently
> declined moving his frigate.

Latter returned to the frigate accompanied by several of the British residents, who stated their case to the Commodore.

The information that Lambert had received in Calcutta from Captain Lewis had been amplified on his arrival in Rangoon through the agencies of Kincaid and Latter. It was all of one piece and self-reinforcing. Lambert unquestioningly accepted truth, exaggerations, and blatant lies as facts that damned the Rangoon Governor. Kincaid's account was self-serving. Latter saw every Burmese action as a calculated insult. His accounts were filled with inconsistencies that identify fraud and result from reliance on second- and third-hand evidence. Lambert had been instructed to obtain about £1,000 compensation from the Governor and to remind him of the sanctity of the Treaty of Yandabo. If unsuccessful he was to forward a letter from the President in Council to the King of Burma. Lambert short-circuited his instructions. Twenty-four hours after his arrival he declared the Governor was "a person whose conduct renders him totally unworthy of any respect."[28] Lambert on his own initiative wrote additional letters to the Governor and the King:

> Since my arrival so many more complaints have been made
> by persons residing at Rangoon, who have a right to claim
> British protection that I have deemed it my duty to withhold
> my original demand until I have again made known their
> complaints. . .to the Government of India.

Lambert then forwarded to the King the President in Council's letter, which demanded the Governor's removal. Lambert's own letter to the "Prime Minister" and King of Burma declared that conditions in Rangoon had deteriorated, and this was an insult to the British nation.[29] Lambert allowed the Burmese court thirty-five days to reply before sterner action would be taken.

All this occurred *before* Lambert received the merchants' written complaints, which only arrived on Thursday, 28 November. The document, signed by twenty-eight people headed by Kincaid, was a strange and obvious case of special pleading, encompassing alleged wrongs over the past ten years. While Kincaid had talked of torture, the petition referred only to extortion, restraint of trade, and religious persecution.[30] That same Thursday morning two English residents called on board and warned that the Governor was planning to take the English officers hostage and had moved the meeting place, set for that same day at 11 A.M., from the customs house to his own house, two and one-half miles inland. However, the meeting went off uneventfully, and Captain Tarleton and Captain Latter "received no opposition either going or coming." They did not negotiate, as Calcutta had instructed, but delivered the letter to the Governor and those for transmittal to Amarapura. Latter could not help adding that the Governor was in informal dress, wearing common white clothes, smoking a cheroot, while all undergovernors were in court dress and the European officers were in full uniform. Latter considered this a studied insult.

On Friday, 29 November, the Governor's deputation visited the frigate and denied having harmed British subjects. Lambert again concluded "that the Governor of Rangoon was unfit to be entrusted with the lives and property of British subjects." The meetings with the Burmese were over. Latter went to Calcutta to render a personal account of events.

Lambert wrote privately to Dalhousie to justify his actions:

> As I feared on my arrival I found a most worthless character
> to deal with in the Governor who was not only prepared to put
> every obstacle in the way of adjustment but ready to offer
> personal insult to me. . . . I feel convinced I should have had
> the greatest difficulty in bringing this man to terms and this
> is not saying that in one of his fits he would not have carried
> out one of his many threats he has made of murdering all the
> Europeans in Rangoon.

Privately Dalhousie approved Lambert's bypassing the Governor and his instructions to negotiate, though he was not happy with the independence he displayed.[31] The Government of India had disallowed Bogle's review of old complaints. It was uncomfortable and inconsistent now to be tied to the argument Lambert had accepted, so it was ignored. The emphasis consequently was placed on the Rangoon Governor's rigidity rather than Lambert's unwillingness to negotiate. Two members of Council wanted Lambert censured.[32] Dalhousie opposed this. Dalhousie's practice of censuring as little as possible had derived from his elitist concept of the public interest and service. Government must not be exposed to ridicule or public opprobrium, especially one's own government. Moreover, the military should be kept cautiously at arm's length. This explains Dalhousie's attitude when Lambert ran amuck in January 1852 and explains his kindly treatment of the septuagenarian General Henry Godwin, charged with the Burmese campaign, whose stubborn traditionalism was tolerated in the public interest. Dalhousie cautioned Lambert to avoid war with honor. The treasury was exhausted from a succession of wars. "Even were war obviously inevitable we could not safely engage in it *now*" because of the season. "A war with Burmah would be indeed a great calamity, and a conquest would be a calamity greater still."[33] But the Government of India had to make a show of force lest Britain's reputation in the Orient slip into decline. Not only must the Governor be removed, but a British agent should be established in Rangoon with fifty troops, as the Treaty of Yandabo stipulated. Failure to comply with these demands would result in a river blockade. Lambert was specifically enjoined from bombarding or occupying Rangoon or Martaban.[34]

On 1 January 1852, a day before the expiry of the thirty-five day deadline, letters arrived from Amarapura which heralded a new Governor and promised to satisfy the Government of India's demands. If Lambert had been mischievous in November, it had had good effect. The Burmese were conciliatory. Lambert wrote: "I am of the opinion that the King is sincere, and that his Government will fully act up to what he has promised."[35] Lambert would have an interview with the new Governor and then return to Calcutta to talk over Burmese trade prospects with the Governor General.[36] Latter arrived in Rangoon on 2 January and rejoined Lambert's staff. Immediately the tenor of despatches became vitriolic. Latter had no interest in conciliation and compromise. Latter recorded that the ex-Governor appeared in town inflamed with wine and threatened to murder all Europeans on shore and endeavored to burn down the town. A merchant set up a stockade and mounted a small cannon. On Saturday, 3 January, a fleet of boats with about three thousand men was sighted. Surmising that this was the new Governor, Latter felt the lack of formal announcement "a discourteous or even contemptuous act." Crisp reported that the new Governor's first orders were to prevent communications with the squadron. The penalty for violation, said Crisp, was death.[37] The Governor also wanted the gun and flagpole removed from the merchant's stockade. Lambert insisted the merchant keep the pole and gun for a distress warning but that they be removed from notice.

Arrangements were made to meet the new Governor. Tuesday, 6 January 1852, was an eventful day. Lambert was again to be swept up by an indistinguishable patina of truth and falsehood and cast a second mold from which there was no extrication but war. Captain Fishbourne of H. M. S. *Hermes* and second in command under Lambert, Captain Latter, Edwards, and the American missionary Kincaid set out to call on the new Governor and deliver the latest letters from Calcutta. Why Kincaid accompanied the official delegation of British officers is unclear; however, he got along well with the officers and was probably considered an asset as an additional translator. Everything seemed to go wrong, almost as though it were planned. Edwards went ahead to see the new Governor and to announce that the deputation was coming and that the reception should be informal. Edwards claimed when he arrived at the foot of the outer steps one of the Governor's men drew a dagger on him. There is no corroborating evidence, and the internal logic suggests that it may have been a fabricated and embroidered story designed for maximum effect with Lambert and Calcutta. Edwards added that he saw the Deputy Governor, told him that his life had been threatened and that the man was punished in the usual Burmese manner. He was "taken by the hair of the head, swung around three times, his face dashed to the ground, himself dragged out by the hair, and pitched down the stairs." The Governor wanted to receive the letter from Edwards, but Edwards said it would not be fitting. The rest of the party landed at noon and obtained horses from the merchants' stockade. The deputation then proceeded to ride into the Governor's courtyard. In a country where it was customary to unshoe on approaching a superior's quarters, this equestrian approach appeared the height of insult. Whether it was studied insult or indicative of British ignorance of Burmese custom is unclear. What is clear is that the British manipulated the incident to make the Burmese appear the offending party. The deputation wanted to deliver the letters personally to the Governor. The Deputy Governor and his translator said the new Governor was sleeping but that Edwards would be allowed to deliver the letter.

The new Governor had been insulted. His courtyard had been violated by men on horses. He was asked to receive a deputation of inferiors. "To be asleep" in Burmese etiquette might well be the same as "not at home" in English. The Governor may have been trying to insult the English or he may seriously have doubted the propriety of receiving the deputation of inferiors. The *Chronicle* explains that Edwards announced that Commodore Lambert himself was coming. But then only Edwards, Kincaid, and other junior officers arrived. The Governor was willing to receive letters from Edwards, whom he could safely disregard as a mere messenger, but not from the deputation, who, theoretically, would have to be accorded the respect of equals.[38]

Captain Fishbourne wanted to wait on the Governor's verandah until he awoke. Latter intoned that it was patently obvious that the Governor was not asleep and that to stay on the verandah was an insult. The Deputy Governor and Fishbourne conferred, and the British deputation decided to stand under a shed. But this again was insulting to Latter, who said the shed was an assemblage point for commoners. So the deputation stood in the sun for fifteen minutes and then returned slowly to the squadron. Latter remarked that "what occurred was as gross an insult as could have been devised."

Latter, Edwards, and Kincaid were all deeply interested in causing a confrontation. Fishbourne, who was somewhat more detached, was the only one to demonstrate moderation and conciliation, but he was disregarded. On returning to the squadron they again bent their efforts to capturing Lambert's ear. Latter and Kincaid were highly regarded by Lambert. Both were time bombs about to explode, trying to draw the full weight of the British into the conflagration. Kincaid remarked to Lambert "that he burned with indignation at seeing British officers so grossly insulted."[39] Later that afternoon a Burmese delegation came on board and asked if the Commodore would visit the Governor. But the Commodore had other plans. That evening the Commodore and his advisers decided to seize the "Yellow Ship," one of the King of Burma's royal barges. Only five days after Lambert had attested to the pacific sincerity of the Burmese, two or three hours after the deputation had gone to see the Governor, and after fifteen minutes of standing in the sun, Lambert declared: "In consequence of the deep insult thus offered by the representative of the Burmese Government to an officer of rank in the British Navy, I have considered it my duty to suspend all further communications with that functionary."[40] Lambert set up a blockade and offered asylum to British merchants and all those desiring British protection. Two American and French missionaries placed themselves under

British protection.[41] Curiously enough the British merchants remained in Rangoon until late January.

The next day, Wednesday, at 7 A.M., a boarding party overpowered the skeleton crew of the King's ship.[42] Fishbourne and the *Hermes* took the King's ship in tow, thus producing their own *casus belli.* Later that day the Dalla Governor, a devout Buddhist and pacifist, visited Lambert. The Commodore told him that confrontation could be avoided if the Rangoon Governor came on board and apologized. The Dalla Governor visited Lambert several more times, relaying messages and letters. His aim was restitution of the King's ship. Lambert extended the period for the Rangoon Governor's visit from noon of Thursday to sunset. At sunset a messenger arrived with a letter from the Governor recounting the Governor's goodwill and the bad faith of the British, who had violated the rules of etiquette:

> Edwards was intoxicated and I was truly asleep. When
> you stole the ship, I did not attack and when your frigate
> struck the shore near Dallah I did not molest or destroy them.
> . . . [I] acted worthily to these unworthy men; and I now
> represent this conduct of Commodore Lambert to the
> English ruler's who came from one country to another,
> and behave in a manner unbecoming an Ambassador.[43]

Last-minute negotiations were attempted. But even the peaceful Dalla Governor said he would have to fire on the British if they attempted to take away the King's ship. On the morning of 10 January 1852 the British moved southward, toward the sea. The Burmese fired the first shots but were quickly silenced by the frigates' broadsides, which did "great execution." So started a war that Dalhousie had tried hard to avoid. Latter was again sent to Calcutta to personally represent or misrepresent events. The major British merchants did not remove their valuables from Rangoon until late January, when boxes of gold, silver, and jewels were transported from the stockade to the *Fox.*[44]

Dalhousie was furious yet impotent. The deed had been done. Despite precise instructions, which sanctioned only a blockade, Lambert had taken action that had forced a war. Lambert arrived in Calcutta on 17 January and dashed off a personal explanation to the Governor General: "Had I quitted Rangoon without some demonstration to show my determination to have our demands complied with these ignorant boasting people would have immediately declared it was from want of prowess." They would have become even more insolent. Dalhousie's plan "of pursuing such a policy that all the world shall be satisfied such a war has [been] forced upon us" lay in ruins.[45] Dalhousie's usually measured, neat, erasure-free hand collapsed as he wrote in a rage to John Hobhouse (later created Lord Broughton), the President of the Board of Control:

> This precipitate act was very flamable [sic]. But I am ~~always~~ reluctant to censor hardly an officer who is ~~hard~~ xxxx in trying circumstances, especially an officer of XXX rank in H.M. Navy who is not under my orders. . .accordingly I have let him down as as I could. . .These commodores are too combustible for negotiations. His rank however was so high that I could not put any [censure on] him in the first instance, without a slight which was the more to be avoided that Commodore Lambert was described to me from Calcutta as a steady, sensible, discreate man.[46]

Dalhousie vented his frustration in his minute:

> [Dalhousie] regret[ted] that any disregard of ordinary and proper forms on our part should have left to the Governor of Rangoon a colourable pretext for any part of his conduct. But while the conduct of the Burmese authorities justified the termination of all communications. . .no such justification can be pleaded for the act of the Commodore in seizing the ship which belonged to the King of Ava. [Lambert had exceeded his instructions and] took a step which naturally —almost necessarily—led to an act of hostility by the Burmese [and] it is my duty to express the deep regret with which I view this act of reprisal and to withhold from it my approval.[47]

Other members of Council were harsher, but they all agreed that Britain must retain the upper hand. War could still be avoided if the Governor of Rangoon wrote a letter of apology to Captain Fishbourne, paid compensation to captains Sheppard and Lewis, and accepted an agent in Rangoon. In return Britain would send an officer of rank to negotiate, return the King's ship, and lift the blockade. The memorandum was an ultimatum: "If these demands shall be refused, the British Government will thereafter exact for itself the reparation which is due for the wrong it has suffered."[48] Lambert was to deliver this message and simply pass the reply on to Calcutta. He was not to communicate independently. Lambert returned to Rangoon on 31 January. He was greeted by a volley of cannon. Though this surprised the unprepared squadron, they silenced the shore battery within three minutes. Lambert forwarded the memorandum to the Governor and included a letter of his own expressing surprise at being fired on. If it occurred again Lambert swore he would silence the guns and destroy the stockade. The Governor agreed to pay compensation to Sheppard and Lewis and receive a Resident, but he saw no reason to apologize to Captain Fishbourne.[49] The ultimatum of the British had been rejected. The Governor General could see "no alternative but to extract reparation by force of arms," and he proclaimed a state of war between the two countries. War could only be avoided if the Burmese accepted the previous conditions and paid an increased fine of Rs. 1,000,000 in consideration of expenses incurred by the expedition and of compensation of property.[50] Dalhousie hoped that a knockout blow would put some sense into the Burmese and bring them to heel.[51]

The Burmese court and the Rangoon Governor were understandably confused. They had met the initial demands of the English by replacing the Governor. But the English constantly escalated their demands. Had Lambert been sent to dispose of the merchant question or to begin a war?[52] The Burmese court tried to avoid communication with or through Lambert at Rangoon. They addressed their missives to Commissioner Bogle. They asked to be allowed to send two high court officials to Calcutta to discuss the issues. Bogle was sympathetic to the Burmese court's dilemma and earnestness and recommended that Calcutta accept this offer to bridge an ever-widening gulf. Dalhousie was unsure whether these letters were "an olive branch. . .or a hum," designed to gain time. He decided on taking a high tone as having the greatest chance of success.[53] Dalhousie reinforced the illogicality of war, commenting that if Britain were driven out of Burma, Cousin Jonathan (i.e., America) was sure to step in.[54] Bogle was directed not to reply as the Governor General was counting on a rapid military blow to bring hostilities to a quick conclusion and make the Burmese sue for peace.[55]

The fleet arrived in the Rangoon River on 2 April 1852. Captain Latter, under a white flag of truce, approached the stockade to see if any letter had arrived from the King. He was fired on. After Latter extricated himself the fleet returned fire and succeeded in blowing up the powder magazine and "destroying many men." [56] By the end of the second week in April Rangoon and Martaban were in British hands. By the end of May the British held Bassein. The knockout blow had been struck. In addition, Lambert successfully blockaded and seized the annual grain shipment to the capital. But this did not bring Burmese submission. If Dalhousie was frustrated by Lambert's initial disobedience, it was nothing compared to his inability to bring the Burmese to terms. He wrote a friend, "The beasts don't give in. . . . *I Can't get a result. They give and take no terms.*"[57] Similar statements of exasperation are found in Dalhousie's correspondence for the next several months.

As late as May Dalhousie conceived of holding Rangoon until the Burmese submitted. If they did not submit by November, he would march on Amarapura and be under its walls in February 1853. Continued Burmese resistance to negotiate prompted Dalhousie to think of holding Rangoon and the adjacent area in perpetuity, rather than march on Amarapura. By late May Dalhousie was still talking about desiring to avoid the annexation of Pegu. [58] By late June Dalhousie had decided to extirpate the "intolerable arrogance" of the Burmese and planned an extensive November campaign. Burma could only avert this disaster if she immediately paid Rs. 1,500,000 and ceded Negrais and Diamond Islands and the district of Martaban. It was unlikely that the Burmese court would receive this proposal, let alone accept it. Dalhousie, who had blanched at war and conquest, now thought that avoidance of conquest "would be a calamity greater still."[59] He minuted sorrowfully:

> If any adequate alternative for the confiscation of territory
> could have been found by me, or had any been suggested to
> me, my mind would most readily have adopted it. . . . But after
> constant and anxious reflection, through the months during
> which hostilities have been in progress, I can discover no escape
> from the necessity.[60]

Though the necessarian argument is inherently weak, Dalhousie did not have many options open to him. In projecting the future course of the war, guided by the pillars of security and economy, Dalhousie outlined five alternative policies and the individual advantages: (1) victory and withdrawal had the disadvantage that the Burmese would not understand and would say they had won the war because the British had left; (2) victory, withdrawal, but maintain Martaban; (3) victory and retain Rangoon and Martaban; (4) retain Martaban, Rangoon, and Bassein. Alternatives 2, 3, and 4 were all poor choices as the area would not provide sufficient revenue to support the protective garrison that would be necessary. The fifth and final proposal, and the one that Dalhousie favored, was the annexation of Pegu Province, including Martaban. This would vest control of the Irrawaddy River and its trade in British hands and join Arakan and Tenasserin; Pegu was expected to produce sufficient revenues to be self-supporting. Members of Council concurred with Dalhousie. The early annexation of Pegu was considered a point of honor, conscience, and paternal responsibility. Pegu had been occupied during the first war. The Taliens had assisted the British against their Burmese overlords and then faced reprisals when the British withdrew following receipt of the reparations payments. One member of Council recommended the Governor General issue a peremptory proclamation annexing Pegu.[61] While Dalhousie favored unilateral annexation without treaty, he did not "feel confident that the policy recommended by the Governor-General in Council, in regard to Pegu, would certainly be adopted in England."[62]

When Dalhousie closed his private diary for 1852 he wrote, "God he knows how fervently I desired to avert this necessity of war."[63] In great part this was an honest appraisal of Dalhousie's role. The early decisions were out of his hands. Kincaid, the American missionary, invoked God to another purpose. Lambert, the man on the spot on the distant frontier, became the tool of vested missionary and merchant interests. Calcutta found it more difficult to rebuke and censure a single naval officer than to go to war with a foreign nation. The war was a product of intense human factors rather than any overriding economic motivation. It was the result of policy creation spinning centrifugally from Calcutta to the frontier. It was the result of conscious exploitation of diverse cultures.

NOTES

1. Maung Htin Aung, *A History of Burma* (New York: Columbia University Press, 1967), p. 225; and *The Stricken Peacock: Anglo-Burmese*

Relations, 1752-1948 (The Hague: Martinus Nijhoff, 1965), p. 41.

2. K. M. Panikkar, *Asia and Western Dominance* (New York: Collier Books, 1969 [orig. publ., London, 1959], p. 83.

3. William Lee-Warner, *The Life of the Marquis of Dalhousie, K.T.*, 2 vols. (London: Macmillan, 1904), 2: 123.

4. D. G. E. Hall, "Anglo-Burmese Conflicts in the 19th Century: A Reassessment," *Asia* 6 (Autumn 1966): 66.

5. Walter S. Desai, *A Pageant of Burmese History* (Bombay: Orient Longmans, 1961), p. 196.

6. Anil C. Banerjee, *Annexation of Burma* (Calcutta: Mukherjee, 1944), p. 55.

7. Dorothy Woodman, *The Making of Burma* (London: Cresset Press, 1962), p. 127.

8. John Gallagher and Ronald Robinson, "The Imperialism of Free Trade," *Economic History Review*, 2d ser. 6 (August 1953): 1-15.

9. Dalhousie to George Couper, 21 October 1851 and 1 February 1852, in J. G. A. Baird, ed., *Private Letters of the Marquess of Dalhousie* (Edinburgh: William Blackwood, 1910), p. 179 and 189-90.

10. Halliday to Secretary with the Governor General, 15 August 1851, IPF/199/42.

11. Halliday to Elliot, 10 October 1851, IPF/199/46. Halliday went on extended sick leave in early 1852 with Dalhousie's blessing. Dalhousie to Couper, 27 January 1852, in Baird, ed., *Private Letters*, p. 210.

12. Note by the Officiating Undersecretary, "Existing Relations of the Government of India with Ava," A. R. Young, 8 September 1851; and Halliday to Elliot, 10 October 1851, IPF/199/46.

13. C. J. Bartlett, *Great Britain and Sea Power, 1815-1853* (Oxford: Clarendon Press, 1963), p. x; and Gerald S. Graham, *The Politics of Naval Supremacy* (Cambridge: Cambridge University Press, 1965).

14. Edmund Fremantle, *The Navy As I Have Known It, 1849-1899* (London: Cassell, 1904), p. 63.

15. Nicholas Tarling, *British Policy in the Malay Archipelago, 1824-1874* (Kuala Lumpur: Oxford in Asia, 1969 [orig. publ. 1957]), p. 152.

16. Lambert to Dalhousie, 4 October 1851, IPF/199/52.

17. Lambert to Dalhousie, 11 October 1851, Dalhousie Muniments, Scottish Record Office, 6/531.

18. Halliday to Dalhousie, 11 October 1851, Dalhousie Muniments, GD/6/152.

19. Dalhousie to Lambert, 18 October 1851, Dalhousie Muniments, 6/531.

20. Minutes by Dalhousie, 29 and 30 October 1851, ISP/171.

21. Dalhousie to Lambert, 29 October and 3 November 1851, Dal-

housie Muniments, 6/531.

22. Phayre to Dalhousie, 9 April 1853, in D. G. E. Hall, ed., *The Dalhousie-Phayre Correspondence, 1852-1856* (London: Oxford University Press, 1932), p. 53.

23. Lambert to Dalhousie, before 18 November 1851, Dalhousie Muniments, 6/531.

24. Richard S. Dobbs, *Reminiscences of Life in Mysore, South Africa, and Burma* (Dublin: G. Herber, 1882), pp. 196-8; Latter to Lambert, 10 February 1852, in *Parliamentary Papers*, 1852, 36, "Papers Relating to Hostilities with Burma," C. 1490, presented 4 June 1852 (hereafter cited C. 1490), pp. 216-7; Phayre to Dalhousie, 9 April 1853, in Hall, ed., *Correspondence*, p. 53; and Garnet Wolesley, *The Story of a Soldier*, 2 vols. (Westminster: Archibald Constable, 1903), 1: 54.

25. Bogle to Halliday, 23 March 1852, Dalhousie Muniments, GD/45/6/171; and Hall, ed., *Correspondence*, p. 50.

26. Kincaid to Corresponding Secretary, 28 November 1851, Kincaid Papers, American Baptist Foreign Missionary Society, Valley Forge, Pa. (microfilm).

27. Ibid.

28. Latter to Halliday, 6 December 1851, ISP/171; Narrative of Events at Rangoon, 10 January 1852, ISP/173; and Lambert to John Littler, 28 November 1851, C 1490 (1852), p. 167.

29. C. 1490 (1852), p. 168, Lambert to Governor of Rangoon, 27 November 1851; President in Council to King of Ava, 17 November 1851; and Lambert to Prime Minister of King of Ava, 28 November 1851.

30. Merchants Resident in Rangoon to Lambert, 28 November 1851, ibid., p. 25.

31. Lambert to Dalhousie, 28 November, and Dalhousie to Lambert, 20 December 1851, Dalhousie Muniments, 6/531.

32. Reprinted *in extenso* in Woodman, *Making of Burma*, pp. 127-8.

33. Dalhousie to Lambert, 20 December 1851, Dalhousie Muniments, 6/531.

34. Halliday to Lambert (extract), 27 December 1851, in C. 1490 (1852), pp. 175-6.

35. Ibid., p. 178, Lambert to John Littler, 1 January 1852.

36. Lambert to Dalhousie, 2 January 1852, Dalhousie Muniments, 6/531.

37. C. M. Crisp to Young, 13 January 1852, ISP/173.

38. U Tin (of Sagaing), *Kòn-baung-zet Maha-ya-zawin-daw-gyi* [Great royal chronicle of the Kon-baung dynasty], 3 vols. (Mandalay: Hanthawaddy Pitakat Press, 1922-3), 3: 94.

39. Lambert to Halliday, ISP/173, in Woodman, *Making of Burma*, pp. 545-6.

40. Lambert to Halliday, 9 January 1852, in C. 1490 (1852), p. 180.

41. Lambert to Dalhousie, 9 January 1852, Dalhousie Muniments, 6/531.

42. Ship's Log, *Fox*, Public Record Office, Admiralty, 4467.

43. Governor of Rangoon's letter, translated by Latter, in C. 1490 (1852), pp. 184-5.

44. Ibid., p. 185, Lambert to Halliday, 10 January 1852; and Ship's Log, *Fox*, 29 January 1852, PRO, Admiralty, 4467.

45. Lambert to Dalhousie, 19 January 1852, and Dalhousie to Lambert, private, 23 January 1852, Dalhousie Muniments, 6/531 and 6/82.

46. Dalhousie to Hobhouse, private, 23 January 1852, Broughton Papers, Add. Mss. 36477.

47. Minute by Dalhousie, 22 January 1852, ISP/175, in Woodman, *Making of Burma*, pp. 540-5.

48. Memorandum from the President of the Council of India to the Governor of Rangoon, C. 1490 (1852), pp. 196-7.

49. Lambert to Halliday and Lambert to Governor of Rangoon, 31 January 1852, and Governor of Rangoon to Halliday, 2 February 1852, ibid., pp. 198-9 and 206-7.

50. Minute of Dalhousie, 12 February 1852; and Governor General to King of Ava, 18 February 1852, ibid., pp. 207-11 and 218-9.

51. Ibid., p. 211, Halliday to Lambert, 13 February 1852; Dalhousie to Mountain, private, 17 August 1852, and Dalhousie to E. Ellice, private, 4 September 1852, Dalhousie Muniments, GD45/6/14.

52. Kincaid to Corresponding Secretary, 22 December 1851, Kincaid Papers; and Burmese Minister to English Government, C. 1490 (1852), p. 213.

53. Dalhousie to Couper, 21 February 1852, in Baird, ed., *Private Letters*, p. 192.

54. Dalhousie to Hobhouse, private, 23 February 1852, Broughton Papers, Add. Mss. 36477.

55. Minute by Dalhousie concurred in by the Board, 25 March 1852, C. 1490 (1852), pp. 225-7.

56. Godwin to Secretary of the Government of India, 6 April 1852, in *Parliamentary Papers*, 1852-3, 69, "The Burmese War, Further Papers," C. 1608, presented 15 March 1853 (hereafter cited C. 1608), p. 366.

57. Dalhousie to Couper, 30 May 1852, in Baird, ed., *Private Letters*, p. 203 (original emphasis).

58. Dalhousie to Couper, 2 and 30 May 1852, ibid., pp. 199 and 203-5.

59. Dalhousie to Couper, 27 June 1852, ibid., p. 208.
60. Minute by Dalhousie, 30 June 1852, C. 1608 (1852-3), pp. 393-406.
61. Minute by Frederick Currie, 1 July 1852, and Minute by Mr. Lowis, 2 July 1852, ibid., pp. 406-7.
62. Minute by Dalhousie, 30 June 1852, ibid., p. 406.
63. Lee-Warner, *Dalhousie*, 1: 446. See also Cyril Philips, "Dalhousie and the Burmese War of 1852," in C. D. Cowan and O. W. Wolters, eds., *Southeast Asian History and Historiography* (Ithaca: Cornell University Press, 1976), pp. 51-8.

4
WAR AND POLITICS IN BRITAIN:
PARTIES, PERSONALITIES,
AND THE PRESS

Governor General Dalhousie's relations with London concerning the war were awkward. Dalhousie was a Peelite, a product of the Conservative party schism over Sir Robert Peel's advocacy of Corn Law repeal in 1846.[1] The Peel ministry, wracked from within, fell over the Irish Coercion Bill. The new Prime Minister, Lord John Russell, a Whig, wanted to incorporate the ex-Conservatives, now Peelites, into the Whig party. Russell first offered Dalhousie the presidency of the Railway Board, but Dalhousie would not accept it "unless there [was] reserved entire freedom of action." The offer came to naught as Lord John was unwilling or unable to assent to this condition.[2] When the Governor Generalship of India was offered to Dalhousie, he accepted. Russell was not as concerned about the exercise of Dalhousie's independence thousands of miles from the House of Lords. Dalhousie wrote to Sir Robert Peel:

> In making this proposal they left me entire independence of political action, and gave me full assurance that my acceptance of the office would be clearly understood not to imply separation from the party with which I have acted. . . . Under these circumstances I felt that I should not be justified either on public or private grounds in declining the appointment.[3]

Dalhousie was an uneasy partner to the Whigs. He found Palmerston's rambunctious foreign policy distasteful.

In February 1852 the unreconstructed Tories, led by Edward Stanley, the Earl of Derby, and Benjamin Disraeli, replaced the Russell ministry. John Herries replaced Lord Broughton as President of the Board of Control. Derby's Cabinet was a makeshift patchwork of second-rate politicians, referred to popularly as the "Who, Who? Ministry." Herries was considered overcunning by the Peelites.[4] He was seventy-five years old and unwell and would have preferred to have been Chancellor of the Exchequer. Instead, he was offered the Colonial Office, Board of Trade, or Board of Control. He took the Board of Control, "being averse to the labour" he believed the other offices entailed.[5]

Changes of party government in London did not affect the Governor General's generally accepted tenure of four years. Though Indian questions were in the arena of party politics, India's governance was looked upon as a trust, and continuity among Governor Generals was desirable. Dalhousie had an agreement with the Whigs that permitted him independence. Dalhousie had no such agreement of political independence with his new masters, the Derby ministry. He wrote: "Though some difference of opinion exists between us on the home politics—no such difference I hope will be found on matters connected with this empire."[6] The Burmese war was to divide them equally on home and Indian affairs.

Dalhousie's Burma policy was assailed in London by the ultraconservatives and the radicals. Their aims transcended a mere attack on an isolated instance of unregulated British expansion. Instead they anticipated the forthcoming debates over the renewal of the East India Company charter in 1853. Lord Ellenborough and Richard Cobden both hoped to restructure the Company.

Immediately Herries had to deal with Burmese affairs; he turned to Lord Ellenborough and the ageless Duke of Wellington for advice. Ellenborough pointed out his 1829 despatch on Burma to Herries. Herries saw Wellington at a levee and passed on the 1829 despatch for his opinion. Herries in turn referred Dalhousie to the "despatch of 29 September 1829 for some interesting guidance."[7] This must have galled Dalhousie, who considered Ellenborough, whose hostility he attributed to jealousy, his "chief assailant" in the House of Lords.[8] Lord Ellenborough opposed the war in light of the costs and casualties of the 1824-26 campaigns. The advantages gained had not been worth the effort, and the 1852 war would meet with the same ill-starred success. Ellenborough felt the less contact with Burma the better. The bitter and disappointed ex-Tenasserim Commissioner H. M. Durand was feeding Ellenborough highly colored reports on Burmese affairs:

> I suspect that Lord Dalhousie had found out that mercan-
> tile interests are very influential in Calcutta, that there is
> a greed for the valuable teak forests of Pegu—a greed the
> keener because the forests in our provinces have been waste-
> fully exhausted—that Bogle and Halliday, popularity hunting
> pulled with the press, and that the claim for £900, by which
> we are plunged into this war, is a most questionable one. Lord
> Dalhousie is said to be in a very surly humour on the whole
> matter.[9]

Halliday and company had conspired to make the Commodore "irremedi-
ably compromise" the Governor General into war. Annexation of Burma
would create a common border with China and lead doubtless to further
unfruitful and expensive annexations.[10]

Ellenborough used Parliament to indict his personal hate objects:
avaricious, speculative timbermen, and the Indian press, as well as East
India Company officials.[11] Ellenborough periodically raised questions in
the House of Lords about the Pegu "pacification" program.[12] In Ellenborough's eyes Lambert was the image of a Palmerstonian filibusterer.
When he arrived in Rangoon "the Don Pacificoes pushed off their boats,
and went on board with representations of the damage which they say
they had sustained." May Flower Crisp was one such individual who did
not deserve British protection. His craven duplicity of selling arms to the
Burmese and advising Commodore Lambert was a travesty. Ellenborough
wanted the anomalous position of the Royal Navy in the Eastern Seas
effaced and "that monstrous job the Indian Navy" replaced by a unified
fleet.[13]

Herries talked to the Duke of Northumberland at the Admiralty. He
concurred on Lambert's culpability. Public criticism was to be avoided.
The Derby government, to please the Admiralty, agreed to "omit the pas-
sages touching on the differences between the Governor General and Commodore Lambert" when it came time to present the Parliamentary Blue
Book. The publication of the Blue Book would be closely timed to the arrival of victory news from Burma.[14]

Beyond the confines of the Cabinet it was Richard Cobden, radical
M. P. for Manchester, who carried the Burmese question into the public
arena.[15] Radical Cobden objected to the war for much the same reasons
as arch-Tory Ellenborough. They agreed England had been brought into a
war by agents beyond London's control. However, they differed in their

solutions. Ellenborough wanted control vested in a Cabinet minister, while Cobden looked to the "public" and "maintain[ed] that the people of this country, through their representatives ought to have the opportunity of expressing their opinion on so important and portentous a proceeding."[16] Cobden took his cue on Burmese affairs from Reverend Henry Richard, Secretary of the Peace Society. Both men loved peace, desired international arbitration of disputes, and thought England, through free trade, could peacefully and bloodlessly conquer the world.[17] The Reverend Richard was appalled that a war was started to avenge an insult to what he described as a fifth- or sixth-rate English officer.[18] Cobden hoped at the 1853 Company charter debates to do away with double government and "mysterious responsibility," which shrouded the Secret Committee in London, the Governor General in Calcutta, and the frontier military commander. The radicals wanted a "Minister for India" in the House of Commons instead of having a Board that never sat.[19]

The "editing out" of important material in the Blue Books infuriated Cobden.[20] The Parliamentary Papers, to paraphrase Cobden, were masterpieces of judicious extracts and abridgements that dispelled blame and reinforced the fighting man's esprit de corps and a Palmerstonian spirit of nationality. Richard Cobden opposed Britain's succession of "little wars" and blamed the military for the Burmese war: "The war was totally unnecessary [and] . . . grew out of the violence of the naval envoy." Cobden also suspected the machinations of American missionary Kincaid.[21] When the Derby ministry was replaced by the Whig-Liberal Aberdeen coalition in December 1852, Sir Charles Wood became the President of the Board of Control. Wood complained to Herries about an "attack made by Cobden . . . in the most unjustifiable manner. He had told me he thought something must have been left out." Wood told Cobden that he could not answer about what he did not know.[22] However, it is obvious from Wood's private correspondence that he knew full well the entire story and had advised that even permanent Cabinet secretaries be excluded from seeing the complete documents.[23] Cobden did not know where the "double government" of India and the duplicity of the Home government stopped or started. Spurred on, he produced his own version of the two government Blue Books—*How Wars are Got up in India: The Origin of the Burmese War*[24]—which appeared at the height of the Government of India Bill debate. It was a catalog of British irresponsibility, illustrating a capricious system unresponsive to public opinion.

The press followed the Burmese war and shifted editorial positions as events dictated. War was bad, but a war badly prosecuted was worse. The *Times* compared Burma to incursions into the Punjab, Scinde, and Afghanistan and commented critically:

> It seems. . .that the ingenuity and perseverance of our Indian authorities have been so successfully exercised as not only to discover an entirely new enemy in a most difficult country, but actually to revive opportunities of the most arduous conflicts in which our Eastern armies were ever engaged.

The editor hoped that rather than answering the call of every border skirmish with overpowering force that the Imperial government would "do all that is required for the security of Bengal without extending our territorial dominions from Beloochistan to Siam."[25]

The *Manchester Guardian,* though emanating from the same locale as the Reverend Richard's Peace Society, took a stridently offensive tone. They strongly opposed the "pacifists." It was "one of the necessities of an empire like that of British India, that all aggressions of the ignorant barbarians by who it is surrounded should be promptly and signally punished."[26] The *Examiner* made comparisons to recent South African experiences. It "would be a repetition of the Caffraria blunder."[27]

As the war progressed the newspapers took up two themes, a grudging acceptance of the war and criticism of war management. There was much to criticize, especially the "superannuated" Commander in Chief, General Godwin. Dalhousie's initial plan for a quick war with few objectives turned into an extended war. It became an "inglorious" and "unpopular" war in which British forces did as little as possible with largest force. Annexation became the overriding issue. The *Guardian*, a missionary newspaper, recalled Britain's mission:

> We cannot evade our responsibility. If it be the will of providence that the British race should have entrusted to its civilising powers a still larger continent than now bows beneath our sceptre—if it be our mission to preach Christianity not only to our subjects in India but the millions beside in Burmah. . .it would ill become us to quail before this career of usefulness attended though it be with an awful responsibility.[28]

The India press was more robust. They looked upon conquest as a positive good. The *Bombay Times, Calcutta Englishman,* and *Friend of India* were papers produced in a frontier environment and the staunchest forward-movement supporters. The editor of the *Friend of India,* John Marshman, produced an inconsequential pamphlet in rebuttal to Cobden.[29]

The vital question to cost-conscious Victorians was Pegu's ability to pay its own way from current revenues. The second consideration was the future stability and security of new borders. If it would lead to further wars frontier extension should be avoided. The *Times* envisioned neither profit nor security from this venture and stated that

> What we have done is to adopt a wide and vulnerable frontier
> in a half-occupied and unsubdued country, exposing our-
> selves in perpetuity to all the perils against which we last
> year assembled an expedition, and taking a new Caffraria
> upon our hands with worse climate, a less productive coast,
> and a hostile monarchy opposed to us.[30]

The radicals had an ally in the *Times.* In light of the Government of India Bill debates the annexation of Pegu was hailed as "a mystery of the double government and must remain an enigma" that "annihilates acountability."[31] Thorough reform of Company rule would have to await the aftermath of the 1857 Mutiny.

The Aberdeen coalition was able to shrug off responsibility for pro-secution of the Burmese war. Aberdeen diverted Ellenborough's query in Lords thusly: "It should be remembered that this war was commenced under the late government and we are as yet not fully apprized."[32] In May 1853 radical M. P. John Bright asked Sir Charles Wood if there were plans for further annexation. Wood replied, "Most decidedly not." Short-ly thereafter the Government of India announced that it was no longer on a war footing and that the blockade had been raised.[33] In London the 1853 session of Parliament was closed with the words of the Lord Chancel-lor, the Earl of Granville. He had been

> commanded [by the Crown] to congratulate you [the
> Parliament] that by the united exertions of the naval and
> military forces of Her Majesty and of the East India Com-
> pany, the war in Burmah has been brought to an honorable
> and successful issue; the objects of the war having been ful-

ly obtained, and due submission made by the Burmese government Peace had been proclaimed.[34]

The background of Tory party schism added a personal dimension to Dalhousie's relations with London. Dalhousie suspected his best interests were not being served in London. Herries wrote the Prime Minister: "Dalhousie is no friend of our party. In the present state of affairs, he and those with whom he acts here, may have views and hopes peculiar to their own interests or designs."[35] While Dalhousie wrote that he felt "duty bound to apply for your [London] orders when time and circumstances admit of it," he employed tactics that made it impossible for London to implement its policy. Although Dalhousie ostensibly "pray[ed] for explicit instructions" he delayed sending his Five Proposals to buy time for his own unapproved plans.[36]

Herries felt the minute of 30 June 1852 so important that he had it printed and circulated for Cabinet comment. Dalhousie chafed at the delay Cabinet comment took and the uncertainty it caused him.[37] Dalhousie's friend, Sir James Weir Hogg, Chairman of the Court, wrote: "I think it is to be much regretted that the last mail did not take out the opinion of the Secret Committee as to the Burmese policy—I am afraid delay may embarrass the Governor General." Herries replied that the mail arrived late, the Cabinet was dispersed because of summer vacation,[38] and that the head of government had taken time to make a "final determination which is to be *most explicit.*" Herries wrote privately to Dalhousie that proposal five would most likely be approved.[39] Derby, however, turned to the aged, deaf, and senile Duke of Wellington, who would die within three weeks, for advice.

Wellington's letter was illegible, and even his private secretary had to guess at what was written. Wellington, without a map and with an imperfect recollection of the first war, opined that all conquered territory should be retained and that war should continue "til the Sovereign of Ava will be convinced of the necessity of signing a treaty [which cedes territory] or till the state of Ava will be destroyed. [If there is a treaty] the sovereign must be made to pay the expenses of war."[40] The Duke was thinking in terms of 1826. Derby and Herries had been willing to unilaterally annex Pegu, as Dalhousie had recommended, but were influenced by Wellington to support a formal treaty. The government then pressed Wellington's views on the Governor General: "We have. . . not adopted the course rather hinted than expressly proposed in your Minute, of confining our military operations to the expulsion of the Burmese from Pegu and then leaving them to do the worst they can against us."[41] London wanted an aggressive policy.

By the time Herries' important instructions arrived in October 1852 Dalhousie had visited Rangoon and reinforced his own plans. He conferred with Lambert and Godwin and issued orders on his own responsibility *not* to march on the capital. On 21 July 1852 he argued that he could wait no longer for London's instructions and left for Rangoon on that day, returning to Calcutta on 6 August 1852. The Governor General's movements outside India technically required London's prior approval. His decision to travel inadvertently or by calculated "oversight" missed the earliest mail to London.[42] Dalhousie was delighted to "settle in five days what otherwise w[ould] take five months" and avoid the "hum and haw" of the court.[43]

Herries referred Dalhousie to "the poor Duke's memorandum [which] leaves no doubt upon" proper policy and hoped Dalhousie would "alter his arrangements if not his opinions." The Prime Minister told Herries to remind Dalhousie of his instructions.[44] Herries referred to public opinion and the press, which

> cry now for conquest and annexation. The mer-
> cantile and manufacturing interests begin to anti-
> cipate the advantages which they may derive from
> our possession of the seaboard of Burma. Although
> you may have set your own plans afoot they have been
> so successful that you are now in a position to carry
> out the rest of *our* wishes.[45]

Dalhousie asked Herries to trust his judgment and experience. He had annexed the Punjab because he was convinced it was indispensable and profitable. He had done so almost against the orders of London.[46]

Dalhousie thought that Pegu was the prize, and by November 1852 it was under British control. Beyond Pegu's northern frontier town, Prome, Burma was neither profitable nor indispensable. Capture of the capital was not synonymous with Burmese defeat. Going beyond Prome would risk all that had been gained and cause the war to last until at least January 1854.[47] Dalhousie prepared another fait accompli for London.

On 29 December 1852 Arthur Purves Phayre, Dalhousie's personal choice as civil administrator for the conquered province, issued a unilateral proclamation annexing Pegu.[48] The war was over, but Pegu would still have to be pacified by police action and "dacoits," or nationalists would continue to disturb the British in Pegu for several more years. The same day the unilateral proclamation was issued a letter was sent to King Pagan Min which prayed he would see the error of his ways and sue for peace. The letter went undelivered, as Amarapura was in revolt. What could London officials do but approve? If they censured or disagreed too loudly, Dalhousie might resign. Not only would he be difficult to replace, but he would become a political threat in England. Herries complained that Dalhousie "is a difficult man to manage. . . . We should have been in Ava long before. . .if our instructions had been obeyed."[49]

While Dalhousie was crossing pens with London, he also had trouble with General Godwin, Commander of the Burmese campaign. The Government of India was a marriage of civil administration and the Indian army. It was never a happy marriage. Ultimate power in the parallel hierarchies was vested in a political appointee, the Governor General. Ambitions clashed, interests were different. Sound administration was synonymous with stable frontiers. But expanding frontiers was the raison d'etre of the military. The military expansionists sided with London's urging of greater conquest.[50]

Dalhousie had appointed General Godwin to head the Burmese campaign. Godwin had served in the First Anglo-Burmese War. Despite his seventy years he was reported to be still active in body and mind, intelligent, and judicious. Initially he desired to follow the contingency plan developed in the late 1830s of an overland expedition against Burma. Dalhousie, after much argument, brought Godwin around to supporting amphibious warfare.[51] Amphibious operations demanded close cooperation between the army and the navy. Godwin disliked steam and naval power. He preferred to have fifty thousand soldiers in the field to five thousand dependent on naval cooperation.[52] To these dislikes were added a personality and command clash. Commodore Lambert, younger and junior in rank, as officer in command of the fleet had precedence over Godwin of the army.

By the end of 1852 Dalhousie had lost all confidence in Godwin, whom he thought gallant but bound by the past. Godwin was jealous, obstinate, and prejudiced. Worse still, Godwin agreed with London thinking that peace could only be found by marching on the capital of Burma. However,

Dalhousie refused to remove him, being solicitous of the General's reputation. In 1853 the General visited India to confer with Dalhousie on questions of war and peace and while there died, thus removing an obstacle in Dalhousie's personal Burma policy.[53]

NOTES

1. See James B. Conacher, "Peel and the Peelites, 1846-1850,"*English Historical Review* 73 (1958): 431-52; and *The Peelites and the Party System, 1846-52* (Newton Abbot: David and Charles, 1972).

2. Dalhousie to Russell, 24 August 1846, and Russell to Dalhousie, 28 August 1846, Russell Papers, Public Record Office, 30/22/5, in Conacher, "Peel and the Peelites," pp. 440-1.

3. Ibid., Dalhousie to Peel, 28 July 1847, Peel Papers, British Library, Add. Mss. 40559.

4. Ibid., p. 445.

5. Edward Herries, *Memoir of the Public Life of the Right Hon. Charles Herries,* 2 vols. (London: John Murray, 1880), 2: 230 and 245.

6. Dalhousie to Herries, private, 24 April 1852, Herries Papers, British Library, 46; Dalhousie to Couper, 2 May 1852, in J. G. A. Baird, ed., *Private Letters of the Marquis of Dalhousie* (Edinburgh: William Blackwood and Sons, 1910), p. 199; and William Devereaux Jones and Arvel B. Erickson, *The Peelites, 1846-1857* (Columbus: Ohio State University Press, 1972), pp. 68-9.

7. Herries to Ellenborough and Herries to Wellington, 4 March 1852, and Herries to Dalhousie, confidential, 8 March 1852, Herries Papers, 78.

8. Dalhousie to Couper, 20 March 1852 and 5 March 1858, in Baird, ed., *Private Letters,* pp. 195 and 409.

9. Durand to Ellenborough, 26 March and 13 May 1852, Ellenborough Papers, PRO 30/12/21/6.

10. Durand to Ellenborough, 26 March and 18 June 1852, Ellenborough Papers, PRO 30/12/21/5 and PRO 30/12/26.

11. Ellenborough in House of Lords, *Parliamentary Debates,* 127, 6 June 1853, C. 1199-1206; and Dalhousie to Wood, 28 March 1853, Wood Papers, India Office Library and Records, F78/17.

12. Ellenborough in House of Lords, *Parliamentary Debates,* 125, 15 April 1853, C. 1187.

13. Ellenborough in House of Lords, *Parliamentary Debates,* 119, 16 February 1852, C. 120, 535-8; 25 March 1852, C. 56-8; and 5 April 1852, C. 658.

14. Herries to Dalhousie, 8 April, Herries to Dalhousie, 24 May, and Herries to Northumberland, 29 May, 1852, Herries Papers, 78.

15. William D. Grampp, *The Manchester School of Economics* (Stanford: Stanford University Press, 1960); and J. S. Galbraith, "Myths of the 'Little England' Era," *American Historical Review* 67 (1961): 34-48.

16. Cobden in House of Commons, *Parliamentary Debates,* 127, 20 May 1853, C. 431-2.

17. See Norman McCord, *The Anti-Corn Law League* (London: George Allen and Unwin, 1958); and Bernard Semmel, *The Rise of Free Trade Imperialism* (Cambridge: Cambridge University Press, 1970).

18. *Manchester Guardian,* 16 May 1853, speech to workingmen's group; and Cobden to Henry Richard, 14 May 1852, in John A. Hobson, *Richard Cobden, The International Man* (London: T. Fisher Unwin, 1919), p. 86.

19. Joseph Hume in House of Commons, *Parliamentary Debates,* 124, 23 February 1853, C 662.

20. Cobden in House of Commons, ibid., 127, 17 June 1853, C. 377.

21. Cobden to Richard, 10 August 1852, in Hobson, *Cobden,* pp. 86 and 95.

22. Wood to Herries, 20 June 1853, Herries Papers, 61.

23. Wood to Herries, private, 8 January and 16 February 1853, confidential, ibid.

24. London: W. and F. G. Gash, 1853.

25. *Times,* 3 February 1852.

26. *Manchester Guardian,* 6 March 1852.

27. *Examiner,* 6 March 1852.

28. *Guardian* (missionary newspaper), 15 April 1852.

29. *How Wars Arise in India: Observations on Mr. Cobden's Pamphlet "The Origin of the Burmese War"* (London: N.p., 1853).

30. *Times,* 18 January and 23 May 1853.

31. Ibid., 1 August 1853.

32. Aberdeen in House of Lords, *Parliamentary Debates,* 124, 24 Feb-

ruary 1853, C 535-44; J. B. Conacher, *The Aberdeen Coalition, 1852-1855* (Cambridge: Cambridge University Press, 1968); and C. H. Stuart, "The Formation of the Coalition Cabinet in 1852," *Transactions of the Royal Historical Society,* 5th ser., 4 (1954): 45-68.

33. Wood in House of Commons, *Parliamentary Debates,* 127, 20 May 1853, C. 435-6; and *Times,* 17 August 1853.

34. Earl of Granville in House of Lords, *Parliamentary Debates,* 129, 20 August 1853, C. 1827.

35. Herries to Derby, confidential, 14 June 1852, Herries Papers, 78.

36. Dalhousie to Herries, confidential and private, 3 July 1852, ibid., 46.

37. Herries to Derby, 19 August 1852, ibid., 44; Dalhousie to Couper, 7 August 1852, in Baird, ed., *Private Letters,* p. 215.

38. James W. Hogg to Herries, 26 August 1852, Herries Papers, 45; and Herries to Dalhousie, 7 September 1852 in Herries, *Memoir of the Public Life,* 2: 257.

39. Herries to Hogg, 29 August, and Herries to Dalhousie, 24 August 1852, Herries Papers, 78.

40. Memo by Duke of Wellington, 24 August 1852, ibid., 92.

41. Derby to Herries, private, 27 August, and Herries to Dalhousie, 7 September 1852, ibid., 44 and 78.

42. Secret Committee to Governor General of India in Council, 6 September 1852; Minute by Dalhousie, 10 August 1852; and Governor General of India in Council to Secret Committee, 19 July 1852 in *Parliamentary Papers,* 1852-3, 69, "The Burmese War, Further Papers," C. 1608, presented 15 March 1853 (hereafter cited C. 1608), pp. 52-4 and 19-24.

43. Dalhousie to Couper, 10 July 1852, in Baird, ed., *Private Letters,* p. 213.

44. Herries to Derby, 5 October, and Derby to Herries, 6 October 1852, Herries Papers, 78 and 44.

45. Herries to Dalhousie, 25 October 1852, ibid., 78; and Secret Committee to Governor General of India in Council, 23 October 1852, in C. 1608 (1852-3), p. 433.

46. Dalhousie to Herries, 8 November 1852, Herries Papers, 46.

47. Dalhousie to Herries, 21 August 1852, ibid.; and Dalhousie to C.B. Tucker, 8 June 1852, Dalhousie Muniments, GD45/6/14.

48. Printed in D. G. E. Hall, ed., *The Dalhousie-Phayre Correspondence, 1852-1856* (London: Oxford University Press, 1932), pp. 4-5.

49. Herries to ?, early 1853, in Herries, *Memoir of the Public Life,* 2: 269.

50. One of Dalhousie's prime antagonists in the latter 1840s wrote, "I pray for the total annexation of Burma." Charles Napier to Dalhousie,

20 October 1852, Dalhousie Muniments, GD45/6/155.

51. Dalhousie to Broughton, private, 8 March 1852, Broughton Papers, Add. Mss. 36477; and Godwin to Dalhousie, 19 March 1852, Dalhousie Muniments, 6/115, pt. 1.

52. Dalhousie to Couper, 2 October 1852, in Baird, ed., *Private Letters*, p. 227.

53. Dalhousie to Herries, private, 23 November and Godwin to Dalhousie, 20 October 1852, Herries Papers, 46 and 97; and Dalhousie to Couper, 25 March and 30 October 1853, in Baird, ed., *Private Letters*, pp. 250 and 270.

5

WAR, REVOLUTION, AND RECONSTRUCTION IN BURMA

The war was a catastrophe for the Burmese. The Burmese may honestly have tried to avert war by complying with the wishes of the British and replacing the Rangoon Governor. Prince Mindon, head of the *Hluttaw*, is reported to have sent a letter to the Governor urging utmost caution. The new Governor was the sole arbiter, and there was a limit to the humiliation to which he would submit. The British in the Rangoon River took advantage of this. After Lambert's seizure of the King's ship, the Rangoon Governor had little choice but to try the fortunes of war.[1] The court pondered Rangoon events and concluded that "the government of India had sent Commodore Lambert, General of the English fighting ships, to cause trouble between the two countries." Deceit and cunning were the hallmarks of the British as they continually escalated their demands. The King, as commander in chief, ordered mobilization. War commenced with an air of bravery and naïveté as the King proclaimed to a silent, bowed audience:

> Pagan Min's order at the beginning of the Second Anglo-Burmese war to the Army marching to Hanthawaddy [Rangoon]. The Governor goes from capital with 20,000 men. 11,438 have been mobilized in the south. Names of commanders. Enumeration of equipment. Capture and defeat the English. Troops should be honest in their progress and not even confiscate fruit or vegetable leaves. No

inauspicious words [swearing], no intoxicating Liquors,
etc., or gambling should be tolerated. Be alert. Hold con-
sultations continuously. Propitiate the Nats and pray to
them to overcome the English who endanger the Buddhist
religion. Consult as to whether fighting or wisdom will
overcome English. Plan your strategy carefully. Fight at
the proper time. Deploy troops well on offensive or defensive position as demanded by circumstance. Keep King
informed by horse or boats. Disloyal troops should be
punished. Those distinguished in fighting should be re-
warded by the King. If they serve this way the English
will be captured, Soldiers can have spoils. When objective
achieved the Commander-in-chief should not come back
to King until called and then he should bring up the spoils
for the King with him. Everyone would think of my orders
day and night and serve accordingly. Faithlessness will be
punished without listening to excuses.

Issued on the 14th day after the
full moon of Taboung, 1213, to
the troops on the frontier.[2]

The futility of the war was soon apparent. The Burmese immediately
felt the taste of defeat with the fall of Rangoon. Burmese forces were
constantly on the defensive. Dismayed, Pagan Min changed several of
his advisers and military commanders, but to no avail. Retreats were
followed by defections. General Bandula was a mere shadow of his
father, Maha Bandula, hero-strategist of the First Anglo-Burmese War.
His army of seven thousand men dwindled to two thousand. He surrendered on 15 October 1852. All along the British line of advance
Burmese local officials had to make the same difficult decisions: to
flee, join the British, or set up private liberation armies. The Governor
of Rangoon fled, while his wife and son chose to come into Sir John
Cheap's camp.[3]

The continuous losses polarized Burmese politics into "bitterenders"
and the peace faction, who supported the ruling line of Pagan Min or
his younger half-brother, Prince Mindon. Mindon was born in 1814 to
a lesser wife of Tharrawaddy; his claims to the Golden Throne were
distant, but fratricidal strife brought this goal closer and closer as the

years went by. He received an extensive religious education and was noted for piety and knowledge. He emerged into the secular world after his father's coup in 1837, serving first as a minor member of the *Hluttaw* and then as its head in the late 1840s. He was able to borrow other men's ideas as his own, ingratiating the giver to himself, rather than creating resentment. Prince Mindon had disassociated himself from the war.[4] Though head of the *Hluttaw* and leader of the moderates, he made no headway against Pagan Min, Maung Bwa, and the military's entrenched power. Pagan Min and his advisers were inextricably tied to narrow tradition and war. They could not count on the luck of Bagyidaw, who lost a war yet retained the throne. The experience since 1837 had been too tumultuous to rely on complacency. Opposition to the war posed a threat to the regime.

There is striking similarity between the revolts of 1837 and 1852. There were rumors that Pagan Min was insane, though there is no evidence for such assertions. Pagan Min relied on Maung Bwa, who was a childhood playmate, foster brother, and son of his nurse and head of the war party. The kinsmen were jealous of Maung Bwa's ascendancy and disliked the war with the English, which they blamed on him.[5] The kinsmen were not alone in their dissatisfaction. Officials whom Pagan Min had displaced when he came to the throne and more recently discarded because of failure to bring victory were vocal supporters of Mindon and his younger brother, Kanaung. Opposition to Pagan Min was developing along the lines of court connections, kinship, and attitudes toward the war. Popular discontent added another dimension to the polarization at court. The British blockade cut off the traditional southern Irrawaddy rice supply. The military call-up reduced the tilled acreage. Rice was in short supply and commanding high prices. Burmese soldiers at Prome were subsisting on ponies and plantains.[6]

By November 1852 the factions had sufficiently polarized for Maung Bwa to search for a pretext to suppress Mindon and Kanaung. The sister of the King's nurse (and therefore a kinsman of Maung Bwa) was robbed. Some of Kanaung's retainers were spuriously indicted. Mindon was accused of harboring criminals in his household. Pagan Min's followers were taking all opportunities to put the half-brothers out of the way. Mindon initially was reluctant to believe this and even more reluctant to take precautions. The Kanaung Prince and other advisers tried to convince Mindon of the danger. Mindon replied as had Tharrawaddy in 1837. He looked upon his elder brother, Pagan Min, as father. Pagan Min had given him and Kanaung cities, and they owed the King submission. Kanaung convinced Mindon that, despite Pagan Min's benevolence, his advisers were false. They were circumventing the usual channels of law, the *Hluttaw* and the *Byetaik*, and were taking action in secret. Kanaung wanted Mindon to flee and follow the advice of his friends, all ex-officials. Various auspicious omens were invoked to support this plan of action.

On 18 December 1852 Mindon and his three-hundred-strong household left Amarapura.[7] Kanaung was in charge of the military operations and in the revolt's early stages made the important decisions. Mindon traveled with the women, children, and servants. He was unsure of his next move. He contemplated fleeing to Manipur, but his advisers, especially Maung Po Hlaing and Maung So, who were later appointed *Wungyis*, suggested he make his stand at Shwebo, the seat of the dynasty.[8] The Shwebo Wun was unpopular, and the populace would fight for Mindon. Moreover, a retreat to Manipur would alienate his followers. It was decided to attack Shwebo, and on 22 December 1852 Mindon successfully entered the city.

Pagan Min was in an awkward position. His troops were deployed in an unpopular war against the British. He had few reserves to put down the revolt. Kanaung and Mindon could rely on natural disaffection to raise recruits. Pagan Min placed his half-brother, the Hlaing Prince, Tharrawaddy's youngest son by a Siamese dancer, in charge of the campaign against the rebels and created him *Einshemin.* Mindon appointed Kanaung commander in chief and *Einshemin.* Dispirited, Pagan Min, after consulting with his religious advisers, decided to abdicate. When Pagan Min's emissaries to Mindon were refused entry into Shwebo, he then decided to resist. In expectation of siege he fortified Amarapura, shut the gates, and mounted cannons on the wall. By mid-January 1853 Pagan Min's forces were experiencing mass desertions among troops fighting the British and those directed against the rebel half-brothers. Fighting between the rival brothers became bitter, with heavy losses on both sides. Mindon urged an active siege on Amarapura. Despite desertions the Hlaing Prince was able to make successful incursions against the rebels. But Mindon and Kanaung used guile as well as military force. Mindon was in secret communication with high officials within the capital.

On February 1853 this bore fruit. The Kyaukmaw Wungyi, later
created the Magwe Wungyi, had secretly won over some of the royal
troops and suddenly proceeded to arrest several top advisers of Pagan
Min and open the gates to Mindon's troops. The Hlaing Prince was
overpowered and killed in the crossfire. The capital was in the hands
of the rebels. Immediately Kanaung gathered all insignia of rank and
sent them to Mindon. The rebels were now the rulers.[9]

Once Mindon and Kanaung had captured the capital they set to
work reconstructing the government. Kanaung controlled the royal
city while Mindon remained at the ancestral seat of Shwebo. His regal
entry into the royal capital occurred in December 1853. Power stabiliza-
tion entailed dealing with ex-King Pagan Min, reinforcing Mindon's
familial claim to the throne, appointing ministers, satisfying the claims
of Prince Kanaung, and dealing with the British.

Pagan Min had eighteen wives. Seventeen of them were still alive in
early 1853. Eleven wives were immediately abandoned when Pagan Min
lost the throne. They also lost their fiefs, which were redistributed among
Mindon's own followers or newly acquired wives. Most of Pagan Min's
deserted wives remarried lesser officials. His reduced household was
given a small new palace, built at the behest of Mindon, and he continued
to live in peace and obscurity until he died of smallpox at the age of
seventy in 1881, outliving Mindon by three years. Maung Bwa was allowed to live and probably died of old age.[10]

Mindon secured his hold on the throne in the traditional manner, via
royal, official, and territorial marriage alliances. Mindon, as prince, had
at least six wives, the first of whom he married as early as 1836. Immediately following the revolution he took at least eight more wives.
By 1866 he had forty-two wives and at his death in 1878 fifty-five wives.[11]
The royal marriages in 1853 were to daughters of Tharrawaddy and
Bagyidaw. The former were Mindon's own half-sisters; the latter were
cousins.

Mindon took as his principal Queen his half-sister, the eldest daughter
of Tharrawaddy, who was a renowned astrologer. She had been reserved
to marry the next King. The marriage ceremony, the laying of hands,
occurred in April 1853. She was forty years old and destined to bear
no children. Her importance lay in her links with the past, her intelligence, and her powers as an astrologer. She had exerted great influence

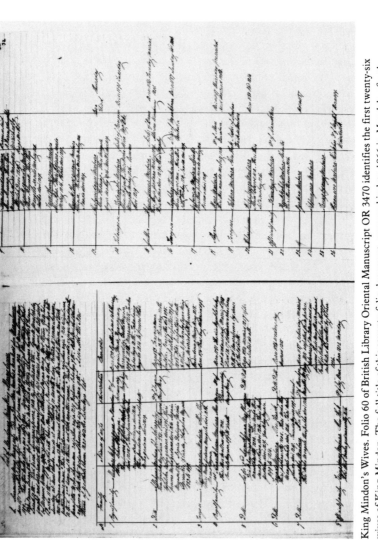

King Mindon's Wives. Folio 60 of British Library Oriental Manuscript OR 3470 identifies the first twenty-six wives of King Mindon. The full title of this seventy folio document, prepared in late 1866 in Mandalay for the Commissioner of British Burma, A. P. Phayre, is "A Historical Memorandum on Burma Minters [kings?] Family from Beginning to the Present 1228. AD 1866. Collected from Burman History and Various Parts. Best Corrected by Various Prince and Queen and Old Officials of the Burman."

with her father, Tharrawaddy, in 1837 prophesying and interpreting favorable omens for the revolt. She had warned Mindon in late 1853 that Pagan Min was plotting against him. Official marriages were made to the daughters of prominent provincial officials and to his own central advisers. Territorial marriages with non-Burmese were made with Tavoyans, Shans, Yuthians, Assamese, and Khantee. Through marriage Mindon forged new links between the heartland and periphery. The wives bore 110 children, about equally divided between male and female offspring. Following Mindon's accession to the throne he "generally [had] an addition to his family. . . once or twice a month." As the reign progressed the rate of natural increase in the royal family dropped, and at his death in 1878 he had about thirty-seven wives and fifty children. Several of the latter died in the 1879 massacre.[12]

Patronage was an important concern, as Mindon had to fill various central bureaucratic positions, including *Wungyis* in the *Hluttaw, Wundauks,* and *Atwinwun* in the *Byetaik.* While monarchy, even in coups, was hereditary, crown officials' positions were filled by royal patronage generally from retainers rather than kinsmen. A prime qualification was service in the Prince's household, loyalty, opposition to his deposed half-brother, Pagan Min, and assistance in the coup. The Prince's household was insufficient to fill the numerous royal positions.

Pagan Min's officials could survive into the new reign with power if they demonstrably aided Mindon in the revolt. Thus the Kyaukmaw Wungyi under Pagan Min, who had won over some royal troops to Mindon's side at a crucial juncture of the coup of 18 February 1853 and opened the palace gates to the rebels, became Mindon's leading minister in the *Hluttaw* with the new title Magwe Wungyi. He was in his mid-fifties and politically adept, having served in Bagyidaw's palace guard and as an *Atwinwun* under Tharrawaddy. Magwe was most knowledgeable about the British, and his discussions and correspondence included scientific subjects, European affairs, America, and maps.[13] His attitude toward the British was that of a man who had burned his fingers badly and learned his lesson. He wanted peace, complied with most reasonable requests of the British, and applied himself to constant surveillance of the frontier.

U Yan We had been Prince Mindon's *saya* at Bagaya monastery, where he also taught U Gaung (later created Kinwun Mingyi). U Yan He was seconded to Prince Mindon's household in 1850 as *Akyidaw*. This teacher-disciple relationship was not unusual, and his student on becoming King promoted U Yan We to Pakhangyi Wungyi.

While this form of recruitment was certainly neither novel nor necessarily reformist, greater care than usual seems to have been paid to appointing experienced, moderate, and intelligent officials. While they may have been the proverbial favorites they were also among the best qualified. The architects of the lost war were purged. *Wundauks* and *Atwinwuns* at the center and the *myosas* and provincial governors were drawn from the Prince's household, willing fathers-in-law, previous court officials, and those who had helped in the revolt.[14]

Non-Burmese advisers also frequented the court. Most important was Camaretta, who had been Tharrawaddy's adviser, fallen out with Pagan Min, and been reinstated by Mindon. Camaretta was employed primarily as a foreign policy adviser. Foreigners were frequently employed at frontier posts. They had the necessary multilingual facilities, and they lacked an independent local power base, making them entirely dependent on the crown for authority. Care was taken to appoint judicious men to marching regions. Mindon's early diplomatic success, concluding a de facto peace with the British without signing a humiliating treaty ceding Pegu, resulted from a message indicated by his patronage policy. Aggressive frontier officials were removed, and the border army was demobilized and replaced with police.[15]

Prince Kanaung was created heir and received new titles, new fiefs, and an expanded household. He married the Hlaing Princess, daughter of Tharrawaddy and his own half-sister. Mindon built a new palace for Kanaung. Kanaung's household became the locus of technological advancement and the cultural center of independent Burma until his death. The Hlaing Princess was a poet and served as patroness to the foremost Burmese literateur, U Pon Nya.

British intelligence first got wind of the November 1852 revolt through imperfect rumors in early January 1853.[16] Rumor was reinforced by a curious phenomenon. As the revolt spread the British found their troops facing no enemy, as Burmese troops were withdrawn to go up to the capital to take sides. It was a happy coincidence that Dalhousie's determination on limited annexation and peace and Mindon's rise were simultaneous.

Shortly after Phayre became Commissioner of Pegu, reliable intelligence increased. Unfortunately, reports were routed by Captain Latter. Despite Latter's alarmism, the import of the message was clear: the new rulers of

Burma wanted peace.[17] Mindon was so keen on peace that he released all European prisoners of war in the areas he controlled. Mindon opened up communications with the British well before he captured Amarapura or was King. He deputized two Italian Catholic missionaries, fathers Domingo Tarolly and Paula Abbona, to deliver a letter of peace. The British received it on the Irrawaddy on 27 January 1853.[18]

The prospective King, through his emissaries, addressed the advancing conquerors frankly. He pleaded that "the business of taking and governing country [revolution], the umbrella and palace is exceedingly onerus, varied, and extensive." War was the result of misgovernment at the hands of ministers and nobles who had served his elder brother, Pagan Min. Mindon hoped that the English rulers in India wanted peace as much as he.[19]

The British had determined on annexing Pegu. They now had to mark a boundary including as much valuable teak forest as possible and conclude a treaty of peace and cession with the Burmese. However, the latter was not attained. Mindon proclaimed Pegu his "ancestors' property." The area from which Mindon derived his name, Mindon Province, was part of the annexed territory. The new King was dejected at the British taking it. He would not formally cede Pegu, but informally he made it clear that he would do nothing militarily to redeem the area.[20]

By the end of January 1853 Phayre had decided that Meaday should mark the boundary. Prome was unhealthy, and the extended boundary would enclose further valuable teak forests. The discussions about peace, a treaty, and boundaries proceeded on the frontier from the end of January to early May 1853.

The four-man Burmese delegation was headed by the principal *Wungyi*, who had opened the gates to the rebels. They met the British commission in early April. Phayre carried with him a draft treaty. The treaty was doomed, not so much because of Burmese hesitancy, but because Godwin and Lambert, the other members of the commission, all but sabotaged any chance of success.

The British Commissioners were not of one mind as to the boundaries. In fact, one of them was almost out of his mind. General Godwin's smouldering resentment against Lambert's superior rank and Phayre's civil appointment exploded at the conference with the Burmese over the boundary. He took an independent line. Godwin argued that the Burmese should be allowed to retain Pegu, since the term was so vague. On alternate days he would propose marching on the capital of Ava and annexing the entire country if a treaty was not concluded. Even Lambert joined in this chorus.[21] Dalhousie, with some foresight, had anticipated problems with a three-man commission and had secretly given Phayre powers to sign a treaty without concurrence from Lambert or Godwin. But this performance had obviously weakened the British bargaining position. Phayre was exasperated. Dalhousie was livid and considered censure. The Burmese held out for more concessions, stating that they would accept Toungoo as the northernmost extremity of British territory vice Meaday. This would mean a shift about thirty miles southward. As a desperate measure to secure a treaty Phayre convinced Dalhousie to accept Prome plus ten miles as a minimum British frontier, about the same as the Burmese were requesting, even though it meant the loss of valuable timbershed.[22] But the Burmese hemmed and hawed, and Dalhousie and Phayre lost patience. When on 9 May the Burmese envoy announced that he was not empowered to sign a treaty negotiations were terminated. Phayre handed the Burmese envoy the Governor General's contingency minute, declaring the boundary fixed at six miles north of Meaday.

A few months later Dalhousie paid a personal visit to the frontier to demonstrate that this decision was unalterable. Phayre observed, sucking sour grapes, that perhaps a treaty was not worth the effort. "I believe the king, having just come to the throne after a revolution, is afraid to incur the odium of signing away the lower provinces of his kingdom. He may, however, silently acquiesce in our occupation and be ready to enter into a commercial treaty." Perhaps this was a lesser crime for Mindon and a facesaving gesture for the British. Phayre asked Dalhousie, "In such a case I should be glad to know what your Lordship's orders will be."[23] Dalhousie replied emphatically, "Under no circumstances will I now recede from Meaday, Ava may become ours, but Meaday never will become theirs again." Furthermore, there could be no commercial treaty that omitted mention of territorial cession. He requested Phayre to send him a map of his new domain.[24]

Mindon sensed that the British would not advance farther than six miles north of Meaday and that they had almost given up obtaining a treaty.[25] The Burmese acquiesced, having neither the power nor the will to resist. Just as London had been presented with a fait accompli not to their liking, so the Burmese were faced with an unalterable fact, unpleasant as it might be.

The Kyaukmaw Wungyi (Magwe Wungyi), after returning to Amarapura, wrote to the British that he had presented the Governor General's minute to the King and that Mindon desired peace. Orders had been issued to Burmese frontier commanders to respect British claims to Meaday and Toungoo. All English prisoners had been liberated, and foreign merchants were given permission to leave the country. The Government of India declared a unilateral peace. The army, though not immediately withdrawn, was taken off a war footing.

Dalhousie and Mindon had accomplished their aims. The Governor General had successfully resisted pressure for larger conquests, even though he had not obtained a treaty. Mindon had accomplished a cessation of hostilities on his own terms, without being personally humiliated. Was it a firm peace or merely a truce? The answer to this question lay in the manner the leaders of the two countries would work out their future relationship and how well the weaker of the two understood its fragile position.

NOTES

1. Narrative of Moung Shoay Ngyouin in letter to Phayre, 23 January 1853, British Library, Phayre Collection, Oriental Mss. 3469; and C. M. Crisp to Young, 23 December 1851, ISP/173.

2. U Tin (of Sagaing), *Kòn-baung-zet Maha-ya-zawin-daw-gyi* [Great royal chronicle of the Kon-baung dynasty], 3 vols. (Manadalay: Hanthawaddy Pitakat Press, 1922-3), 3: 96-8; and Taw Sein Ko, *Selections from the Records of the Hluttaw* (Rangoon: Government Printers, 1889), pp. 28-31.

3. Governor General of India in Council to Secret Committee, 19 July 1852, in *Parliamentary Papers,* 1852-3, 69, "The Burmese War, Further Papers," C. 1608, p. 415; and Lambert to Dalhousie, 29 October 1852, Dalhousie Muniments, 6/531.

4. James George Scott [Shway Yoe], *The Burman: His Life and Notions* (New York: Norton, 1963 [orig. publ. 1882]), p. 140; Godwin to Grant Allan, 6 January 1853, ISP/181.

5. Phayre to Secretary of the Government of India, 18 January 1853, and Latter to Allen, 26 January 1853, report by a Mohammedan trader, Muhammud Hussain, ISP/181.

6. Lambert to Dalhousie, 25 August 1852, Dalhousie Muniments, 6/531; and extract from letter to Captain Neblett, 11 September 1852, Herries Papers, 46.

7. Statement of Nga Shwe taken at Prome, 19 February 1853, enclosed in Phayre to Secretary of Government of India, 19 February 1853, ISP/181.

8. J. G. Scott and J. P. Hardiman, comps., *Gazetteer of Upper Burma and the Shan States,* 2 pts., 5 vols. (Rangoon: Government Printers, 1900), pt. 1, 1: 67.

9. Latter to Phayre, 25 February 1853, and Father Domingo's statement to Phayre, 28 February 1853, ISP/181.

10. J. G. Jacob to Edwards, 11 October 1853; Spears to Phayre, 11 September 1854 and 21 January 1855, in D. G. E. Hall, ed., *The Dalhousie-Phayre Correspondence, 1852-1856* (London: Oxford University Press, 1932), pp. 110, 249, and 295.

11. Phayre Collection, Oriental Mss. 3470; and Scott [Shway Yoe], *The Burman,* p. 59.

12. Spears to Phayre, 17 March 1855, in Hall, ed., *Correspondence,* pp. 308-9; and Scott [Shway Yoe], *The Burman,* p. 59.

13. Mission Diary, 24 September and 4 October 1855, in Henry Yule, *A Narrative of the Mission sent by the Governor General of India to the Court of Ava in 1855* (Kuala Lumpur: Oxford University Press, 1968 [orig. publ. 1858]), pp. 100 and 127; Ma Kyan, "King Mindon's Councillors, *J.B.R.S.* 44 (1961): 43-60; and U Khin Mg. Kyi and Daw Tin Tin, *Administrative Patterns in Historical Burma,* Institute of Southeast Asian Studies, Southeast Asian Perspectives no. 1 (Singapore, 1973), pp. 53-4, notes that *Wungyi* survival from reign to reign was not unusual. Four served five consecutive kings; six served four; nine served three; and twenty-four served two.

14. Yule, *Reports of the Mission to Ava in 1859* (Calcutta: Government Printers, 1856), pp. 248-9.

15. Spears to Phayre, 18, 20, and 28 February, 18 March, and 6 August 1854, in Hall, ed., *Correspondence,* pp. 39, 140-1, 158, and 230.

16. Godwin to Allen, 6 January 1853, ISP/181.

17. Latter to Phayre, 25 February 1853, ISP/181.

18. Phayre to Government of India, 28 January 1853, in Hall, ed., *Correspondence,* pp. 19-22.

19. King of Burma to English General, dated no later than 23 January 1853, enclosed in Phayre to Government of India, 28 January 1853, ISP/181.

20. Father Domingo, Statement to Phayre, 28 February 1853, ISP/181

21. Phayre to Dalhousie, 9 April 1853, in Hall, ed., *Correspondence,* p. 53.

22. Dalhousie to Phayre, 25 April 1853, ibid., p. 56.

23. Phayre to Dalhousie, 11 May 1853, ibid., p. 66.

24. Dalhousie to Phayre, 21 May 1853, ibid., p. 69.

25. Phayre to Dalhousie, 21 July 1853, ibid., p. 84.

6

BURMESE MODERNIZATION: ADMINISTRATION AND ECONOMY (1853-66)

The loss of Pegu was the second truncation of Burma by the British within living memory. The common frontier with the British was now longer and closer to the heartland. Mindon and Kanaung perceived an obvious threat. There was no reason to expect that Western exploration, trade, military, and missionary ambitions would stop and leave Upper Burma, or North Burma, to remain independent. Burma was now landlocked, and there were predictions even as the second war tailed off in 1853 that it was only a matter of time before the remnants of sovereign Burma would disappear. Mindon and Kanaung turned themselves to averting this fate.

Mindon felt the war was caused by "the officials in whose charge the provinces at the extremities of the empire were placed" and not by central authorities.[1] Burmese exclusivism exacerbated the problem that led to national disaster. In response to defeat Mindon strengthened control in the remaining kingdom through a program of limited "defensive Westernization." He meant to be the ideal Buddhist monarch, fusing politics and religion, and assumed that innovations would not breach tradition, that modernization policy could be harmonized with Buddhism, and that there was a particular Burmese road to development.

Mindon concerned himself with administration, the economy, Buddhism, and the avoidance of unequal diplomatic contacts and treaties. Sound administration throughout his domain would be the necessary minimum to forestall any further British advance. Mindon had a Buddhist vision of a better-fed, healthier, and happier Burmese society. This could be achieved through the exercise of traditional royal prerogatives, including monopoly. Kanaung devoted himself to technological development, the military, and patronage of the arts. During the first part of Mindon's reign, 1853-66, the brothers committed themselves to transforming the traditional Burmese state into a viable, nineteenth-century nation. Their policies were interdependent. This fruitful partnership ended with the assassination of Kanaung in 1866. Thereafter Burmese policy lost much of its animation and confidence.

ADMINISTRATIVE REFORM

Mindon aimed to increase national integrity by demanding greater accountability and communications within the central administrative structure. He applied a cohesive, sustained, and interacting policy that affected patronage, the judiciary, revenue collection, the military, and infrastructure. Mindon's first edicts had the effect of settling disturbances by reaffirming eminent domain, providing recourse to the *Hluttaw* for grievances, and punishing false claimants to official appointments.[2] The revolution purged the architects of failure. Mindon placed his followers throughout the country, taking extraordinary pains to appoint judicious men along the British border. Insubordinate or corrupt officials were quickly removed.[3]

Burma's judicial system was decentralized. The Burmese proverb, "More money wins the case," indicates its entrepreneurial orientation. Contemporary British descriptions are less flattering.[4] Recourse to higher courts consumed time and funds. Mindon, as Tharrawaddy before him, opened the reign with traditional appeals against bribery and corruption. Mindon warned judges against accepting rewards and presents that would interfere with pending or future cases. Fee taking in excess of regulations and extortion were forbidden. Mindon's concern ran deeper than his father's. The second war could be traced indirectly to the Rangoon courts presided over by an avaricious Governor. The traditional system stood condemned. Mindon's response was to attack successively central and local corruption, introduce regulations, divide the law into civil and criminal jurisdictions, formalize appeal procedures, limit local hereditary officials to civil cases, and ultimately to replace local officials with royal appointees. The results included better justice, more money for the central treasury, and increased patronage for the crown.

In April 1853 Mindon issued judicial guidelines for *Hluttaw* and provincial officials. They established set legal tariffs or fees for at least thirty-three legal procedures. Central officials were remunerated by the crown, though not through actual salaries, thus removing the need to make a living from fees. Penalties for malfeasance depended on the rank of the offender and included reimbursement, fines, detention, strokes with the lash, imprisonment, loss of insignia and rank, and dismissal. Because of distance, provincial officials were more difficult to control, and the regulations, therefore, provided for punishments for first, second, and third acquittals. The central courts were divided into three jurisdictions: civil, land and inheritance, and criminal.[5]

In May 1860 local officials lost the power to impose the death penalty without confirmation of the *Hluttaw.* In spite of the schedule of fees and penalties for bribery and corruption Mindon's injunctions had limited effectiveness. In response to complaints additional schedules of judicial fees were issued to the provinces. The forces of modernizing centralism were struggling with the Burmese "gentry." The local hereditary *Myothugyi* and *Taikthugyi* had substantial responsibility for law and order. For generations they had existed symbiotically with the center. In times of war they marshaled troops, food, and money; they were less forthcoming in times of peace. Overexaction from the center could result in local rebellion. Oppression by local officials could result in complaints to the center or the aggrieved migrating to another province.[6]

The center meant to destroy the practice of sharing court fees with provincial officials. In April 1865 a custodian of judicial fees with a staff of at least fifty-two was appointed. They were to supervise the collection and audit of local judicial fees. In 1866 the custodian of court fees was directed to send the money either monthly or quarterly to the capital. Punishment for bribery and corruption was increased again. Shortly thereafter officials were placed on salaries.[7]

In 1865 the local courts were restructured. Local officials were limited to handling only civil cases. Criminal cases would be referred to district courts. The new judges were to report regularly to the *Hluttaw* on irregularity or malpractice among local officials, general economic conditions, the state of cultivation, and law and order. In 1867 local officials lost their civil legal jurisdictions, and judges were dispatched to offer their impartial services without delay to litigants. Subsequent legal reforms included the

establishment of judges in distant regions in 1870, a clearer definition of
civil and criminal jurisdictions in 1871, and the institution of an oath of
office in 1873.[8]

Despite bureaucratization Mindon continued to exercise his prerogative
of benevolent interference. An early habit was his fortnightly progress
around the capital, visiting the *Hluttaw* and other courts to hear appeals
of dissatisfied litigants. In cases where Mindon reversed judgments, officials were fined. Kanaung, as head of the *Hluttaw*, on more than one
occasion had to pay a 150 *tical* fine. The *Wungyis* were fined 50 *ticals*.[9]
Ill health during the 1860s reduced the frequency of Mindon's appearances
in the law courts. His early "accessibility" became "an almost uninter-
rupted seclusion."[10] After the revolt in 1866 and Kanaung's assassination
Mindon hardly ventured out of the Golden Palace.

Increased British and French economic interest in Upper Burma during the 1860s meant more commercial visitors and concession hunters
coming to the capital. This led to the issuance of contracts and consequent
litigation. Concession arrangements were generally made with the King
or his ministers, who were often accused of "defaulting." From 1854 onward the British maintained an agent in Amarapura, initially on an informal basis and during the 1860s at an increasingly formal and political
level. European merchants applied to the British political agent for redress of alleged grievances, with mixed success. Agent Clement Williams
suggested that the political agent act as mediator or judge in cases involving British subjects. The Burmese, however, wanted ultimate appeal
to the *Hluttaw*, and Williams thought this negated any benefit, as it was
"all powerful to delay, confuse, and hopelessly entangle" suits submitted
to it.[11] Williams's successor, Edward Bosc Sladen, noted that "the office
of judge, to which a mere nominal salary is attached, is only worth holding on account of the means it affords for the receipt of bribes from parties to suits for the purpose of biasing the judgment in such suits."[12]
Perhaps Sladen's opinion was jaundiced by having to argue unsuccessfully
in support of several fraudulent British claims. He wrote further: "I
state my opinion that the law courts of this place may correctly, though,
perhaps, figuratively, [be] described to be mere sinks of iniquity, oppression and extortion."[13] Some adjustment in the favor of British interests
was provided in the 1867 treaty, which established a joint judicial commission.[14]

Mindon's interests in justice for his people and accountability from his officials had several effects. Jurisdictions were defined, cash flow regularized, and anachronistic courts abolished. More judgeships were created. The direction of change was toward greater specificity and definition of function. At the beginning of Thibaw's reign (1878) it appeared this trend would continue. The Kinwun Mingyi wrote a Western-style constitutional-legislative code. Thibaw issued more regulations against corruption. Courts were further streamlined.[15]

Mindon's aim in civil administration was to reform and rationalize revenue collection. Theoretically the court could levy any tax it desired. The traditional sources of revenue included road and river tolls, 5 to 10 percent forest duties, mine-product duties, bazaar or market tolls, export duties, import duties, and cultivator taxes, also known as *Thathameda* or tithe.[16] The last produced the greatest amount of revenue and touched the greatest number of people. In theory it was a tax on incomes justified by the *Dhammathats* and apocryphal laws of Manu. In practice it was a household or family tax based on possessions and calculated at about one-tenth of the agricultural produce. There was no uniformity in assessment, and non-Burmese were exempt. Some paid heavy taxes, others none. Some paid in cash, others in kind or periodic labor. Resistance to paying taxes was not unusual. Leaks in the collection of revenues occurred. Application lacked uniformity, and the capital only received a fraction of what the agriculturalists paid. British officials at mid-century and in 1866 estimated that local officials retained two-thirds of the collected revenue.[17] This was an inevitable byproduct of a decentralized system where unsalaried local officials served as the revenue agents.

Mindon first regularized the *Thathameda*. The grosser abuses were attacked in 1857 when a tax of 1 silver *tical* per household was levied. The tax was gradually raised to 10 silver *ticals* by 1866. Uniformity was not absolute. A sliding scale was introduced to take into account land type, wet or dry cultivation, village or town. The rate, settled every year, was calculated on the amount of trade, industry, and level of prosperity—information supplied by judges. It was a flexible system designed to provide the traditional 10 percent but in a more orderly manner.[18] A tax and military service census was carried out in 1864. Payment was made in cash and kind. Officials still took their portion. In 1866 Mindon put all officials on salary and further turned the agriculturalists toward a cash economy by demanding silver rather than kind for taxes. By this time Burma's own mint was in operation. Mints existed before Mindon, but from mid-1854 Mindon was set on getting a technologically advanced operation. The French and British made various offers to design a mint, and in November 1865 a mint and building along British lines started to produce silver rupees of the British Indian Standard. Salaries for *Wungyis* had been discussed as early as 1855 and some officials, such as the Collector of Customs on the Burmese border with Pegu, were salaried.[19] After 1866 the salaries were paid monthly. *Wungyis* received Rs. 1,000; *Wundauks*, Rs. 500; *Atwinwuns*, Rs. 660; Court Announcers, Rs. 200; and *Myowun*, Rs. 100-200. Salaries were often in arrears and the problem of misappropriation of funds was not wholly eliminated.

The shift to salaried officials had several effects. Royal revenues increased. Patronage increased, and as many as six hundred new revenue officials may have been created. *Thathameda* reform and salaries increased central control and allegiance and diminished the power if not the titles of the local hierarchies. Local officials, now more than ever, were agents for the center rather than autonomous commanders.[20]

In the early part of the reign frontier officers and ex-Pegu officials, who had fallen on hard times, sent petitions to court for permission to reopen hostilities.[21] They continuously fed bazaar rumors. Mindon, realizing the potential for disaster, withdrew the troops from Meaday and Toungoo and soon demobilized them. Only a police contingent remained on the frontier.[22]

The army was a traditional feudal institution suitable against traditional foes. In peacetime the *ahmudan* worked the royal lands, giving one-quarter of their produce to the crown. During wartime all males ages seventeen to sixty were liable to military service. The King would pass the word to the *Hluttaw* and it, in turn, to Provincial Governors, *Myothugyis*, and *Taikthugyis*.[23] All civilian distinctions fell away, and government officials became military officers. Sleepy villages were called upon to supply two soldiers per sixteen family dwellings, along with supplies of rice and money. River towns provided warboats and crews instead of troops.[24]

Signs of military decay were evident during Bagyidaw's reign. To acquire revenue several permanent officers were calling up inhabitants of their districts to armed drills. Recruits would pay money to avoid muster.[25] Royal call-up of troops was often resisted. The provinces resented the myriad of taxes and balked. Mindon's revenue reforms had as one object the alleviation of distress and discontent in the provinces. Under Mindon local officials were prohibited from calling muster and accepting cash payments in lieu of attendance. Military obligations were to be based on the censuses of 1773 and

1782. A new census for taxation and military service was taken in 1864.[26] The lot of the common soldier was improved; higher pay, enlistment bonuses, and lighter *ahmudan* conditions made military service more tolerable. The idea of service lands was abandoned in 1872, when soldiers became salaried.[27]

Mindon reduced the size of the standing army somewhat after 1852, but pressure for greater internal control caused expansion. The approximate size of the army in 1862 was:[28]

soldier *ahmudan*	40,000
boat *ahmudan*	10,000 (?)
mahout (elephant) *ahmudan*	3,000 (?)
horse *ahmudan*	3,000
artillery *ahmudan*	1,000
blacksmith, tailor, etc. *ahmudan*	300

The artillery was an inefficient amalgam of recent imports and weapons captured from the Portuguese in the sixteenth and seventeenth centuries. Prisoners of war became a hereditary gunner class. Deserters were induced to leave the East India Company's service by the lure of cash payment, a Burmese wife, and a subsistence allowance.[29]

Nations tend to associate independence and control of their own destiny with armaments. In an age of rapidly developing technologies, backward countries had to import these symbols of modernity and tools of autonomy. The British viewed any armaments as offensive and discounted their role in internal security and national status. Before the Second Anglo-Burmese War the British had tried to control arms imports to Burma by having shippers leaving Calcutta with arms give assurance that they would not unload powder, flint, or sulfur at Rangoon. However, an illicit gun trade, British and American, operated out of Singapore, the center of the most loosely controlled of the Indian presidencies. Four thousand stand of arms were reported imported into Rangoon in late 1844. After the loss of Pegu Britain controlled the entrance to the Irrawaddy, the vital supply line of high technology to the heartland. This gave the British substantial diplomatic leverage. One lure held out to the Burmese to conclude a treaty was the free import of sulfur and flints, though Dalhousie still refused powder, muskets, or cannon.[30] The Burmese refused to be held over a barrel and turned to developing their own resources.

Saltpeter was abundant, but initially sulfur was found only in limited quantities in the Shan states and Yunnan. Sulfur was later extracted in sufficient quantities from oil shale obtained from the ravines near oil wells; so the Burmese no longer needed British supplies.[31] The British doubted Burmese self-sufficiency and thought sulfur was being smuggled through Arakan over the Aeng Pass, and the Arakan Commissioner was instructed to cut off this supply. The British wanted to "make them feel their dependence on us for that article."[32] By early 1855 an Armenian was directing a gunpowder factory on the outskirts of Amarapura. Production and quality gradually increased.[33] The question of sulfur supply was not raised again except insofar as Mindon was willing to lease out the sulfur concession to the highest bidder.[34]

The Burmese were not as successful in breaking the British weapons monopoly. The Pabai Wungyi was in charge of the King's ironworks. By mid-1855 the Burmese were producing their own arms in a limited quantity, and Pegu Commissioner Phayre was unable to obtain a treaty in 1855 even after threatening to prohibit arms importation. The royal family took a keen interest in the "Prince's Foundry which turned out very fair rifles. . . percussion caps. . .and gunpowder."[35] A British observer noted an increase in noise and perhaps efficiency.[36] French, British, and Italian military instructors and engineers were employed in the small arms factory and gunpowder mills and to drill troops and design forts.[37]

Domestic weapons production could not replace the need to import the latest weaponry and large quantities of standardized arms available only from technologically advanced manufacturers. Burma occasionally made weapon requests of the British. While on a visit to Mandalay in 1859 Commissioner Phayre permitted the import of 1,650 new flint muskets and flints for the King's personal guard.[38] Later the British, after much wrangling, allowed the import of two Whitworth guns. The Burmese were informed that special permission was not likely to be granted again for cannon imports. This annoyed Mindon and the *Wungyis,* who argued correctly that the recently concluded commercial treaty of 1862 did not prohibit weapon imports. In early 1865 the Governor General showed "indulgence" and allowed the import of 2,000 muskets.[39] When the 1867 treaty was being negotiated the Burmese requested an article on weaponry imports as a right rather than a privilege. The British negotiator, Albert Fytche, agreed, adding the rider "on good behavior." However, this article was deleted by Calcutta in the final treaty version.

Improvements in transport and communications were closely linked
to the administrative and military programs. Mindon dabbled in steam
navigation, railroads, telegraphs, and road improvements. The Burmese
navy comprised about two hundred war and ceremonial oar-powered
craft. River trade was carried on by innumerable dak boats. Closest to
Mindon's heart, and most expensive and prone to end in litigation, was
the introduction of modern steam vessels. The Burmese had acquired
a small steamer in the early 1840s, but it appears to have been used only
as a novelty. Mindon employed the steamers to draw barges.

Several steamers were ordered during the reign. As the steamer had to
pass through British territory, permission for delivery and to ply the Irrawaddy on a regular basis had to be obtained from the British. The
British placed no obstacles on these early requests. By 1857 two small
steamers traveled regularly between Amarapura and Rangoon. During
the 1870s the Government of India objected to British merchants selling
gunboats to the Burmese.[40] Requesting British permission humiliated
Mindon. He toyed with the idea of making treaties with Sardinia, France,
and America which he hoped would have the effect of making the Irrawaddy an international river. Mindon dreamed in vain of regaining
Pegu and acquiring a seaport.[41]

During the 1860s the steamers plunged Mindon into interminable
wrangles. Contracted steamers often did not meet specifications, and
prices seemed to rise as completion and delivery approached. The steamers were built in British territory, and the King's deposit was held, giving the builder a lien on the Burmese government. Builders were adept
at cost overruns. Several steamer contracts had to be turned over to
arbitration.

The steamers served both commerce and the military. In the rebellion
of 1866 steamers were instrumental in Mindon's victory. By 1870 the
King had eight or ten steamers that an observer noted lay idle and neglected.[42]

The telegraph was first introduced to the Burmese in 1854, when a
Burmese mission went to Calcutta. American missionary Kincaid, who
visited the capital in 1856, took a small model to the court. In mid-1857
Mindon sounded out the Government of India for British assistance to
connect Pegu by telegraph to Mandalay. The Pegu Commissioner recommended aid.[43] Mindon asked repeatedly for information, but Calcutta
dragged its feet; and in the early 1860s Mindon considered offering the

French a seventy-year monopoly that would involve a road from Bhamo to China and an electric telegraph and railroad linking Mandalay to Chiengmai and Bangkok. Nothing came of this scheme, except perhaps to frighten and rekindle British Francophobia and prompt the British agent to prepare a telegraph cost estimate for Mindon in May 1863. The Shwepyi Wun wrote a Morse code in Burmese.[44] Missionary Kincaid also took a model steam railway to Amarapura. During the 1860s the idea of a railway through Burma to tap the Yunnan-western China trade was being popularized in London.[45] As Mindon preferred traditional river traffic, he opened the railroad scheme to concession seekers. Various routes were proposed, and several agents squabbled over the concession. Richard Sprye, the London propagandist, was represented by Mr. Barlow. They complained that Halliday, Fox and Company, the King's steamer agents, were sabotaging railway negotiations.[46] Doctor Marfels, a German physician who served as Mindon's supervisor of forests, interceded in Barlow's behalf. In May 1864 a concession was granted to build a railway to the Chinese frontier. The King was to receive 10 percent of the net profits. The contract lapsed when the concessionaires could not raise the capital and begin work within the specified time limit. No help could be expected from the British government, which felt generally that railways in Burma could only lead to trouble.[47]

Administrative reform was well advanced by 1866. The central government had adopted several pragmatic reforms and experienced difficulty enforcing them. This did not alter Mindon's resolve. Rather, it intensified the necessity to push on. After Mindon's death the Kinwun Mingyi continued the reform program. Officials were still not completely salaried in 1880. The army was found wanting in 1885, though as a guerrilla force it proved formidable. The steamers were expensive and probably not put to the best use. A telegraph line was erected but from all reports was inefficient. The railroad was a British dream, and they built it after the conquest of 1886.

ECONOMIC POLICY

Administrative and judicial reforms and military and infrastructure development were matched by simultaneous efforts in the economic sector. The Burmese-controlled economy was marked by the creation of national policy in the fields of agriculture, mineral resources, industrialization, and foreign trade.

British possession of wet zone Pegu after 1853 posed serious economic problems to the Burmese. The heartland in the dry zone was not self-sufficient in rice supplies and had traditionally imported rice from the southern wet zone.[48] Two types of farming were practiced, irrigated and non-irrigated, wet and dry. After 1853 there was a disparity between rice's retail cost in the south and the north since production costs were lower in the south. While this was not unusual it now had political and demographic ramifications. Peasants and workers might move southward to the land of cheaper food. In early 1854, because of poor rainfall, the price of rice in Amarapura was three times the cost at Prome, near the frontier. Mindon built special boats to carry over one hundred thousand baskets of rice from British-held Pegu to the Burmese heartland during 1854. The rice was then sold at below-cost prices. State food subsidies were stopgap measures. The only way to increase local rice production was to expand the amount of land under irrigation by repairing old and creating new systems.

Mindon and Kanaung set themselves the task of freeing Burma from the necessity of external aid in foodstuffs.[49] The first irrigation schemes were repayment of political debts. The Shwebo district canal systems had been started by Alaungpaya and fallen into disrepair after his death. Mindon was indebted to this district for assistance when he was fighting for the throne, and it received his early attention.[50] Irrigation to the north of the capital was concerned primarily with repairs to old systems. It was in the south that totally new regions were for the first time linked by canal to river water. Wet rice cultivation was extended about twenty-five miles southward.[51] Mindon was proud of the large tracts of land brought under cultivation. Chronicles and stone inscriptions commemorate irrigation expansion as *karma*-worthy acts. Current needs were being met, and Mindon hoped in a year or two to be able to export rice, a projection a British observer found "incredulous."[52] Progress was impressive but perhaps illusory. Although the British observed that "Upper Burma is each year becoming less dependent than formerly on the Lower Provinces,"[53] progress was due only in part to irrigation. Rainfall in the period 1854-57 was particularly good. In the years of abnormally poor rainfall, 1858-60, however, the rivers were too low to feed the canals and sluices. Kanaung ordered a steam engine from Calcutta in 1855, but this was an impractical way to raise water for widespread irrigation. No amount of irrigation could rectify this, and land lay unused. Shortages had to be met at great expense from Pegu, and prices fluctuated widely. Mindon interposed himself into the supply-and-demand market, even at a loss to the royal treasury. It was more important that the people get moderately priced food than for hawkers to make huge profits on the open market. Mindon had definite ideas about legitimate profits. He declared that debts with interest, which caused distress, were contrary to justice and caused the forfeiture of the double merit in the present and future existence.[54] Mindon's agents bought the limited supply of rice and retailed it at a moderate price. It sold out quickly to only a fraction of those desiring it. A black market arose, prices soared, and the King would contribute more money to buy more paddy. Irrigation projects continued to have high priority during the 1860s in an attempt to overcome the food-supply problems.[55]

Burma's valuable mineral resources, timbershed, and agricultural commodities had a ready export market[56] and were subject to royal monopolies. Royal control of export and customs were the most often discussed "Burmese problems" in British circles. In the early years of the reign Mindon personally exercised his right to exploit resources. Foreigners clamored for a share. By the early 1860s Mindon began to contract out monopolies for limited periods to the highest bidder. He reaped revenues without managerial responsibilities or capital outlay. Farms were eventually granted in coal, iron, copper, sulfur, wheat, gram (chickpeas), cotton, tea, teak, and cutch (a drug derived from acacia tree gum).[57] Mindon interfered in the sale of exports, determining prices, and customs fees, thereby maintaining price levels and revenues. The most successful of the concessionaires was an Indian merchant, Moolah Ibrahim. By the mid-1860s he held large contracts in teak, oil, cotton, teel seed (sesame seed), and managed the King's steamers and controlled customs. Mindon created him Governor of the Mohammedan community.[58]

The early search for sulfur for munitions development set in motion a national treasure hunt. Deposits of lead, coal, copper, rubies, oil, amber, iron ore, and gold were also discovered. At first known sources were exploited, and then new deposits were prospected with the assistance of European adventurers. Mindon intervened in purchase and export. Lead came from the Shan States. The King paid the *Sawbwas* Rs. 5 to 8 cash per hundred *viss* of lead and then resold it to eager merchants at Rs. 15 to 20.[59] Mindon later sold lead directly to Calcutta and presumably used his own shipping fleet to transport it. While lead output was good, Mindon tended to exaggerate forthcoming amounts, and projected quotas were rarely met. Copper was also a lucrative export.[60]

Coal was used domestically for steam engines, and the British were ready buyers for their own fleets. The Kanaung Prince took a personal interest in prospecting and sold to the British in bulk at Prome. Britishers found dealing in coal difficult, as Kanaung's agent had cornered the market. Price fixing guaranteed the Prince's profits, which were put into his personal treasury.[61]

Burma's "earth oil" was legendary and literally bubbled to the surface in the Yenangyaung area. Mindon purchased it and resold it at 100 percent above the wholesale production cost. As English demand increased continuously, so did the Burmese price.[62] Britain retaliated by raising the customs duty. A French adventurer and self-styled general, D'Orgoni, won the oil contract in March 1865 for a year and controlled all oil marketed south of Yenangyaung. He was to pay the King Rs. 120,000 in monthly installments of cash, kind (oil), and manufactured products, such as muskets, swords, and pistols. D'Orgoni died shortly after the contract became operative. Though his wife argued she had testamentary rights to the contract, the Burmese government let the contract to Moolah Ibrahim for Rs. 15,000.[63]

A large high-grade iron deposit was discovered by the French, who claimed it was capable of making steel as good as that in England. Mr. Blayse, who had been D'Orgoni's secretary, also discovered gold and offered to work the mines for the King at 20 percent of the profits if the King would pay the expenses; alternatively for 50 percent of the gold Blayse would finance the project. The plan was deservedly stillborn.[64] Mindon also received revenue from silver mines, but it appears that this was neglected during the reign due to the Yunnan rebellion disrupting the supply of skilled Chinese and Panthay workmen.[65] The traditional prohibitions on the export of jewels and bullion continued in force, and travelers were liable to search. Silver coins from the new mint in Mandalay were also prohibited exports.

Burma had invaluable forest resources. Mindon, like his father, perpetually interfered with price and export. British merchants were eager for fresh teak sources since local forests were denuded and Pegu was not as bountiful in timber as had been anticipated. Contracts were granted in terms of number of trees or geographical area; leases after 1862 included at least nine forest areas. A merchant traded two steamers and 250 cases of piece goods for all the timber on the Toungoo frontier; another delivered a steamer in return for 1,000 pieces of Chindwin timber.[66] Rangoon and Calcutta commercial houses sent several agents to

the Burmese capital to fill the insatiable timber requirements created
by the rapid expansion of the Indian railway network. Mindon was on
the lookout for new forests to work. Shan timber revenues, which had
previously gone to provincial chiefs, were transferred to the crown as
part of Mindon's program of extending peripheral control.[67]

British merchants complained about royal interference. British officials
acknowledged that "the forests belong to His Majesty" to do with them
as he saw fit, as long as he abided by Article 7 of the 1862 treaty. Mindon cooperated with the Pegu Commissioner by informing him when
the royal demand for teak would be greatest in an effort to discourage
cantankerous agents from coming to the capital.[68]

The British looked to Burma for wheat and chickpeas for its troops.
The Lower Burma supply was small, and Bengal imports were expensive.
The King controlled the crops by granting advances to peasants. A
merchant representing the Pegu government offered to buy the King's
crop, and Mindon generously let the British determine the price. Mindon had second thoughts and set a price for delivery at Prome of Rs.
250 per hundred baskets of wheat and Rs. 200 for gram. While the
price was a little high, it was not thought too much to pay to ingratiate
Mindon to the British. Mindon overestimated the amount available, but
the British took what they could, after some delays and misunderstandings,
and hoped for a better price in 1855.[69] British goodwill soured when Mindon would not lower his price. Phayre wrote:

> The King it appears, refuses to sell wheat and gram at a lower
> rate than last year; and as he does so quite in the spirit of hag-
> gling trader. . .it will be better to show we are not dependent
> upon him, and refuse to give a higher price than what has been
> offered—namely Rs. 220 per 100 baskets for wheat and Rs. 180
> for gram.[70]

Pegu, Tenasserim, and Arakan turned to more costly Bengal wheat. Thereafter Mindon sold to private British traders.[71]

Cotton was a traditional dry-zone crop, and the surplus was sold to
western China. Britain had vaulted herself to world economic supremacy
in textiles and had an insatiable appetite for cotton and was always on the
lookout for new supplies. Sensing the importance of cotton Mindon monopolized it in early 1854. The bountiful years of 1854-58 produced good
cotton crops. A free market would have placed clean cotton at about 25

ticals per 100 *viss*. The King kept the price artificially at 35 *ticals* by pro-
hibiting its sale at a lower price. Mindon made large advances to cotton
cultivators. Demand was so great in 1855 that the price went up perhaps
100 percent over the previous year, with substantial profits accruing to the
royal treasury.[72] The American Civil War induced a cotton famine and
drove prices even higher. The King controlled various sectors of production.
He advanced cultivators Rs. 5 per prospective 100 *viss* of cotton. His
buyers paid Rs. 35 to 40, and it was exported at Rs. 150 to 200 either to
China or Rangoon, 600 to 800 percent over the 1854 price. These fabulous
profits did not continue long. In late 1865 there were unseasonably heavy
rains, which reduced the cotton crop. With the conclusion of the American Civil War the world price of cotton dropped. Other royal interests included tea, hemp for twine and fishnets, cutch, and teel seed.[73]

Prince Kanaung directed the selective adoption of European technology.
The major innovations—gunpowder mills, foundries, and communications
systems—have already been noted. In addition, shipbuilding yards were
established. The government made capital investments in imported machinery for consumer goods, including sugar-refining mills, cotton-cloth mills,
sawmills for finished timber, and pottery- and carpet-making equipment.
After Kanaung's assassination in 1866 several of these projects were terminated.[74]

Monastic and Western secular education were encouraged. Several
youths from Kanaung's household went to Calcutta to study.[75] A French
diplomatic mission visiting Mandalay in 1859 returned to Paris with three
youths from the Prince's household. During the 1862 treaty negotiations
Mindon announced that his and his officials' children were being taught
English, French, and "Hindoostanee."[76] The Burmese valued education
highly, and these foreign-educated Burmese found a ready place in central
government.[77] Mission societies were welcomed if their programs included
establishing schools. In 1868 the Reverend John Marks of the Society for
the Propagation of the Christian Gospel established a mission school at
Mandalay.[78] When Thibaw ascended the throne he planned a university in
Mandalay, specializing in Burmese and foreign-language studies.

Customs and tariffs were the most controversial and troublesome aspects
of the Burmese-controlled economy. They served as significant supplements
to state revenue to finance the high costs of modernization and ward off
financial crisis. The thrust of British mid-nineteenth-century international
trade was toward "free trade." Tariffs and monopolies were looked upon
as a hindrance to trade and economic growth. Free traders maintained

that tariff abolition created new incentives, greater industrial output, and expanded government revenue in other areas. Burma looked upon her customs and tariffs differently. Burma's national goals diverged from the British. Buddhist benevolence and the state-controlled economy were Burmese aims, not capitalism, profits from free trade, or mercantile individualism. The British dream had no place in the Burmese eschatology. The Burmese trod two paths simultaneously: they attempted to please the British in form and satisfy the revenue needs of the government in reality. Irrigation, technology, European managers, military hardware, and steamers were expensive. The traditions of a large royal family, religious charities, building pagodas and monasteries, and building the new capital of Mandalay also sapped the treasury. Unexpected expenses, such as Shan wars, created periodic financial crises.[79] Mindon appeared to live from hand to mouth and from concession to concession.

Private and official British agents naturally desired ease of access to Burmese territory and markets. They differed in the degree of pressure they could or were willing to bring to bear. Between 1853 and 1860 the British relied on limited informal and friendly contacts. The British were still pacifying Pegu and recovering from the 1857 Mutiny. However, after 1860 various economic interests became increasingly aggressive, attempting to secure a formal treaty that would allow them to pursue their economic goals unhindered.

In 1860 the British informally asked Mindon to reduce his tariffs to one-eighth of their former charge, which was between 6 and 12 percent, and to standardize them. The request was virtually ignored.[80] At the 1862 treaty negotiations tariffs were discussed more seriously. Mindon stated "that his revenues are now scarcely sufficient for his expenses."[81] Nonetheless, Mindon acceded to Article 8 of the 1862 commercial treaty, which committed Burma to reciprocating Britain's lowering of tariffs in the near future. British merchants, however, expected the Burmese to comply. Mindon took a different path altogether. Needing greater revenues he farmed out the customs. The British argued unsuccessfully for customs reductions. Commissioner Phayre recognized that Burma, for the immediate future, could not do without her frontier customs. The Burmese consistently evaded giving a regularized tariff schedule, as required by Article 4 of the treaty, and continued to levy unofficial rates. Complaints of irregular assessments were legion.

In 1864 the British agent, Williams, persuaded the Burmese to reduce customs to 6 percent ad valorem on all articles except piece goods, which would bear 2½ percent, and monopoly commodities. [82] To compensate for the lost revenues due to the 6 percent schedule the Burmese government in August 1864 imposed a royalty and a weighing charge on all goods at the frontier. These levies had previously been imposed only on European traders and were now extended to all traders. The printed schedule of 6 percent therefore was actually upward of 10 percent. Williams complained ad nauseam and lashed out:

> The present system is irregular, harassing, and oppressive to traders, but because, in the slipshod, thriftless mode of Burmese finance, the present appears the most profitable system for the King, he does not try to remedy the evil and realize his promises by a reform. [83]

From the British point of view things went from bad to worse. They accused the major customs farmer, Moolah Ibrahim, of extortion and manipulating the tariff upward. After several complaints the Burmese published another tariff list. [84] At about the same time the customs farm was again sold to Moolah Ibrahim for Rs. 400,000. In response to the badgering of the British political agent, the *Wungyis* pleaded national penury. They hoped that the *Thathameda* reforms would alleviate the problem. [85]

At this point the British tried another tactic and pointed to the prosperity in Pegu Province under free trade. The *Wungyi* asked, "How is it your taxes are lighter than ours, and yet you get more revenue?" This was no doubt because Pegu residents were paying almost the highest income-tax rates in the British Indian Empire. [86] Agent Sladen offered the following suggestion:

> If your fear of abolishing duties is the immediate loss of revenue, reduce your export and import duties at once by one-half, and do away altogether with. . .[royalties and weighing charges] then see after the lapse of one, two, or three years how much your country has benefited and your inland customs revenue *increased.*

Sladen urged Mindon to go to the priesthood for advice. [87] British ambitions and Burmese needs were approaching an impasse. The British felt Burmese finances could be stabilized if a British officer supervised Burmese customs. [88] On the last day of 1865 Sladen broached the idea of a British directed customs house to a *Wungyi.* Burmese reaction was swift.

The proposal was humiliating and out of the question. The Burmese promised once more to look into their customs organization with a view to improvement. Calcutta, more sensitive to Burma's feelings than Rangoon, quietly quashed the idea of a joint customs post.[89] Mindon, desiring to continue traditional revenue-collection practices and placate the British, allowed the British political agent to go into direct contact with Moolah Ibrahim to deal with tariff questions and complaints. The duty was lowered about 1 percent.[90] As royal finances neared a crisis in mid-1866 they were eclipsed by a political crisis that jeopardized the entire program.

CONCLUSION

The objectives of modernized central control and economic planning were the maximization of benefits to the state and private sectors. Buddhist state cosmology fused politics, national pride, economics, self-sufficiency, and social welfare. It is clear that Mindon and Kanaung were taking steps to modernize their country and that this course was taken within the context of Burmese traditional and historical institutions. Their plans were well advanced by 1866. Accountability, increased central control, and bureaucratization were the hallmarks of Mindon's policy toward the administrative, judicial, revenue, and military branches of the state. The British looked on approvingly, with the significant exception of military modernization, which they tried to thwart.

The goal of economic self-sufficiency was approached through increased domestic food production, monopolies, and price controls. Despite irrigation, harvests ultimately depended on rainfall. Postwar prosperity was due to good rains, a psychological ebullience of dynamic leadership, and the limited number of projects set afoot with consequent limited costs. Early British assessment of Mindon's economic programs was favorable. Though Mindon's development plans were not in line with British visions of political economy, he was lauded for instituting more social progress in four years than had occurred during the previous twenty years. His aims were considered worthier than most Eastern kings.[91] Exports and monopolies allowed the temporary lowering of taxes. However well intentioned, this was shortsighted,[92] as a Britisher close to Mindon recorded: "As the King is a very intelligent man, I trust he will soon find out that monopolies in any shape are much more injurious than any other mode of taxation."[93]

State-directed economic growth demanded increased revenues. When expansion in agriculture failed to meet expectations Mindon turned to other primary products and customs to raise funds. Mindon's economic policy conflicted with British India's free-trade policy. During the 1860s British attitudes hardened against Burma's monopolistic trade policy as British merchants became more aggressive. Agents Williams and Sladen did not approach the sympathy or understanding of Spears. A prime example of Burma's difficulty in pursuing domestic policy is seen in the tariff question. Technological modernization also had counterproductive aspects. Imitating Europe led to debts and angry creditors. Maintenance of machinery created service problems. European technicians served as a fifth column. Technological modernization was promoted by one man, the Kanaung Prince. Economic expansion meant a continuing stream of British and French concession hunters to the Burmese capital. No matter how Mindon treated them he was damned. If he withheld contracts he was called a "monopolist." If he granted contracts he was assailed by those who did not bid high enough. Concessionaires turned to litigation when the grant was not as lucrative as they anticipated and complained that the Burmese had not lived up to their part of the bargain.

For over a decade administrative reform and modernization was paralleled by stable monarchy. This was interrupted by the traditional-style revolt of 1866 and the assassination of Kanaung.

NOTES

1. King of Burma to Governor General, dated late April or early May 1853, ISP/182.
2. Edicts of 21 February, 11 and 19 March, and 5 May 1855, in Henry Yule, *Reports of the Mission to Ava in 1855* (Calcutta: Government Printers, 1856), pp. lxxvi, cxxvi, and 362-3.
3. Ibid., p. 137; Spears to Phayre, 25 March 1856; and Spears to Hopkinson, 25 August 1857, Canning Papers, Sheepscar Library, Leeds, 55/28 and 55/2421.
4. John Crawfurd commented, "No prudent person enters into a law suit," quoted in Janell Ann Nilsson, "The Administration of British Burma, 1852-1885" (Ph.D. diss., University of London, 1970), p. 54; and Henry Gouger commented, "Bribery is the mainspring by which all manner of business is moved throughout the country," quoted in John S. Furnivall, *Colonial Policy and Practice* (New York: New York University Press, 1956 [orig. publ. 1948]), p. 19.

5. Edict of 24 April 1853, in Yule, *Narrative of a Mission to the Court of Ava in 1855* (Kuala Lumpur: Oxford University Press, 1969 [orig. publ., 1858]), pp. 363-6; Yi Yi, "The Judicial System of King Mindon," *J.B.R.S.* 45 (1962): 13-15; and Kyin Swi, "The Judicial System of the Kingdom of Burma" (Ph.D. diss., University of London, 1965), pp. 453-6.

6. Yi Yi, "Judicial System," p. 13; Kyin Swi, "Judicial System," p. 158; and Paul J. Bennett, *Conference Under the Tamarind Tree* (New Haven: Yale University Southeast Asia Studies, 1971), pp. 62-4.

7. Yi Yi, "Judicial System," p. 15; and Kyin Swi, "Judicial System," pp. 306 and 448.

8. Yi Yi, "Judicial System," pp. 18-22; Kyin Swi, "Judicial System," pp. 165-6; and Maung Htin Aung, *Burmese Law Tales* (London: Oxford University Press, 1962), pp. 24-7.

9. Spears to Phayre, 30 April 1854, in D. G. E. Hall, ed., *The Dalhousie-Phayre Correspondence, 1852-1856* (London: Oxford University Press, 1932), p. 182.

10. Williams Diary, 10 February and 3 March 1864, IPF/204/72; and 31 December 1864, IPF/204/78.

11. Williams Diary, 13-24 September 1864, IPF/May 1865, in Dharm Pal, "British Relations with Burma (1864-1868)," *Indian Historical Quarterly* 21 (1945): 271-83.

12. Sladen Diary, 1 March 1866, IPF/437/67.

13. Sladen Diary, 2 June 1866, IPP/437/68.

14. Sladen Diary, Message to Abbona, 3 April 1865, IPF/204/78.

15. Kyin Swi, "Judicial System," pp. 167, 178, and 207-11.

16. Barbara J. Stewart, "Administrative Beginnings in British Burma, 1826-1843" (Ph.D. diss., University of London, 1931), p. 54; *Pegu Administrative Patterns in Historical Burma,* Institute of Southeast Asian Studies, Southeast Asian Perspectives no. 1 (Singapore, 1973), p. 31.

17. Kyin Swi, "Judicial System," p. 90; Nilsson, "Administration," pp. 45-51; Ma Mya Sein, *Administration of Burma* (Rangoon: Zabu Meitswe Pitaka Press, 1938), p. 186; James Gray, *The Alaungpra Dynasty* (Edinburgh and London: Ballentyne Press, 1887), p. 163; and Bertie Reginald Pearn, "The Commercial Treaty of 1862," *J.B.R.S.* 27(1937), p. 3.

18. Kyin Swi, "Judicial System," p. 92; Stewart, "Administrative Beginnings," pp. 184-8; and James George Scott, *Burma, From the Earliest Times to the Present Day* (London: T. Fisher Unwin, 1924), p. 294.

19. Spears to Phayre, 13 July 1854, in Hall, ed., *Correspondence,* p. 223; and Yule, *Narrative of a Mission,* p. 257.

20. Williams Diary, 6 August 1865, IPF/204/78; and Ma Mya Sein, *Administration*, pp. 164 and 189.

21. Spears to Phayre, 18 February and 6 August 1854, in Hall, ed., *Correspondence*, pp. 39 and 230.

22. Spears to Phayre, 20 and 28 February, 18 March 1854, ibid., pp. 140-1 and 158.

23. Gray, *Alaungpra Dynasty*, p. 163; and Yule, *Reports of the Mission*, p. 252.

24. William Louis Barretto, *King Mindon* (Rangoon: Burma Union Press, 1935), p. 42; Yule, *Reports of the Mission*, p. 252; Williams to Arthur Grote, 4 July 1862, Elgin Papers, India Office Archives, F78/48/665; and Yule, *Narrative of a Mission*, p. 249.

25. Walter S. Desai, *History of the British Residency in Burma, 1826-1840* (Rangoon: University of Rangoon, 1939), p. 179.

26. Royal Edicts of 25 April and 8 July 1855, in Yule, *Reports of the Mission*, pp. xxxi and lxxxiv; Williams Diary, 6 August 1864, IPF/204/78.

27. R. R. Langham Carter, "The Burmese Army," *J.B.R.S.* 27 (1937): 254-76; Williams Diary, 14 July 1864, IPF/204/75; and Sladen Diary, 14 February 1866, IPP/437/67.

28. Williams to Arthur Grote, 4 July 1862, Elgin Papers, F78/48/665.

29. Allen Report on Burmese Military, 12 November 1855, ISP/181; Phayre to George Edmonstone, 3 May 1856, IPF/201/58; Yule, *Reports of the Mission*, p. 257; and Yule, *Narrative of the Mission*, p. 255.

30. Dalhousie to Phayre, 5 July 1854, in Hall, ed., *Correspondence*, p. 198.

31. Langham Carter, "Burmese Army," p. 262.

32. Phayre to Dalhousie, 30 September 1855, and Spears to Phayre, 23 November 1855, in Hall, ed., *Correspondence*, pp. 383 and 399.

33. Yule, *Narrative of a Mission*, p. 249; and Spears to Phayre, 26 December 1855, in ibid., p. 406.

34. Williams Diary, 23 May 1863, IPF/204/67.

35. Phayre to Dalhousie, 30 September 1855, in Hall, ed., *Correspondence*, pp. 382-3; Phayre to Durand, 21 November 1862, IPF/204/63; and Sladen Diary, 8 August 1865, IPF/204/78.

36. Spears to Phayre, 7 January 1858, Canning Papers, 3270; and Sladen Diary, 21 June 1866, IPF/437/68.

37. Williams Diary, 15-17 June 1864, IPF/204/75; and Sladen Diary, 5 July 1865, IPF/204/79.

38. Phayre to Grey, 13 December 1859, IPF/203/71.

39. Williams Diary, 11 October 1864, and Phayre to Durand, 6 December 1864, IPF/204/78.

40. Owen to Edmonstone, 7 February 1856, IPF/201/46; Shaw to Phayre, 1 May 1856, IPF/201/54; *Pegu Administration Report, 1856-7,* p. 157; and Note no. 100, 20 June 1856, IPF/201/58.

41. Phayre to Canning, 26 April 1856, and Hopkinson to Talbot, 13 July 1857, Canning Papers, 55/28 and 55/3409A.

42. James Wheeler, "Memorandum," 21 January 1871, IPP/760.

43. Spears to Phayre, 12 April 1856, Canning Papers, 55/28; and Spears to Hopkinson, 13 June 1857, and Hopkinson to Talbot, 13 July 1857, Canning Papers, 55/3409A.

44. Williams to Phayre, 30 December 1861, IPF/204/59; and Ma Kyan, "King Mindon's Councillors," *J.B.R.S.* 44(1961): 58.

45. See Ma Thaung, "British Interest in Trans-Burma Trade Routes to China, 1826-1876" (Ph.D. diss., University of London, 1954).

46. Sprye to John Lawrence, 10 December 1863, Lawrence Papers, India Office Library and Records, F90/78.

47. Williams Diary, 15 and 24 May 1864, IPF/204/78; Lawrence to Wood, 14 July 1864, Wood Papers, India Office Library and Records, F78.

48. Cheng Siok-Hwa, *The Rice Industry of Burma, 1852-1940* (Kuala Lumpur: University of Malaya Press, 1968), p. 4; and Michael Adas, *The Burma Delta* (Madison: University of Wisconsin Press, 1974).

49. Spears to Phayre, 7 March 1854, in Hall, ed., *Correspondence,* p. 145.

50. Spears to Phayre, 7 March 1854, ibid., p. 145; and J. M. B. Stuart, *Old Burmese Irrigation Works* (Rangoon: Government Printers, 1913), pp. 11-12.

51. Manning Nash, *The Golden Road to Modernity* (London: John Wiley, 1965), p. 209.

52. Spears to Phayre, 13 August 1854, in Hall, ed., *Correspondence,* pp. 237-8; and Yule, *Narrative of a Mission,* p. 108.

53. *Pegu Administration Report, 1857-8,* p. 138.

54. Royal Edict of 10 April 1853, in Yule, *Narrative of a Mission,* p. 363.

55. Spears to Phayre, 17 October 1858 and 22 February 1859, Canning Papers, 4580 and 55/28.

56. Williams to Grote, 4 July 1862, Elgin Papers, F78/48/665; and Williams to Phayre, 30 December 1861, IPF/204/59.

57. Williams to Phayre, 30 December 1861, IPF/204/59; and Yaw Atwinwun conversation with Williams, Williams Diary, 23 May 1863, IPF/204/67.

58. Williams Diary, 24 May and 16 August 1864, IPF/204/78.

59. Spears to Phayre, 2 April 1854, in Hall, ed., *Correspondence,* p. 163;

and Yule, *Narrative of a Mission,* p. 256.

60. Spears to Phayre, 4 February and 26 December 1855, in Hall, ed., *Correspondence,* pp. 296 and 406; and Sladen Diary, 20 February 1865, IPF/204/78.

61. Spears to Phayre, 8 April, 6 August 1854, and 2 January 1855, and Phayre to Dalhousie, 22 September 1854, in Hall, ed., *Correspondence,* pp. 178, 229-31, 241, and 284.

62. Spears to Phayre, 23 November 1855, in ibid., p. 399.

63. Sladen Diary, 18 March and 1 April 1865, IPF/204/78; Spears to Phayre, 8 April 1856, Canning Papers, 55/28; and Phayre to Edmonstone, 1 October 1856, IPF/202/1. D'Orgoni's given name was Louis Charles Girodon.

64. Williams to Grote, 4 July 1862, Elgin Papers, F78/48/665; and Spears to Phayre, 24 March and 8 April 1856, Canning Papers, 55/28.

65. Sladen Diary, 10 October 1865, IPF/204/79; and Yule, *Reports of the Mission,* App. 59.

66. Charles Lee Keeton, *King Thebaw and the Ecological Rape of Burma* (Delhi: Manohar Book Service, 1974), p. 342; and Spears to Phayre, 2 and 13 January 1855, in Hall, ed., *Correspondence,* pp. 283 and 293.

67. Spears to Phayre, 14 April 1859, IPF/203/50; and Williams Diary, 31 December 1865, IPF/204/78.

68. Phayre to Durand, 7 December 1865, and Williams Diary, 12 January 1865, IPF/204/78; and Sladen Diary, 18 November 1865, IPP/437/66.

69. Spears to Phayre, 13 and 18 February and 24 April 1854, and Phayre to Dalhousie, 10 November 1854, in Hall, ed., *Correspondence,* pp. 136-8, 163, and 257-9; Grant to Phayre, 31 March 1854, ISP/188; and Dalhousie to Couper, 30 March 1854, in J. G. A. Baird, ed., *Private Letters of the Marquess of Dalhousie* (Edinburgh: William Blackwood, 1910), pp. 293-4.

70. Phayre to Dalhousie, 25 January 1855, in Hall, ed., *Correspondence,* p. 281.

71. Spears to Phayre, 2 January and 5 June 1855, ibid., pp. 283 and 340; Phayre to Edmonstone, 15 February 1856, IPF/201/47. Spears to Phayre, 9 March 1856, Canning Papers, 55/28. Phayre to Durand, 29 May 1863, IPF/204/67. Sladen Diary, 18 January 1867, IPP/437/70.

72. Yule, *Narrative of a Mission,* p. 144; and Spears to Phayre, 22 April and 25 October 1854, and 21 January 1855, in Hall, ed., *Correspondence,* pp. 173, 265, and 295.

73. Sladen Diary, 11 and 18 October 1865, IPF/204/78; 1 November 1865, IPF/204/79; 2 and 10 April 1866, IPP/437/67; and Phayre to Durand, 29 May 1863, IPF/204/67.

74. Wheeler, "Memorandum," 21 January 1871, IPP/760, p. 42; C.H.E.

Adamson, *Narrative of an Official Visit to the King of Burma, in March, 1875* (Newcastle-on-Tyne: N.p., 1878), p. 20; and Ma Kyan, "Mindon's Councillors," p. 60.

75. Spears to Phayre, 15 January 1854, in Hall, ed., *Correspondence,* p. 128; and Maung Maung, *Burma in the Family of Nations* (Amsterdam: Uitgeverij Djambatam, 1956), p. 50.

76. Phayre to Durand, 20 November 1862, IPF/204/63.

77. Wheeler, "Memorandum," 21 January 1871, IPP/760, p. 61; and V. C. Scott O'Connor, *Mandalay and Other Cities of the Past in Burma* (London: Hutchinson, 1907), p. 42.

78. John Ebenezer Marks, *Forty Years in Burma* (London: Hutchinson, 1917).

79. Williams Diary, 31 December 1864, IPF/204/78.

80. Office Memo by Phayre, 17 September 1860; and A. J. Camaretta, Collector of Customs at Mandalay, to R. S. Edwards, Collector of Customs, 21 July 1860, IPF/204/26.

81. Phayre to Durand, 16 October 1862, IPF/204/63.

82. Williams Diary, 22 April and 16 August 1864, IPF/204/78; and Phayre to Durand, 4 August 1864, IPF/204/75.

83. Williams Diary, 26 September 1864, IPF/204/78.

84. Williams, 11 October 1864, and Sladen Diary, 21 March 1865, IPF/204/78.

85. Sladen Diary, 11 and 27 July, and 13 October 1865, and Davies to Secretary to the Government of India, 25 October 1865, IFP/204/79.

86. John S. Furnivall, *An Introduction to the Political Economy of Burma,* reprint ed. (Rangoon: People's Literature Committee, 1957), pp. 200-3.

87. Sladen Diary, 11 August and 3 October 1865, IPF/204/79.

88. Davies to Secretary to the Government of India, 25 October 1865, IPF/204/79; Phayre to Secretary to the Government of India, 5 February 1866, and Sladen Diary, 16 December 1865, IPF/437/66.

89. Sladen Diary, 3 January 1866, and Secretary to the Government of India to the Chief Commissioner of British Burma, 20 March 1866, IPP/437/66.

90. Sladen Diary, 15 February and 24 March 1866, IPP/437/67.

91. Hopkinson to Talbot, 4 January 1858, Canning Papers, 55/3074/31; and *Pegu Administration Report, 1856-7,* p. 157.

92. Yule, *Narrative of a Mission,* pp. 193 and 256.

93. Spears to Phayre, 13 February 1854, in Hall, ed., *Correspondence,* p. 137.

7
FAMILY POLITICS AND CIVIL WAR, 1867

At the outset of Mindon's reign his power was unrivaled. It was a period of confidence in which Mindon met dissent with magnanimity. The King directed, and Kanaung and the ministers followed. Kanaung's position of almost equal partnership at the time of the 1853 revolt deteriorated, and he was soon displaced as commander in chief.[1] Kanaung's voice in foreign affairs became inaudible, and his household was watched closely. The "prince bore...[this] like a dutiful subject."[2] However, when Phayre visited the capital in 1855 Mindon took him aside and intimated that he had been opposed by all his ministers in establishing salaries, abolishing court fees, and forbidding money levies.[3]

Following Mindon's official coronation in July 1854 he started to plan the construction of a new capital. There were pressing reasons for a move. Since Tharrawaddy's return to Amarapura in 1837, it had become overpopulated, unsanitary, and it lacked room for expansion. The city contained fifty to sixty thousand people, and the general area around one hundred thousand.[4] Mandalay offered a spacious, clean environment, and a survey was begun in 1855. It was heralded as a decision of Buddhist destiny. The fourth year of Mindon's reign was the 2,400th year after the death of Buddha. The astrologers forecast 15 February 1857 as the most auspicious moment for groundbreaking. When fires broke out during construction astrologers declared them good omens. When lightning struck the new palace spire it was interpreted favorably to mean that Mindon would be victorious over all his enemies.[5] Mindon talked of little else but the new city. Kanaung busied himself with steam-pumping equipment to fill the ditches and manmade lakes designed for beautification and irrigation.[6] Agriculturalists were encouraged to move near the new capital. There were many complaints at the forced move. Amarapura may have been "a nasty hole," but Mandalay was a wretched place, costing far more than it was worth. To counter discontent Mindon threatened to call up troops.[7] In mid-1857 Mindon moved into his new temporary palace, and by 1859 the capital was almost complete.

The King employed Buddhism to enhance his power. He fostered the idea of being the defender of the faith through works of merit and attempted to transform the ecclesiastical order from a passively loyal to an actively loyal institution. He wanted to turn a potentially destabilizing force into a power-supportive asset by conciliation and his own outward *Karma*.[8] Mindon was sensitive to the power of the church and frequently sought churchmen's advice in political matters.[9] By royal edict Mindon opened direct channels of communication between himself and the provincial religious. Many monks were made royal *Sayadaws*. On the representations of local monks Mindon reversed several of his own decisions declaring military and religious lands royal land.[10] Cultivators of religious lands were exempted from new taxes. All this tended to align the church with the crown.

Mindon's personal example of benevolence to the religious is recorded in stone. His religious foundations abounded. Some complained that these were being funded from state revenues rather than the privy purse. Mindon financed lavish ceremonies and expended cash, kind, and laborers' energies.[11] He sponsored religious pilgrimages, which had foreign policy dimensions. One of the holiest pagodas was in British territory, the Shwedagon Pagoda, in Rangoon. A request to re-gild the finial was refused in 1853 unless Mindon signed the treaty. Mindon complained of desecration of holy places in Pegu by British troops in search of loot. Even if Mindon had signed the treaty the British were wary of permitting a Buddhist pilgrimage to the Shwedagon Pagoda, which was a symbol of Burmese nationalism. Dalhousie minuted: "Such a mission would in the eyes of the people of Pegu be nothing less than a triumphal procession symbolizing the future restoration of the king's supremacy."[12] The British regarded Buddhism as subversive.[13] A pilgrimage was again refused in 1856, at which time Phayre objected to the style of the letters requesting permission. By the late 1850s the Burmese obtained permission for a pilgrimage, but by this time they had grander plans and sent missions to southwest Yunnan, Laos, and Manipur.[14] The high point of early pilgrimages was a reciprocal mission between Mandalay and Kandy, Ceylon, the seat of southern Buddhism. Two Cingalese Buddhist priests visited Mandalay in 1858 to seek advice on the religious schism in Ceylon. The Burmese took from Kandy a wax model of the tooth of the famous Buddhist relic there.[15] Mindon enhanced his *karma* by commuting death sentences to lifetime servitude as pagoda slaves, freeing criminals and caged animals, canceling debts, closing law courts for limited periods and therefore putting a stop to arrests and litigation, and putting bans on the slaughter of animals. The British frowned. The freeing of criminals was linked to increased border dacoity, and the prohibition on the slaughter of animals seemed to occur when Europeans were visiting Burma.[16]

The unity that King Bodawpaya's heavy hand brought to the church in the early nineteenth century stood virtually unchallenged until Mindon's reign. In 1853 Mindon appointed a conciliar and traditional figure as *Thathanabaing*, U Nyeya (the second Maungdaung Sayadaw), who had served in this position under Tharrawaddy and had left office during Pagan Min's reign. During the early 1860s controversy fairly raged over the questions of reform, the *Sangha's* political role, and the conflict over monastic luxury and purity. Mindon attempted piecemeal reforms in religious education, revising the scriptures and upgrading monastic education. It is in the political sphere that Mindon was most active with the *Sangha*. Ferguson and Mendelson have described the factionalism and sectarianism that flourished during Mindon's reign, a process he may have encouraged initially but was ultimately unable to control and discipline.[17] The *Sangha* was also used as a political weapon against Mindon. Under pressure from the monks he rescinded land transfers from the church to the state. The British used the *Thathanabaing* on more than one occasion to pressure Mindon on frontier tariffs. By the time of the *Thathanabaing's* death in 1865 the church was rent by schism.[18] Faced with conflict Mindon decided to leave the position unfilled and interpret the middle path himself. An unsuccessful attempt was made to heal the breach at the Fifth Great Buddhist Council, the first meeting of its kind in two thousand years. When Thibaw ascended the throne in 1878 the monastic schism was recognized as irreparable by the appointment of two *Thathanabaing.*[19]

Burma's geography, limited technology, and poor communications allowed isolated pockets of minority peoples to exist with minimum interference from the central state. The minorities occupied the bulk of the land, albeit the poorer and inaccessible parts. During the mid-nineteenth century Burma was on the brink of breaking her traditional technology-communication restraints, and Mindon attempted to shift from informal to formal control of the minorities. Initially the minorities welcomed Mindon. The Shans even joined his camp at Shwebo, paid homage, and assisted in the revolt. Mindon's marriage links were calculated to create fresh bonds between the center and the periphery. But, unlike his forebears, Mindon was not satisfied with salutary neglect. The increasing frequency of ethnic rebellion and the efforts of some chiefs to change their allegiance from Burma to Britain, China, or Siam attest to mounting ethnic alienation. Minorities, organized on a village basis, had little intervening authority between village and Mandalay and were therefore unable to make their ethnic nation felt. It was relatively easy, if somewhat tiresome and expensive, for the Burmese to quell sporadic uprisings.

The Chins had the least contact with Burma. On the western frontier they were uniquely favored, as neither British nor Burmese had interests in crossing their territory to somewhere else, the overland route between India and Burma having been abandoned in the mid-1830s. The wild and volatile Kachins, on the other hand, lived astride the "path of silver and gold" that led to China. When the British wanted to travel north from Mandalay to Bhamo, the King invariably discouraged them. Mindon could not guarantee safety crossing Kachin territory, to which frequent murders and robberies attest. The Pagan *Wungyi* stated: "As to the Burma officials they will not but obey us. We cannot answer for the wild Kakhyeens; those people are half wild, and [obey] orders as they choose."[20] The northern minorities problem was even more confused than usual because of the Panthay Moslem rebellion and subsequent Panthay control of Yunnan from 1855 to 1873. With the demise of Chinese imperial control "the Shans and Kakhyens [were] utterly independent of restraint."[21] Bhamo, the northernmost Burmese town, was alternately under attack from Chinese, Kachin, Shan, or Panthay forces.

The Karens, an ill-defined group along the eastern frontier, provided the most vexing diplomatic problems. The eager amateur ethnologist and East India Company servant, O'Riley, thought that "the whole country is inhabited...by 'wild' or independent tribes of Karens, and for the present I am inclined to think they had better be left to themselves. They never owed allegiance to the Burmese."[22] Mindon, however, claimed overlordship and intervened in Karen affairs when the Karens raided Burmese subjects. The British thought the Burmese were trying to make up the loss of Pegu by extending the southeast frontier.[23] Mindon softened the usually oppressive Burmese policy toward the Karens to counter the success of the Baptist missionaries and allowed Karens for the first time to enter the Buddhist monkhood.[24] From the mid-1850s to the 1870s the Karens were divided among themselves between pro-British and pro-Burmese villages. Karen external posture was secondary to an intra-Karen power struggle,[25] and they had been playing off the British against the Burmese since at least 1838. In 1875 Sir Douglas Forsyth went to Mandalay to solve the Karen jurisdiction dispute.

The Shans were the most politically, economically, and culturally developed minority. Mindon was eager to incorporate them into heartland control. They lived in the China-Siam buffer zone, and much trade passed through their territory or was internally generated. Their valuable resources were timber, sulfur, copper, and lead—all Burmese revenue sources. At the beginning of the reign Mindon faced a serious challenge from the Siamese, who were encroaching on traditional Burmese-oriented Shans, though some of them welcomed the Siamese. Mindon commented:

> They [Siamese] think now that the English have taken nearly half my country, that I have not even power to resist *them,* but they will find themselves much mistaken. The English in taking the lower country have certainly deprived me of a large revenue, but the fighting men have always been drawn from the country still under my charge, Pegu could only supply boatmen, who could be of no use at anytime in a Siamese war.

Within three months Mindon's uncle, in charge of the Siamese campaign, effectively removed the Siamese threat to Kentung.[26]

Mindon mixed conciliation with coercion in extending control to the Shan States. The status of the *Sawbwas* at court was raised.[27] During mid-1863 Mindon became keener on Shan control and made the Shans liable to taxation. He took over the Shan forests to bolster the royal treasury. Previously, Shan customary obligations had been of an extraordinary nature. In time of war they assisted the Burmese with gold, crops, ponies, and men. They paid a nominal annual tribute. Now the Burmese were trying to extend regularized assessment. If the *Sawbwas* resisted they were taken hostage to Mandalay and replaced by a royal appointee, often a Burman. There was a marked increase in the turnover of *Sawbwas.*[28] Shan resistance was serious. Burmese officials were reported massacred in the Shan States adjoining the Toungoo district. Entire Shan communities migrated to British territory. It embarrassed Britain to become a political haven, and she informed Mandalay that the pensions to chiefs were charitable and not political.[29] Shan unrest became so serious that by March 1865 all-out military occupation of the Shan States was contemplated because the local populations refused to accept Burmans as *Sawbwas.* In early 1865 Mindon gave up trying to install one of his nominees as the troops were needed elsewhere in the Shan States.[30] When five thousand troops were sent to the Shan States, the British political agent commented: "These disturbances in the Shan States have of late years assumed a chronic shape, and only disappear for a time whilst held in check by the presence of superior forces."[31]

The succession problem was Mindon's most serious concern. There had been several minor succession disputes before 1866 but no serious threats. In May 1854 the last remaining son of Setkya Min revolted. No executions resulted, and all conspirators were set free as an act of charity at Mindon's coronation.[32] A short while later another conspiracy was uncovered but caused hardly a ripple in Mindon's firm control. This time the object had been to restore Pagan Min to the throne. Again within a month all conspirators were released. In 1855 there was a Mohammedan disturbance.[33] The first ten years of the reign saw relative peace within the royal family. As the reign progressed, however, politics at the center focused increasingly on the royal family, with its ever-growing number of squabbling wives and mature sons, which culminated in the revolt of 1866.[34] Foreign observers incessantly predicted that strife was imminent in the form of a coup by Kanaung or one of the King's growing sons.[35] The impasse many considered inevitable took time to develop.

Mindon himself was aware of the problem and its causes. He prohibited ministers from having large families, which caused expenses, irregularities, and oppression. At the same time, in late 1859, Mindon

was celebrating the birth of his fifty-third and fifty-fourth children.[36]
By the early 1860s Mindon was keeping a close watch on his eldest sons,
limiting their movements outside the palace.[37] In 1863 Mindon's son,
the Thonze Prince, fled Mandalay to British territory. It was rumored
that he had talked about succeeding his father and given gifts to various
palace guard officers. He arrived in Rangoon without money, expressing a wish to go to the Shan States with a pension. After receiving letters from his mother and the *Thathanabaing*, promising to forget the
past, he returned to Mandalay.[38]

During 1866 several problems converged, indicating a politically
and economically discontented nation. This was followed by prophecy
and finally revolt. People had been leaving Burma for British territory
because of taxes, the price of rice, stiffer Shan policy, and the lure of
wage labor in Rangoon.[39] The Pakan Wungyi had superseded the
Magwe Wungyi and the former's ill health introduced a degree of ministerial instability. One of Mindon's *Atwinwuns* had brought frequent
scandal on the court for his Westernized habits and disregard for Buddhist precepts.[40] The Burmese treasury was having cash-flow difficulties,
and only the granting of monopolies staved off bankruptcy.[41] The
death of the *Thathanabaing* was another loss to stability. Mindon's
own health was deteriorating, and he took less direct interest in the affairs of state.[42] Problems concerning customs posts, duties, border dacoity,
concession seekers, creditors, and law courts had, in the eyes of some, reduced Mindon to a mean trader, subservient to the British. Squabbles within the royal family were notorious, as wives sniped at one another or took
lovers. Unrest among the ethnic minorities was increasing.

The final element of convergence was prophecy. The months before
the revolt had been tinder-dry and intensely hot around Mandalay. The
city was in dire danger. By March two fires had destroyed one-fourth of
the city and almost three million baskets of rice.[43] At the commencement
of the Burmese year 1228 (April 1866) astrologers forecast an evil year for
the state of Burma. Death of the monarch and fire had been part of the
prophecy. Mindon attempted to evade this "curse" by benevolence. He
distributed gifts, even to the astrologers, and contemplated moving Mandalay away from the river. The worst fire in living memory occurred on
15 April 1866. The best areas of Mandalay were destroyed. The fire was
carried by a breeze that became a whirlwind or fire storm. The official
toll was nearly ten thousand houses destroyed. Calamities had not run

their course: two weeks after the devastating fire a hurricane hit Mandalay. Hurricanes were unusual and were further verification of the prophecy.[44]

By the mid-1860s several of Mindon's and Kanaung's sons were restive and had aspirations of their own. The leaders of the early stages of the 1866 revolt-cum-civil war were the Myigun Prince and his younger brother, the Myingundaing Prince. Both were in their early twenties, and their mother was a lesser queen of Mindon's. They professed that their uncle, the Kanaung Prince, had treated them badly, and they resolved to put him to death. Kanaung was in charge of all royal sons, and although they frequently complained of harsh treatment, a Britisher noted that Kanaung was very good to his nephews, nursing them when they were ill as though they were his own children. But Mindon's elder sons were inclined to be wild and unruly, especially the two princes who revolted first.[45]

At noon on 2 August 1866, to signal their revolt, the two rebel princes set fire to part of Mandalay. The Kanaung Prince was conferring with the ministers near the *Hluttaw*. The princes attacked the assembly, and within minutes the Kanaung Prince, the Myadaung Wungyi, and three princes lay dead. Kanaung's head was paraded about by the Myingundaing Prince. Several officials were left for dead. The Pakan Wungyi and several *Wundauks* and *Myowuns* escaped. The rebel princes swore they wished no ill to the King. However, their actions belied their words. The rebels headed for the King's temporary summer palace. The commotion and uproar that preceded them gave Mindon a few minutes' advance warning. His most trusted officers created a diversion while he and about fifty of his family fled to a fortified position in the city palace. Political agent Sladen and Dr. Williams, who had returned to Mandalay in late May 1866 as an agent for the Irrawaddy Flotilla Company and Todd Findlay and Company, were in the audience hall with the King when the revolt began and found themselves surrounded by the insurgents. Sladen temporized with the man carrying Kanaung's head. Sladen and Williams were allowed to escape to the Residency.[46]

The evening of the revolt was filled with inconclusive firing. The insurgents looted but were brought to a halt by loyal contingents. Having lost the element of surprise the young princes realized they had little chance against the King's superior forces. The next day they captured one of the King's steamers and with about two hundred followers steamed southward. They captured several river towns, including the Burmese border customs post, which they sacked and then paused to plan anew. Hoping to foment rebellion in the south and then attack Mandalay, they solicited aid from the British at Rangoon. When Commissioner Phayre received a letter from the princes requesting delivery of Mindon's two steamers in Rangoon, Phayre politely and firmly refused.[47]

Several of Mindon's and Kanaung's sons fled Mandalay on 3 August for fear of their lives. As many as four princes may have harbored their own plans for revolt. Most returned within a few days, with the notable exception of the Padein Prince, eldest son of the assassinated Crown Prince, Kanaung. He fled north, capturing Shwebo, which rallied to his support, having been his father's fief. Mindon implored Padein to return and promised to create him heir. But Padein, advised by Kanaung's household *Atwinwun*, decided to try for the throne. At this juncture Mindon considered abdicating to Padein rather than shedding blood to retain the throne.[48] Mindon was dissuaded from this course by his wives. The chief queen read omens favorable to Mindon's cause, and the King turned to the offensive.

Mindon wanted the British steamer in Mandalay. Sladen had already requested it from Williams for evacuating the European population. The King's discussions with Sladen and Williams about the steamer broke down on 7 August. Sladen wanted a guarantee for European lives and property and assurances that the ship would not be used offensively. Williams wanted to profit from Mindon's use of the steamer and demanded a special rental as well as compensation for delays. The two Britons fought bitterly between themselves. Williams resented his replacement by Sladen as British agent at Mandalay, and the crisis of revolt brought these feelings out into the open and gave them tangible form. Burmese forces quietly and bloodlessly seized the steamer. On the following day, 8 August, Sladen felt that life and property were insecure, as Burmese officials were sending their valuables and families to the Residency for safety. The steamer had been used offensively against the Padein Prince. Sladen was extremely nervous about Mindon's tenure and Sladen's own personal security. He weighed the diplomatic consequences of withdrawal.

> The King if he remains in power, which is almost impossible, will doubtless, be angry at my having taken the steamer from him, but I had no other course left. The Padyne Mentha, if he becomes King, will not forget that the steamer was used against him.[49]

Sladen decided to recapture the *Nerbudda* and flee to British territory. The vessel was easily taken later that day and reached Rangoon safely on 15 August.[50]

The threat to Mandalay was most serious from 15 to 20 August. Padein faced the capital from the north, east, and west. On the south, along the Irrawaddy highway were the Myingun and Myingundaing princes. Mandalay inhabitants were thoroughly demoralized. Provisions were scarce, and food prices skyrocketed. Slowly the royal troops were deployed and placed at strategic points under the command of the returning princes. Mindon placed supreme command of the twelve-thousand-man force in the hands of a general who had distinguished himself in 1853 and then left public life. The royal forces were superior in number and materiel. By the end of August the threat from Padein had been greatly reduced. A third threat emerged at the beginning of September in the form of provincial officials to the south of Mandalay, coalescing with ten thousand men under Padein's banner. The movement of all contestants was hampered during September because of unusually heavy rains. Padein's forces suffered from lack of supplies, internal dissension, and during the beginning of October loss of several important engagements. The Shans, under one of Mindon's sons, rose and threatened the Padein's rear. Padein attempted to sue for peace, but his adviser diverted the mission.

Mindon's two steamers at Rangoon were sent to Mandalay by the British on 23 September with an armed guard of loyal troops sent down by the Burmese frontier governor. They attacked the two rebel princes, who then fled to British territory. On 6 October the two rebel princes turned themselves over to British custody and told the British officers they had been forced to revolt because of Kanaung's aggrandizing power. They hoped the British would intercede on behalf of their wives and children and reconcile them with the King.[51] The three steamers then returned to Mandalay on 13 October. This had a salutary effect. Padein's officers and men melted away. His major adviser fled to Shwebo on 24 October. The following day Padein took sanctuary in a monastery and awaited his arrest by royal troops. He was led captive into Mandalay on 2 November. The civil war was over. Mindon was still on the throne.

Unlike earlier revolts of similar scale in 1837 and 1853, Mindon continued on the throne. In great part this survival was due to improved central control. The revolts of 1866 marked a turning point in Burmese history. The prospect of renewed monarchical instability and succession strife loomed on the horizon. Recognizing the need to take security precautions for the princes Mindon provided them with a rotating armed guard and limited the size of their permanent retinues.[52] Within less than three months of the quelling of the civil war, three more princes rose in unsuccessful bids for the throne. Despite the British political agent's intercession in their behalf, several of the conspirators, including the Padein Prince, were executed.[53] There were no further rebellions or widespread bloodletting until Thibaw's accession in 1878, though a small conspiracy was uncovered in 1870.[54]

Mindon's grasp of state affairs was clearly shaken, and national self-interest was redefined. Internal modernization was deemphasized, and Burma's diplomatic contact with the outside world assumed greater importance. The revolt changed Burma's political personnel and Britain's attitude toward Burma. The Kinwunmingyi rose in power as did the Pangyet Wun, the latter being recalled from his engineering studies at the Sorbonne shortly after Kanaung's assassination. Both men were modernizers, became Mindon's confidential advisers, and would develop an international aspect to Burmese state policy. Burma's weakened internal position following the revolt provided an opportunity for Britain to attempt once more the enforcement of paramountcy in the treaty negotiations of 1866 and 1867.

NOTES

1. Spears to Hopkinson, 10 August 1857, and Hopkinson to Talbot, 4 September 1857, Canning Papers, 55/2330 and 2421; and Georgios Calogreedy to Edwards, October 1857, ISP/215.

2. Spears to Phayre, 18 March, 2 and 16 April, and 26 May 1855, in D. G. E. Hall, ed., *The Dalhousie-Phayre Correspondence, 1852-1856* (London: Oxford University Press, 1932), pp. 160-4, 323, and 338.

3. Henry Yule, *Reports of the Mission to Ava in 1855* (Calcutta: Government Printers, 1856), p. 137.

4. Maung Maung Tin and Thomas Owen Morris, "Mindon Min's Development Plan for the Mandalay Area," *J.B.R.S.* 49 (1966): 29-34; and Howard Malcom, *Travels in South-eastern Asia,* 2 vols. (Boston: Gould, Kendall, and Lincoln, 1839), 1: 101.

5. Thaung Blackmore, "The Founding of the City of Mandalay by King Mindon," *Journal of Oriental Studies* 5 (1959-60): 82-98; J. G. Scott and J. P. Hardiman, comps., *Gazetteer of Upper Burma and the Shan States,* 2 pts., 5 vols. (Rangoon: Government Printers, 1900), pt. 1, 1: 40-4; and Charles Duroiselle, *Guide to the Mandalay Palace,* 2d ed. (Calcutta: Government of India Publications, 1931), p. 13. "Prophecies, Omens, and Dialogue: Tools of the Trade in Burmese Historiography," presented by Michael Aung Thwin at the 31st annual meeting of the Association for Asian Studies, Los Angeles, 1979, analyzes the role of cosmology as a legitimating, stabilizing and literary device in Burmese history and politics.

6. Spears to Hopkinson, 13 June, 10 and 25 August 1857, Canning Papers, 55/2330 and 55/2421.

7. Spears to Hopkinson, 23 July 1857, and Spears to Canning, 24 December 1857 and 7 January 1858, Canning Papers, 55/2320 and 3270-1; and Spears to Hopkinson, 23 July and 16 November 1857; and Calogreedy to Edwards, October 1857, ISP/215.

8. Melford E. Spiro, *Buddhism and Society* (London: Allen & Unwin, 1971), pp. 438-43; and J. A. Stewart, *Buddhism in Burma* (Rangoon: N.p., [1939?]), pp. 3-6.

9. Phayre to Durand, 20 November 1862, IPF/204/63.

10. H. R. Spearman, ed., *British Burma Gazetteer*, 2 vols. (Rangoon: Government Printers, 1880), 2: 2.

11. *Inscriptions Collected in Upper Burma* (Rangoon: Government Printers, 1900), pp. 432-5; and Stewart, *Buddhism,* p. 6.

12. Minute by Dalhousie, 25 November 1853, in Hall, ed., *Correspondence,* p. 105.

13. Albert Fytche, *Burma, Past and Present,* 2 vols. (London: Kegan Paul, 1878), 2: 76-7; Wheeler, "Memorandum," 21 January 1871, IPP/760, pp. 35-7; Maung Htin Aung, *Burmese Monk's Tales* (New York: Columbia University Press, 1966), pp. 14-31; and C. J. F. S. Forbes, *British Burma and Its Peoples* (London: Murray, 1878), p. 325.

14. Janell A. Nilsson, "The Administration of British Burma, 1852-1885" (Ph.D. diss., University of London, 1970), p. 101; and *Pegu Administration Report, 1859-60,* p. 174.

15. C. E. Godakumbura, "Relations Between Burma and Ceylon," *J.B.R.S.* 49 (1966): 156; and Niharranjan Ray, *An Introduction to the Study of Theravada Buddhism in Burma* (Calcutta: Calcutta University Press, 1946), pp. 244-9.

16. Wheeler, "Memorandum," 21 January 1871, IPP/760, pp. 43-5.

17. E. Michael Mendelson, *Sangha and State in Burma,* ed. John P. Ferguson (Ithaca: Cornell University Press, 1975), pp. 28, 40, 79, 82, 113, and 359.

18. Ray, *Theravada Buddhism,* pp. 246-50; *Lower Chindwin Gazetteer* (Rangoon: Government Printers, 1912), p. 2; Stewart, *Buddhism,* pp. 6-13; Nilsson, "Administration," p. 167: Sladen Diary, 7 November 1865 and 24 May 1869, IPF/204/79 and IPP/438/66.

19. Maung Htin Aung, *Monk's Tales,* p. 26; and Maung Maung, *Burma in the Family of Nations* (Amsterdam: Uitgeverij Djambatan, 1956), p. 48; Stewart, *Buddhism,* p. 7; and Wheeler, "Memorandum," 21 January 1871, IPP/760, p. 48.

20. Quoted in Ma Thaung, "British Interest in Trans-Burma Trade Routes to China, 1826-1876" (Ph.D. diss., University of London, 1954), p. 259.

21. Williams Diary, 19 May 1864, IPF/204/78.

22. They were called variously Karens, Kayins, Karenni, and Red Karens. Phayre to Dalhousie, 12 June 1855, in Hall, ed., *Correspondence,* p. 279.

23. Palm Leaf letter received 16 April 1856 from Burmese fort officer at Mobai, IPF/203/40; and *Pegu Administration Report, 1856-7,* p. 158.

24. Theodore Stern, "*Ariya* and the Golden Book: A Millenarian Buddhist Sect Among the Karens," *Journal of Asian Studies* 27 (1968): 297-328.

25. Spears to Phayre, 13 January 1855, in Hall, ed., *Correspondence,* p. 292.

26. Spears to Phayre, 1 June 1854, ibid., p. 195; and William Louis Barretto, *King Mindon* (Rangoon: Burma Union Press, 1935), p. 5.

27. Scott and Hardiman, comps., *Gazetteer,* pt. 1, 1: 289-90; and Spears to Phayre, 30 April 1854, in Hall, ed., *Correspondence,* p. 181.

28. Statement of Moung Naw Pha, *Sawbwa* of Neoung Yuay, 6 May 1864, Phayre Collection Oriental Mss. 3466; Williams Diary, 29 October-18 November 1864, and Phayre to Durand, 16 September 1864, IPF/204/75; and Williams Diary, 6 August and 31 December 1864, IPF/204/78.

29. Wheeler to Phayre, 20 April 1864; Davies to Durand, 20 April 1864; and Phayre to Durand, 6 May 1864, IPF/204/73.

30. Williams Diary, 17 April 1864, 27 January, 27 February, and 5 March 1865, IPF/204/78.

31. Sladen Diary, 20 January 1866, IPP/437/67.

32. Spears to Phayre, 12 May and 25 June 1854, in Hall, ed., *Correspondence,* pp. 187 and 207; and Spears to Phayre, 22 February 1856, Canning Papers, Misc. 6.

33. Spears to Phayre, 11 September, 11 October 1854, and 25 July 1855, in Hall, ed., *Correspondence,* pp. 248-9 and 363.

34. Henry Yule, *Reports of the Mission,* pp. xli and 135; and Yule, *Narrative of a Mission to the Court of Ava in 1855* (Kuala Lumpur: Oxford University Press, 1969 [orig. publ. 1858]), p. xxxix; Scott and

Hardiman, comps., *Gazetteer*, pt. 1, 1: 65; James George Scott [Shway
Yoe], *The Burman* (New York: Norton, 1963 [orig. publ. 1882]), p. 467;
and Sladen Diary, 27 March 1866, IPF/204/78.
For ramifications of the illegitimacy scandals see Paul J.
Bennett, *Conference Under the Tamarind Tree* (New Haven: Yale University Southeast Asia Studies, 1971), and for a fictionalized account see Maung Htin
Aung, *Burmese Drama* (London: Oxford University Press, 1937).
  35. Calogreedy to Edwards, October 1857, ISP/215; Sladen Diary,
22 November 1865, IPP/437/66; and Williams to Davies, 23 October
1867, IPP/438/3.
  36. Journal of Events at the Capital of Burma, 11-12 November 1859,
by A. P. Phayre, 30 December 1859, IPF/203/71.
  37. Williams to Grote, 4 July 1862, Elgin Papers, 48/665.
  38. Phayre to Durand, 4 May and 23 July 1863, and Davies to Durand,
27 July 1863, IPF/204/67.
  39. Williams Diary, 11 October 1864, IPF/204/78; and Sladen Diary,
11 August 1865, IPF/204/79.
  40. Sladen Diary, 14 May 1866, IPP/437/68.
  41. Sladen Diary, 22 December 1865, IPP/437/66; and 24 March 1865,
IPF/204/78.
  42. Sladen Diary, 24 March 1866, IPP/437/67.
  43. Sladen Diary, 7 March 1865, IPF/204/78.
  44. Sladen Diary, 20-27 April 1866, IPP/437/67; and 24 December
1866, IPP/437/70.
  45. L. Allen Goss, notes appended to *Parliamentary Papers* 50 (1867),
"Papers on the Late Rebellion in Upper Burma," presented 4 April 1867.
Goss was in Mandalay during the revolt, and his personal copy of the Parliamentary Paper is in the Library of the School of Oriental and African
Studies, London. See also Scott and Hardiman, comps., *Gazetteer,* pt. 1,
1: 53-4.
  46. Sladen to Phayre, 5 August 1866, in "Papers on the Late Rebellion"
(1867), p. 4.
  47. Phayre to Secretary to Government of India, 14 August 1866, and
Memo by Phayre, 13 August 1866, in ibid., p. 3.
  48. Sladen to Phayre, 7 August 1866, in ibid., p. 4; and Scott and Hardiman, comps., *Gazetteer,* pt. 1, 1: 58.
  49. Sladen to Phayre, August 1866, IPP/437/68.
  50. Phayre to Government of India, 22 September 1866 and 20 October
1866, IPP/437/69. For the acrimonious correspondence between Williams
and Sladen see *Private Copy of Portions of Correspondence between Dr.*

Clement Williams and Officials of the Indian Government, in Reference to Injuries Sustained on Account of the Conduct of the Political Agent in Upper Burmah (London: N.p., 1868); Blackmore, "Dilemma of the British Representative to the Burmese Court After the Outbreak of a Palace Revolution in 1866," *Journal of Southeast Asian History* 10 (1969): 236-52; Williams to Sladen, 3 August 1866, IPP/437/69; and Williams to Davies, 23 October 1867, IPP/438/3.

51. Memo of conversation with Myingun Prince at Thayetmyo with Capt. H. T. Duncan, 6 October 1866, IPP/437/69; and Phayre to Sladen, 6 October 1866, Sladen Papers, India Office Library and Records, E290/1A.

52. Sladen Diary, 12 December 1866, IPP/437/70.

53. Sladen Diary, 10 May 1867, IPP/437/71.

54. Wheeler, "Memorandum," 21 January 1871, IPP/760, pp. 66-7.

8
DIPLOMACY, TRADE, AND POLITICS (1853-67)

British officialdom and private individuals pursued their individual policies with varying intensity, resulting in the subordination of Burma to a Calcutta-Rangoon-based political *and* economic hegemony. Britain used her geopolitical leverage, won in the two wars, to control landlocked Burma. Upper Burma was part of Britain's informal empire. The Burmese monarch was forced to deal with the Governor General in Calcutta, rather than Queen Victoria and the Foreign Office in London, as Mindon wished. Britain could also exert influence over Burma's relations with other foreign powers. The major Burmese foreign policy consideration was the omnipresence of British power and the staving off of further demands and encroachments on her sovereignty. Movement to formal empire was slow and halting but not inexorable or inevitable.

Personal ambitions; mercantile pressure emanating from London, Calcutta, and British Burma; exploration of the overland trade route to western China; and the threat of French activities in Indochina spilling over into Burma governed the creation and application of Britain's Burma policy, which fell into four phases. Between 1853 and 1860 relations with Burma were informal and low-key. The Government of India employed Thomas Spears, a merchant, as unofficial newswriter in the Burmese capital. His replacements were government officials. Dr. Clement Williams and later Edward Bosc Sladen were both more aggressive and

less sympathetic to Burmese problems than Spears. They transformed
the nature of Anglo-Burmese contact. These political agents interfered
in Burmese politics and between 1860 and 1867 strove to carve out
special rights for the English. The treaties of 1862 and 1867 went far to
establish Britain as virtual paramount power over Burma. From 1868
onward relations deteriorated, and official contact was broken in 1878.
Formal annexation into Britain's Indian Empire was achieved by force
in 1886 following the two-week-long Third Anglo-Burmese War.

INFORMAL CONTACT

Dalhousie kept his resolve of quick victory, minimum conquest, and
allowing time to heal relations. Peace was assured, but a treaty was wanting. In the remaining years of Dalhousie's governor generalship the conclusion of a treaty was London's constant request, but not one of Dalhousie's vital aims. His major efforts were directed toward creating a
secure frontier, a viable economy, and suppressing civil disturbances in
the newly annexed province.[1] The new Pegu Commissioner, A. P. Phayre,
was instructed to employ a newswriter to replace the discredited and
murdered Captain Latter.[2] Phayre settled on Spears, and a new era of
friendly informal contact opened that lasted as long as Spears remained
in Burma. He acted as messenger, negotiator, and adviser to both the
British and Burmese. As relations normalized various drafts of treaty
proposals were sent up to Mindon. Dalhousie, however, did not want
Phayre to negotiate personally, as it would appear that the British were
overanxious. The Burmese broached the idea of a goodwill mission to
Calcutta. Phayre and Dalhousie welcomed the idea.[3] Dalhousie was prepared to offer retrocession of some border areas and free import of powder
and sulfur in exchange for a treaty. The Burmese envoys arrived in Rangoon in early October 1854. The mission was soon in jeopardy as the envoys' letters of greeting and introduction were deemed offensive by Phayre.
The envoys stayed in Rangoon until late November awaiting further instructions and fresh letters of introduction from the capital. The envoys
spent three weeks in Calcutta exchanging platitudes with the Governor
General and arranging a return British mission to Burma. Just before departing Calcutta, the envoys, at a private interview, pleaded for the return
of Pegu. Dalhousie replied "that so long as the sun shines, which they see,

those territories will never be restored to the Kingdom of Ava.'"[4] Dalhousie
was unable to conclude a treaty, and the Burmese envoys returned to
Amarapura with slightly ruffled feathers.

As the British return mission was being planned French, Sardinian, and
American interests were converging on Burma. In September 1854 the King
of Sardinia's Consul in Calcutta approached King Mindon to sign a commercial treaty. Mindon saw a draft and balked at the article providing for
a Consul at Amarapura, as it might provide the thin edge of the wedge the
British were looking for.[5] Mindon rejected the treaty, preferring to rely
on the peace and friendship that already existed between the two countries.
Mindon's adviser, secretary, and translator in much of his European diplomacy was Dom Paula Abbona, a Catholic missionary and representative of
a century-long tradition of papal contact with the kings of Burma. Abbona
wrote newsletters to the Vatican on the status of Catholicism and religious
toleration.[6] While the British thought the Sardinian overtures in 1854 and
later in 1856 absurd, they did not regard French plans so lightly. Between
1853 and 1866 a certain French "General" D'Orgoni attempted, rather
unsuccessfully, to increase French presence in Burma. Louis Charles Giro-
din was a Legitimist, Anglophobe, and an insolvent sugar planter from Ile
Bourbon.[7] He arrived in Rangoon in July 1853 and traveled to Shwebo,
where he offered his services to Mindon as scientist and mechanic. Mindon
employed him making gunpowder. By early 1854 D'Orgoni had persuaded
Mindon to finance a trip to France to investigate treaty possibilities and
recruit artisans. D'Orgoni was a man of many schemes, more interested
in lining his own pockets than furthering Burmese diplomacy.[8] D'Orgoni
returned to Amarapura in June 1855, bringing presents, *not* as an authorized agent of the French government but as their correspondent, similar
in status to Spears. American Baptist missionary Kincaid also tried to open
treaty feelers between Burma and America. He instigated Mindon's writing letters to President James Buchanan and Secretary of State Lewis Cass.
Kincaid's fond hopes for a treaty, however, resulted in little more than
an exchange of letters.[9]

Pegu Commissioner Phayre headed a well-recorded British mission. He
was accompanied by a surgeon, geologist, artist, photographer, military
analyst, and surveyor to draw up comprehensive reports. The budding
orientalist and secretary to the mission, Henry Yule, who was unsympathetic to the Burmese, would write a confidential report, as well as his
well-known *Narrative of a Mission to the Court of Ava in 1855.* Phayre

carried with him a fresh treaty, which did not mention cession of territory and contained only two articles concerning trade and amity. Dalhousie wrote that he had "no expectation of obtaining any treaty."[10] The mission was almost aborted when Phayre, enraged over a border incident, wanted satisfaction from the Burmese before proceeding to Burma. Dalhousie chastised Phayre for not having a sufficiently strong border police and for allowing a trivial incident to jeopardize the mission.[11] When the mission arrived in Amarapura matters of ceremony caused a few awkward moments. The mission argued among themselves about the propriety of taking off shoes when visiting pagodas, an issue that would continue well into the twentieth century. Phayre, the most pro-Burmese of the envoys, wanted to honor Burmese custom. Others found removing the shoes repugnant.[12] The Governor General's official letter of greeting was to be received under a canopy umbrella. Several Burmese officials thought this accorded too much honor to the Governor General. Phayre did not press the point and settled for a British flag being hoisted above the letter.[13] The Burmese herald's phraseology at introductions also caused some difficulty: for instance, at the audience with Kanaung Phayre threatened to walk out if "offering" was not changed to "gifts." There was also the discomfiture of kneeling and bowing.

The main British aim was the conclusion of the treaty. Despite the fact that the treaty did not mention cession of territory or the appointment of a Resident or Consul, Mindon rejected it as unnecessary. Friendship already existed, and he welcomed traders. He added that he might accept a treaty sometime in the future if he could get better terms from the next Governor General, such as the removal of frontier import duties. Phayre declared that if a treaty was not concluded then gunpowder and other warlike stores would not be allowed past the frontier. Undaunted, Mindon declared, "I shall not now want muskets. The Myadaung Mengyi has undertaken to supply me with 10,000."[14] Though an empty boast it marked the end of negotiations. In early October 1855 the British mission left Amarapura with Mindon's good wishes but without a treaty.

British failure to conclude a treaty spurred D'Orgoni to plan a second trip to France to represent his and Burma's interests. In mid-1856 he was received by Napoleon III. The Burmese portion of the mission returned to Burma without D'Orgoni. While the Burmese envoys were waiting in Rangoon for a steamer to the capital, a fire destroyed Napoleon III's letter to Mindon. On reaching the capital the envoys were thrown into irons.[15] In consequence of French Catholic Bishop Paul Ambrose Bigandet's represen-

tations, Count Waleski, French Minister of Foreign Affairs, despatched
Henry de Sercy, a discredited French officer, with a duplicate letter to ex-
onerate the ill-treated envoys and to evaluate D'Orgoni's wild claims about
Burma. De Sercy spent two months in Burma, and when he left he took
with him three young Burmans from Kanaung's household to be educated
in France. De Sercy reported in Paris that a treaty could be concluded.
But the French government was cautious, pointing out the susceptibilities
of the English and the expense experienced establishing consular missions
in Siam and Cambodia. The British Ambassador in Paris kept a watch on
D'Orgoni. The British did not want D'Orgoni to return to Burma but could
find no legitimate pretext to prevent him. He obtained financial backing
from Marseilles and Bordeaux merchants and returned to Burma in early
1859, bringing with him several artisans, his family, two steamers, and a
plan to open a river trade to Yunnan.[16]

Governor General Earl Charles John Canning succeeded Dalhousie in
1856. Canning had little interest in Burma. At the beginning of Canning's
governor generalship Mindon proposed another grand mission to Calcutta.
Phayre thought the visit calculated to get a seaport. Canning wrote: "The
relations of the two governments are thoroughly friendly. . . .No good
result [could] be obtained by" such a visit. Moreover, Canning was "quite
indifferent" to concluding a treaty.[17]

During the course of the 1857 Indian Mutiny Calcutta feared the Burmese would take advantage of the situation and encroach on Pegu. Mindon, however, feared that reduced British forces in Pegu would cause a
Mon rebellion. Kanaung sent men to Calcutta to observe.[18] British fears
increased as Mindon called up his *ahmudan* to build Mandalay. Phayre
was away on emergency leave, and Pegu was in the charge of jittery Henry
Hopkinson. Hopkinson speculated that the twenty thousand "workers"
called up to build Mandalay were in reality an army to regain Pegu. Abbona wrote of Hopkinson that "the English agent troubled night and day,
and even allowed his fear to seep out."[19] British fears were unfounded.
Only the Moslem and Armenian population in the capital were actively
anti-British. This hostility surfaced during the Crimean War and was of
little import. Border headmen's petitions to raid across the frontier were
rejected. Hopkinson concluded that there was a peace and a war party,
and only the King's statesmanlike conduct restrained the latter.[20] An
act of merit, of which the King talked incessantly as an example of friendship, was his donation of £1,000 to the Indian Mutiny Relief Fund.

After the full fury of the mutiny was spent Mindon talked of sending

a mission to England. Phayre had by then returned to Rangoon, and he
thought Mindon wanted to be treated like Siam, whose ambassador
was received by Queen Victoria in November 1857.[21] Phayre wanted to
visit Mandalay. The recent shift in the Catholic missionaries' headquarters
from Sardinia to France had raised his suspicions. Calcutta instructed
Phayre to wait until the northwest provinces were more tranquil.[22] D'Orgoni's arrival back in Burma in 1859 intensified Phayre's desire to visit
the capital. Though Phayre considered D'Orgoni's ideas of trade quixotic,
they coincided with increasing French influence in Indochina. Though
still "entirely indifferent" to a treaty, Canning felt the time right for an
informal visit.[23] Within six weeks Phayre was on his way to Mandalay. At
Phayre's reception Mindon pointedly asked about the health of the
"English Queen and Royal Family" instead of the Governor General.
No doubt this was a reflection of his dealings through D'Orgoni directly
with Napoleon III. Mindon told Phayre that he liked France and England equally and that his sons were being taught the languages of one
or the other. Phayre was given letters addressed to Queen Victoria that
discussed the restoration of Pegu for the sake of Mindon's constant friendship. Phayre immediately replied that this was absolutely impossible.[24]
Phayre evaluated the Burmese position:

> There is a settled conviction among the majority of all
> classes of Burmese that they are completely in our power.
> . . . As to the king's power for evil against us, it is almost
> literally nothing. . . .I am convinced he sees that the only
> safe policy for the kingdom, is to preserve the peace with
> the British government.[25]

Spears took the opportunity of Phayre's visit to announce his intended
departure in 1860. Mindon's description of Spears was apt. Spears was
"like the frog in the fable, that never sat even near the lotus and never
sipped the sweets of the flowers, while you [Phayre] are like the bee,
which though living at a distance occasionally come and did not neglect
to suck the nectar."[26] Rather than appoint a new agent, Phayre preferred
to visit Mandalay himself.[27] Spears left Burma in March 1860. No longer
in British government pay he decided to carry letters from Mindon directly
to the Secretary of State for India in London. These letters requested the
return of Arakan and Tenasserim. Phayre chastised the Burmese for the

irregular procedure, adding that the Governor General or Commissioner of Pegu would have been happy to receive the letters. Of course, the request was out of the question.[28]

GROWTH OF FORMAL CONTACT

The Indian Mutiny had wide-reaching consequences for the organization of Britain's Eastern Empire. The East India Company's charter was terminated in 1858, and the Indian possessions were placed directly under crown control through the Secretary of State for India. A thorough scrutiny was carried out in all the provinces with an eye to economy, security, efficiency, and streamlined organization. A commission was sent to Pegu, Arakan, and Tenasserim to investigate possible reforms. The result was the Bruce Report, which recommended that the army be replaced by a police force, that the three separate administrations be unified, and that the revenue system be revised.[29] Arakan, Tenasserim, and Pegu were amalgamated into British Burma under Chief Commissioner Phayre in 1862.

Amalgamation indirectly affected British policy toward sovereign Burma. The Commission and Phayre objected to tariffs as prejudicial to trade. Phayre tried unsuccessfully to induce the Burmese to reduce their duties.[30] Canning was averse to another attempt at tariff reduction and wrote to a Commission member:

> I do not share your regret that the King of Ava did not sign the Treaty proposed to him in 55. Treaties with states that are semi-barbarous but entirely independent invariably lead to quarrels, especially commercial treaties which effect so many private interests; and they have the further evil that they convert into a national question, and a point of honor, matters which without them would have no such character and would admit to much easier settlement.[31]

At the time Canning wrote this there were already indications that his "kid glove" policy was out of date. Interest in London in the western China trade was reviving. French interests in Burma had to be thwarted. Increased trade and revenue in Pegu and free-trade ideas caused the formulation of a new commercial policy. Aggressive British agents were sent to Mandalay in the place of Spears. Canning's replacement by James Bruce, the 8th Earl Elgin, militated against the continuation of Canning's cautious policy.

In mid-1861 British Burma's revenues showed a large increase, and, in line with free-trade ideas, Phayre contemplated abolishing frontier duties. Duty on teak and control of the export of arms, ammunition, and sulfur would be retained. Canning concurred, "The frontier customs. . . cry for abolition, and I hope to knock them on the head."[32] Phayre wanted to open trade with China via Bhamo on the Irrawaddy River, thereby rivaling D'Orgoni's plans and scotching the Sprye plan of a costly railroad, which would create political difficulties. Phayre also looked to China for a ready supply of labor for Pegu.[33] To accomplish these aims Phayre thought a treaty necessary.

Phayre was too pressed in Rangoon to make the projected visits to Mandalay. With important matters like tariffs afoot and Spears gone, it was becoming increasingly necessary to have a correspondent at the Burmese capital. An unclear and temporary arrangement was made with Dr. Clement Williams of the Indian army. Canning thought the appointment of a correspondent all the more urgent because of a recently concluded treaty with China and the renewed possibilities of trade. Williams, the physician, aspired to be an explorer, trader, diplomat—and rich. He "wanted to do something for science and history without great pecuniary loss."[34] How Phayre chose him is unclear, but a personality more opposite Spears's would be difficult to find. Williams haggled over pay, conditions of employment, and his title. He thought himself a consular agent. Perhaps Phayre reasoned that for the conclusion of a treaty something more than an inconspicuous and unassuming newswriter was necessary. Phayre instructed Williams to smooth the way for a treaty mission.[35] Williams was soon writing at length on Burma's economic potential. He thought that Mindon would gladly hand over resources to France or England for the "sugar plum of *present cash.*" Williams hoped the British would preempt the French and that a company with capital would obtain monopolies from Mindon.[36] Through his medical services Williams ingratiated himself with the Burmese officials.

Since Canning's term of office was about to expire Phayre hoped that the Governor General before he left India would go on record stating the desirability of Phayre going to Mandalay. Canning did not do this; however, the new Governor General needed no prodding. Lord Elgin, fresh from his victories in China, was keen for Phayre to proceed.[37] Elgin hoped that a treaty would open a river route to western China, abolish frontier duties, allow for the free movement of British merchants, provide sufficient Chinese labor, and regularize the opium trade. In return the British would concede imports to Burma via Rangoon being charged one-eighth the fixed tariff value; the elimination of Tariff Article 20 of 1854, which established a 10 percent duty on goods carried on land and river on the British side of the frontier; and unrestricted import of arms to Burma on a cash basis.[38]

At this juncture frontier relations were becoming critical. A British officer was killed with the collusion of local Burmese officials. Phayre did not demand the extradition of the murderers but asked in accordance with friendship that they be punished. The Magwe Wungyi replied that there were bad men on both sides and that he was investigating.[39] Eleven men were shortly confined. Williams urged, "Our government should take action AT ONCE. Mandalay is RIPE." Present British policy was "fiddling, timorous, wonderfully supine." A crisis was approaching. Mindon was nervous about the consequences of the murder and had lost confidence in the Magwe Wungyi.[40] Mindon would have preferred negotiations to take place in Rangoon or Phayre to visit "informally" as he had in 1859. By the time of Phayre's arrival in Mandalay in early October 1862 the Pakan Wungyi had replaced Magwe as paramount *Wungyi*.[41] Pakan in comparison to Magwe was a traditionalist and not as accommodating toward Europeans.

By 13 October a draft treaty was agreed upon. Mindon added an article of "Friendship" to Elgin's five points. The *Wungyis* and Kanaung supported a pro-French policy and argued that the proposed abolition of Burmese frontier duties was a trick designed to disarrange finances, induce the government to make up the loss by direct taxation, excite discontent among the people, and favor the ulterior designs of the British. Mindon's wives opposed the treaty, fearing reduced personal allowances. The treaty looked lost. Phayre induced French Bishop Bigandet and the *Thathanabaing* to surmount Mindon's reservations.[42] Phayre compromised somewhat and allowed four years before frontier duties were to be abolished by the Burmese. Mindon's objections to any mention of opium in the treaty were honored, though he said he would not interfere with transshipped goods. The questions of armament imports and bullion exports were not raised. Mindon was still confident of his internal arms-production capacity and no doubt felt that, as the treaty did not mention arms imports, they were not proscribed. After the treaty was signed Phayre did approve the purchase of one thousand arms. Mindon directed the Pakan Wungyi to complete the formalities with Phayre. Sensitive to Magwe's feelings and his decade of service, Mindon allowed him to sign the long-avoided treaty. At the signing ceremony Pakan asked Phayre if the treaty was made in the

name of Her Majesty the Queen. Phayre replied, "No, but in that of his
Excellency the Viceroy."[43] Pakan perhaps took comfort in knowing that
the East India Company no longer existed and made no further remark.
Phayre recommended the treaty to Calcutta. Its

> great object. . .was to remove obstacles existing to a direct
> trade between Chinese territory, and the seaboard. That has
> been done effectually. The frontier duties are, I submit, of
> secondary importance and I feel convinced that the Burmese
> were not in a condition at once to abolish them. . . .I have
> full confidence that the Burmese will abolish theirs within
> the time specified, namely four years.[44]

Phayre recommended that Father Abbona be granted an assisted passage to
Europe for his services and that Bishop Bigandet be permitted to accompany
Williams on an exploratory expedition to western China. Williams had his
assignment at Mandalay extended and received a pay raise. Phayre himself
was recommended for a C.B.[45] The treaty was ratified in Calcutta and Elgin noted that

> the present engagement was hardly sufficiently comprehensive
> to be called a commercial treaty, but it was without a doubt a
> step towards the development of trade. . .between British Bur-
> mah, Burmah proper. . .and the States of the Southwest Fron-
> tier of China.[46]

King Mindon feared two things resulting from the treaty. Increased
trade and Europeans in the capital could lead to further misunderstanding.
The establishment of a more formal Residency would increase the English
sway, perhaps sufficiently to depose him.[47] Mindon's fears were prophetic.
The establishment of more formal relations created new problems, with
both parties violating spirit and letter of the treaty. That the treaty was not
rigidly enforced and the infractions allowed was due to Lord Lawrence
becoming Governor General upon Lord Elgin's death in 1863. Sir John
Lawrence's policy of "masterly inactivity" and maintaining a tight rein
on local officials was calculated to keep the peace. Caution in Calcutta
was matched in London, where Sir Charles Wood, Secretary of State for

India, kept merchant clamorers at arm's length. But the men on the spot
were difficult to stay, and much of the acrimony in subsequent Anglo-
Burmese relations stemmed from political agent Williams's and later Sladen's
own attitudes and interpretation of the 1862 treaty. They doted on punc-
tilio and spearheaded the rights of Englishmen in Burma. They puffed up
their own status and tended to exacerbate rather than ameliorate relations.

The Burmese were unwilling (so the British thought) or unable (as I
have argued in Chapter 6) to meet the conditions of the 1862 treaty,
especially those articles related to freer trade. The Burmese reluctantly
provided the published fixed tariff schedules but did not adhere to them.
Burmese monopolies, while entirely legal, interfered with Article 7, which
provided the British merchants could "purchase whatever they may require."[48] Tariffs were not abolished. The Burmese were hesitant to allow
free movement by foreigners in Burma. Agent Williams was allowed to
travel to the western China border but not before having to surmount
strenuous Burmese objections.[49] The British explorers Sconce and Watson
were arrested and detained by the Burmese as they attempted to cross
the troubled eastern Shan States. Mindon complained, "There is one
thing I do not like, and this is not right: two officers from [British ter-
ritory] have come to Burmese Shan territory, and at these times, when
we are at war with rebel Shans, for English officials to go there without
my knowledge is not good."[50] The Burmese had good reason to suspect
the intentions of the expedition. The Tenasserim Commissioner, Albert
Fytche, wrote letters of introduction to the dissident *Sawbwa* of Mobyai,
citing the "advantages for the future to receive the officers. . .[and] of
cementing the friendship of the English rulers." The Government of India
admitted its indiscretion and apologized.[51] The Burmese published travel
regulations to qualify Article 9 of the treaty. Unarmed merchants could
travel unhindered, but armed parties had to apply to the Chief Commissioner's agent at Mandalay, who would in turn request permission from
the *Hluttaw*. Travelers were to respect Burmese officials and remove their
hats on meeting them. The observance of Burmese customs by Europeans
created some problems. The Pakan Wungyi was a traditionalist and insisted
that Europeans who were not in government service must sit down in the
street when a Burmese *Wungyi, Wundauk, Atwinwun,* or capital *Myowun*
with escort went by. A Eurasian was beaten for not obeying protocol and
received no redress. As to the custom of taking off shoes, the British envoys
had compromised in 1855, 1859, and 1862 by taking them off just before

a formal royal or ministerial reception commenced. The Pakan Wungyi, however, now wanted them removed on ascending the steps of the building to be entered. Williams accepted unshoeing, arguing that it was not degrading but rather a question of conciliating narrow prejudice. Williams's question was, "*Where* is the limit?"[52] Calcutta newspapers talked of war for national honor. But Lawrence maintained his policy of noninterference and kept the peace.

London and Lawrence were soon voicing dissatisfaction with Williams and blaming Anglo-Burmese misunderstandings on him. Britain was not well served by self-seeking meddlers. H. M. Durand, with his contacts with Ellenborough and Burma going back to the 1840s, held a watching brief on Burma, and marked Williams in the mold of Blundell.[53] Among Williams's projects calculated to irritate the Burmese was a plan to build a fort for the protection of Europeans and establishing a *Register* of British subjects as the first steps to gain extraterritorial rights for Britons. This went beyond the rights accorded Britons in Article 3 of the treaty. Within less than two weeks Williams's own clerk was arrested for gambling. The clerk was released on Williams's request and then dismissed. Williams, however, failed to get extraterritoriality formally acknowledged.[54] Williams was falling under a cloud. Secretary of State for India, Sir Charles Wood, wanted him eased out and declared that a medical officer must practice his profession in government service. Calcutta began to look around for a replacement, despite Phayre's support for Williams.[55] Government's first choice, Captain H. A. Browne, refused the position despite the increased salary of Rs. 1,500 per month. Edward Bosc Sladen, who had volunteered for Burmese service as early as 1862, was government's second choice.[56] Williams resigned from the Indian service in a huff.

Sladen arrived in Mandalay in February 1865. His skin was equally as tender as Williams's, and his diaries read like a register of Burmese-inflicted insults. At Sladen's first interview with the Crown Prince, the new political agent sat on the floor while Kanaung was in a chair. Even pacific Lawrence objected to this. Phayre argued that there was nothing derogatory in the ceremony. Such questions of protocol would become intractable in the 1870s.[57] Mindon attempted to co-opt Sladen by telling him to consider the Pakan Wungyi his father.[58] Sladen had plans of his own similar to Williams. He wrote:

> My opinion is that the safest and most practicable plan of
> securing either international or even treaty rights in Burma

> proper is to gradually strengthen the hands of the Agent at
> Mandalay until he becomes the *sole acknowledged* medium
> of communications between the two Governments.[59]

Sladen, as Williams, planned to press for extraterritoriality as well as
British supervision of Burmese customs collection.

British mercantile interests felt that the 1862 treaty had several glaring
deficiencies. The treaty itself was insufficient, and moreover it was not
enforced. Lawrence and Wood were prepared to tolerate various mercantile pressures and even increased border unrest in preference to opening new negotiations with the Burmese. Over two hundred border incidents were reported between 1861 and 1865. At one point unrest
necessitated the use of cipher between Sladen and Phayre.[60] But when
Cecil R. A. T. Gascoyne, Lord Salisbury, succeeded Wood as Secretary
of State for India in 1866 London policy toward Burma turned to accommodate the demands of British commercial interests. Salisbury ordered
exploration and surveying of trade routes to proceed in projects that
Lawrence preferred kept in abeyance. Salisbury had expansionist ideas of
his own and wished the Shan States were tributary to Britain rather than
Burma. With this encouragement Rangoon merchants talked of forming
a railway company. Salisbury noted that a railroad to Upper Burma was
a necessity and would come "when we, or some other European power,
are masters of Burmah."[61]

Chief Commissioner Phayre was also encouraged by Salisbury's invigorat-
ing attitude. Phayre prepared to go on another treaty mission and cap his
Burmese career in triumph.[62] Objectives were similar to 1862: no duties
above 5 percent, the publication of annual tariff lists and monopolized
items, and the eventual abolition of duties. Phayre admitted the latter
would be a difficult task as the Burmese government needed the money.
In addition, Phayre wanted an agent appointed by the Governor General
to reside at the Burmese customs post to handle British complaints. If
the Burmese were uncooperative Phayre proposed using Britain's geopolitical position to reimpose duties on certain foodstuffs, including rice,
salt, and fish paste. Lawrence had not been anxious to enforce the letter
of the 1862 treaty. Calcutta, after reams of political agents' diaries about
Mindon's impoverishment, did not think duties could be abolished, since
the King lived from hand to mouth.[63] On Salisbury's urging the Government of India put forward a claim for moderate tariffs and some satis-
factory solution to the recent rise in border brigandage.[64] Phayre wrote

privately to Lawrence to impress on him the urgent need for a new treaty. He cited the French presence in Indochina and the possibility that the French Great Cambodia River exploring expedition would soon cross the Shan States into Burma. Though the French had no political aims in Burma, their presence would tantalize the Burmese government, which ever since 1852 had looked to "France as some counterpoise to our overwhelming might." In light of the revolt of August 1866 Phayre hoped to conclude a treaty similar to that which France had made with Cambodia. Britain would restrict Burma's foreign relations in return for guaranteeing Mindon's safety from his enemies. Lawrence appreciated Phayre's not mentioning the French problem in public despatches but did not think they would act against British interests. Moreover, Lawrence was averse to any treaty in which the British propped up the Burmese government. An offensive-defensive treaty would cost the British much and the Burmese nothing. Lawrence displayed a similar aversion to entangling alliances in his attitude toward Afghanistan.[65]

Phayre planned his trip for early September 1866. News of the Mandalay revolt reached Rangoon before Phayre left. He proceeded to the frontier and waited there for the first favorable opportunity to continue the mission.[66] He arrived in Mandalay on 7 November 1866. The Pakan Wungyi welcomed Phayre and thanked him for the timely delivery of the steamers. The capital was still in obvious disarray.[67] This strengthened Phayre's bargaining hand. He hoped to save the Padein Prince's life, secure the safety of the families of the Myingun and Myingundaing princes, and extract more treaty concessions from the Burmese monarch. Phayre reasoned that Mindon would be too weak to resist and decided to press for a British officer to supervise Burmese customs collections, free export of gold and silver, limitation of the items under monopoly, and the establishment of the political agent's jurisdiction in cases involving solely British subjects. Phayre found, however, that the rebellion had not weakened Mindon's resolve against signing unequal treaties. After lengthy debate Mindon assented to a British customs officer. The treaty foundered on the political agent's legal jurisdiction and the relinquishing of certain monopolies. The Burmese would not permit the ultimate jurisdiction of the political agent and demanded that there be recourse of appeal to the *Hluttaw*. They also wanted a Burmese agent to have reciprocal rights over Burmese citizens in Rangoon. Phayre offered the free import of arms (using his authorization of 1862) and a continued no-duty policy on the frontier.

Mindon then agreed to give the British all the jurisdiction they wanted, but not in treaty form. However, Mindon's objections to the abolition of all monopolies except oil, timber, and precious stones after April 1868 were insurmountable. Threaten as Phayre might about consequent unfriendly relations, the Burmese would not budge.[68] After a month in Mandalay Phayre left without the coveted treaty.

Mindon sent Buddhist scriptures to Governor General Lawrence as a symbol of goodwill. Relations, however, had taken a turn for the worse. Lawrence thanked Mindon for the gift but added that he was disappointed that Burma would not relax customs duties and that he was following Phayre's suggestions of stern countermeasures. In June 1867 frontier duties would be reimposed on all imports into Burma. Sladen went to great pains to make the presentation of Lawrence's letter a humiliating experience. He refused to let the Burmese government have a hint of its import or tone and insured it was received personally by Mindon with full honors and read out loud to a public audience. Sladen reported that the King was visibly shaken.[69]

The disappointed and somewhat embittered Phayre had served fifteen years as a Commissioner in Burma and was relieved in normal rotation as Chief Commissioner by Albert Fytche in February 1867.[70] If any Britisher associated with Burma in the nineteenth century can be called an imperialist Fytche would hold the title. His experience with Burma dated from 1839, when he was eighteen. Recalling Tharrawaddy's visit to Rangoon in 1841 he bemoaned that "all our martial hopes of war with the 'Golden Foot'. . .soon vanished into thin air" as the King only cast a big bell.[71] He felt the second war had been brought to a premature conclusion. Burma could easily have been reduced to the condition of a feudatory state. Fytche dedicated his autobiography to his cousin, poet-laureate Alfred, Lord Tennyson. Ralph Fitche, first Englishman to visit Burma (1586-87), was also his forebear. Albert Fytche hoped to leave an equally large mark in history by concluding a treaty that would "bring about a community of interests between Rangoon and Mandalay."[72] Fytche held the Burmese in low esteem. They were inert in everything but usurpation, commotion, rebellions, and massacres.[73] For much of 1866 Fytche had been in England on furlough, during which time he married the daughter of the Liberal M. P. N. G. Lambert and thus acquired a spokesman in his father-in-law to call for the publication of several reports in Parliament at Fytche's suggestion. While in London Fytche kept abreast of Burmese affairs and had an important interview with Salisbury, who declared that

it is of primary importance to allow no other European
power to insert herself between British Burma and China.
Our influence in that country ought to be paramount. The
country itself is of no great importance, but an easy communication with the multitudes who inhabit Western China
is an object of great national importance. No influence superior
to ours must be allowed to gain ground in Burmah.[74]

Salisbury had been disappointed at Phayre's failure to conclude a treaty.
Burma "[wa]s almost the only part of the east this side of Japan where
our trade can hope to find any new market of importance."[75] Fytche
returned to the Indian Empire and while in Calcutta in January 1867
related his conversation with Salisbury to Governor General Lawrence.
When Fytche returned to Rangoon he felt he had Salisbury's cachet to
bring Burma to terms.[76] With obvious glee Fytche wrote to Sladen,
"Colonel Phayre *goes for good.*"[77] But Fytche would soon have to trim
his sails when Salisbury resigned from the Tory Cabinet, and the cautious
Sir Stafford H. Northcote took over the India Office.

Burma's diplomatic bargaining position was weakening. Civil war and
poor rainfall led to a very poor harvest. Duties on imported rice worsened
the situation. Toward the end of January Mindon told Sladen that he had
second thoughts about rejecting Phayre's treaty proposal. Sladen and
Fytche saw the opportunity for applying further pressure. Sladen would
like to have withdrawn the political agent and applied a temporary blockade. Fytche thought "a stern policy [wa]s the only one" calculated to
get results.[78] Mindon had contracted with Williams for two thousand
Enfield rifles, but the guns and the ammunition were seized by customs
at the frontier. Calcutta had, however, overridden this and permitted the
import on a one-time-only basis.[79] Meanwhile, the rebel prince, Myingun,
escaped from Rangoon and raised another rebellion in the Shan States.
Mindon thought the British had assisted his escape. Another younger
prince had been quickly bundled off to the Andaman Islands. The Burmese monarch was getting a taste of overt and inadvertent external pressure on his regime.[80] By mid-February 1867 Mindon was telling Sladen
that Phayre had misunderstood him, and he was surprised at the reimposi-
tion of tariffs. Mindon stated he was not averse to a treaty, but the time
was inappropriate when Phayre visited him after the civil war.[81] Mindon
bestowed on Sladen a twelve-string *tsalwe.* In early March Mindon announced to Sladen that his house was in order and that a treaty was now

possible. Mindon was willing to give up some monopolies and lower frontier customs. At the same time Mindon was making these long-awaited concessions he was awarding another customs contract to Moolah Ibrahim, with the fees designated to finance a mission to France. Lawrence directed Fytche to detain the French mission. Northcote allowed it to proceed but without giving it special attention, facilities, or recognizing it as a sovereign diplomatic mission. The pressure against the French mission mounted, and Sladen got Mindon to recall the mission in May 1867, with consequent loss of influence for Bishop Bigandet and Camaretta.[82]

Fytche, in response to Mindon's offer to relax trade, wrote Sladen, "Before I come to Mandalay I should require to know what the king was prepared to do. Depend upon it, I shall not come on a *bootless*! errand." Fytche wanted a twenty-four string *tsalwe*, equal in number to the Crown Prince. William E. Gladstone had been given sixteen strands on an earlier occasion. As a further earnest of the King's intentions duties could be lowered and monopolies done away with under the provisions of the treaty of 1862.[83] On 16 April 1867 Mindon issued a royal proclamation abolishing monopolies with the exception of oil, timber, and precious stones. Import duties were reduced from 10 percent to 5 percent and export duties from 6 percent to 5 percent. The proclamation had a life of ten years. Fytche found this acceptable and did not object to the exclusion of timber, which Phayre had not included as a legitimate monopoly. The combined monopolies did not amount to more than 14 percent of the trade. The lost revenues, however, were made up by increased local direct and indirect taxes, brokerage fees, and income tax.[84]

While Calcutta was pleased with the turn of events Northcote was now Secretary of State for India, and he felt undue pressure had been applied against the Burmese. He disapproved of the retaliatory measures and wrote on 23 March 1867 that he thought the actions of Lawrence, Phayre, and Sladen were "not those best calculated to conduce the desired end." The reimposed tariff was withdrawn. His letter reached Calcutta in May 1867, and the British tenor changed, but not before the shortlived retaliatory trade policy had taken its toll on the Burmese position.[85] Lawrence wrote to Fytche that he did "not perceive why the King should have been kept in ignorance of the purport of [Lawrence's] letter until it reached his Majesty's ears in the presence of his courtiers." This was derogatory, and Sladen was warned to temper his "harsh and imperious character" in his future relations with the King.[86] Calcutta added if the King of Burma "desire[s] that a new treaty on the basis of that proposed by Colonel

Phayre, should be arranged between the two countries, His Excellency
in Council would be quite prepared to re-enter on the negotiations for
that purpose."[87]

Fytche employed as many arguments as he could think of to get Calcutta's approval for a mission to Mandalay. He often referred to merchant pressure in Rangoon and London.[88] He argued that public opinion,
as reflected by the frequent suggestions of annexation in the press, would
not abate until there was unrestricted trade with Upper Burma. This
made little impression on Calcutta and London officialdom. Lawrence wanted the initiative for a treaty to come from the Burmese.
Fytche cautioned Sladen to make it appear in his official letters that the
initiative was Mindon's. Fytche even tempered his own aggressiveness and
agreed to take off his shoes and press for Phayre's treaty draft.[89] To
Fytche's claim that the mission would strengthen Mindon against the
insurgent Myingun Prince and his band of Shans and Karens, Calcutta
replied that "every moral influence at our command" should be at
Mindon's disposal to dispel the idea that the British had "let" the Prince
escape.[90] Fytche's idea for exploration past Bhamo got a curt refusal.
Calcutta was most interested in stemming the increasing wave of border
brigandage, which in the first six months of 1867 had exceeded all of
1866. Sladen pressed the necessity of preventive measures on Mindon.[91]

On 28 May 1867 Mindon delivered a letter to Sladen for the Governor
General. It contained a draft treaty modeled along Phayre's lines. Duties
would be reduced starting in 1870 rather than 1868. The political agent
would have legal jurisdiction but with recourse of appeal to the *Hluttaw*.
The Burmese would have an agent in Rangoon with jurisdiction, recourse
being to the Chief Commissioner. In addition to the usual war materiel
the Burmese wanted treaty rights to import steamers, frigates, and trading vessels. The Burmese draft pointedly omitted an article regarding
monopolies. Calcutta generally approved of the Burmese draft. Lawrence's
most important modification dealt with the import of arms and maintained "that the permission of the Chief Commissioner must first be pro-
cured." Calcutta's instructions to Fytche circumscribed his scope of action:
"No pressure should be put upon the King to execute a treaty. . . not in
entire accordance with his Majesty's views and wishes."[92]

Fytche was disgruntled with the limitations imposed by Calcutta and
felt that the modifications to Mindon's treaty draft were unsatisfactory
as regarded arms. Fytche correctly foresaw that they would create dif-

ficulties and told Sladen to assure Mindon that he "was not likely to put any difficulties in his way" in the matter of arms purchases.[93] Like Phayre, Fytche harbored plans to restrict Burma's foreign intercourse in exchange for maintaining Mindon on the throne. Sladen reported that Mindon welcomed some sort of offensive-defensive alliance.[94] Again Fytche pressed the French menace, and Calcutta approved his proposed article that "the Burmese ruler engages not to enter into negotiations or communications of any kind with any foreign power, except with the consent, previously obtained, of the British ruler."[95]

The treaty mission left Rangoon in mid-September and arrived in Mandalay in early October 1867. Fytche took off his shoes at audiences. Treaty negotiations snagged on the arms issue. Mindon objected to obtaining the Chief Commissioner's permission to import arms. To counter the ill effect of Calcutta's proviso, Fytche appended the notorious Supplementary Article to the treaty providing that "consent and approval will not be withheld so long as the two countries remain on friendly relations with each other." Fytche's bargaining position had been significantly weakened, and he dropped the article relating to the limitation of Burma's foreign contacts.[96] The treaty was signed on 25 October, and Fytche immediately assented to Mindon's purchase of eight thousand arms. Mindon issued a decree granting royal approval to Sladen's projected mission to western China. The treaty that Calcutta ratified on 26 November 1867 was strikingly different. Appendix A of the treaty, assuring Mindon of permission to import arms while the two countries were friendly, had been deleted. Lawrence, who had never really been in favor of the treaty, no doubt felt that the appended article offered the Burmese too much and that it would be better to have no treaty than allow the free import of arms. The revised treaty was presented to Mindon in January 1868. He objected to re-ratifying the treaty. This had not occurred after Yandabo and 1862. Mindon was bitterly disappointed over the deletion of the Supplementary Article. Nonetheless, he signed the treaty, conscious of the pressure Britain would apply if he did not.[97]

The treaty of 1867 marked a turning point in Anglo-Burmese relations and in Burma's relations with the outside world. Prior to 1867 the impetus for treaties had always come from outside of Burma, from the imperial agents of Britain, America, France, and Sardinia. Mindon held them at bay as best he could, capitulating only to the omnipresent neighbor, Britain. The intensity of Britain's quest for a treaty was governed by various pressures: merchants, local officials, free-trade ideas, and the French threat. While Burma had never trusted the British, duplicity over the 1867 treaty now vindicated her suspicions. In retaliation Mindon indirectly reinstated his monopolies that he had surrendered as a token of goodwill to hasten treaty negotiations. After the 1866 civil war and the 1867 treaty, the Pakan and Kinwun Mingyi replaced the Kanaung Prince as paramount advisers to Mindon. Burma started to take the diplomatic offensive in seeking avenues and powers to circumvent Britain's stranglehold and act as a counterpoise. This was the Indian summer of Burma's independence. Perhaps she was too successful in her diplomatic ventures, as the war in 1885 and annexation in 1886 were in great part due to British fears of a growing French presence in Mandalay.

NOTES

1. Dalhousie to Wood, 14 February, 18 and 28 March, and 30 June 1853, Wood Papers, India Office Library and Records, F78/17.

2. See Latter's Intelligence Report of 18 May 1853, in Phayre to Secretary to Government of India, 25 May 1853, ISP/183; Phayre to Secretary to Government of India, 1 September 1853; Abbona statement, 21 October 1853, ISP/184; and Dalhousie to Phayre, 30 August 1853, in D. G. E. Hall, ed., *The Dalhousie-Phayre Correspondence, 1852-1856* (London: Oxford University Press, 1932), pp. 91-2.

3. Dalhousie to Phayre, 1 May, Spears for *Wungyis* at *Hluttaw* to Phayre, 9 May, and Phayre to Dalhousie, 1 June 1854, in Hall, ed., *Correspondence,* pp. 65, 167-8, and 185.

4. ISP of 26 January 1855, in ibid., p. 269.

5. Spears to Phayre, 11 October 1854, in ibid., pp. 259-60 and 272-5.

6. Dom Paula Abbona for the *Hluttaw* to Kastella, Minister of the King of Sardinia, November-December 1854, and Dalhousie to Phayre, 18 January 1855, in Hall, ed., *Correspondence,* pp. 275-8. See also Vivian Ba, "Some Papal Correspondence with the Kings of Burma," *J.B.R.S.* 50 (1967): 11-19; and Spears to Hopkinson, 13 June 1857, Canning Papers, Sheepscar Library, Leeds, 55.

7. Spears to Phayre, 3 December 1855, in Hall, ed., *Correspondence,* p. 402; and Vivian Ba, "The First Burmese Embassy to France in 1856," *Guardian* 9 (1962): 20-1.

8. Secret Committee, 23 September 1854, L/P & S/5/3/1, pp. 394-5; Spears to Phayre, 7 July 1854, and Phayre to Dalhousie, 18 May 1855, in Hall, ed., *Correspondence,* pp. 216 and 317; Dalhousie to Wood, 8 February, 16 and 19 March 1855, Wood Papers, F78/18/2; and Notes on an interview

between Wood and D'Orgoni sent to Dalhousie, 29 September 1854, Wood Papers, F78/19-20.

9. John L. Christian, "Burma in the American State Papers," *J.B.R.S.* 26 (1936): 110-15; and "A Diplomatic Mission from Burma to America," ibid. 29 (1939): 187-92.

10. Dalhousie to Wood, 21 January 1855, Wood Papers, F78/18/2; and Dalhousie to Phayre, 3 July 1855, in Hall, ed., *Correspondence*, p. 343.

11. Dalhousie to Wood, 18 May 1855, Wood Papers, F78/18/2.

12. D. G. E. Hall, "Phayre's Private Journal of his Mission to Ava in 1855," *J.B.R.S.* 22 (1932): 77; Henry Yule, *Reports of the Mission to Ava in 1855* (Calcutta: Government Printers, 1856), p. 84; and Yule, *A Narrative of the Mission to the Court of Ava in 1855* (Kuala Lumpur: Oxford University Press, 1969 [orig. publ. London, 1858]), p. 61.

13. Mission Journal, 12-13 September 1855, in Yule, *Reports of the Mission*, pp. 91-2; and Yule, *Narrative of a Mission*, p. xxiv.

14. Mission Journal, 25 September 1855, in Yule, *Narrative of a Mission*, p. 103.

15. A. Waleski, French Minister for Foreign Affairs to French Consul, Calcutta, Mss. Valbeyeu, 16 January 1856, ISP/197; and Spears to Hopkinson, 13 June 1857, Canning Papers, 2320, and 4, 6, 7, 32, and 2636A.

16. Simpson to Phayre, 14 January 1858, ISP/215; Vivian Ba, "The Confidential Mission of Count Henri de Sercey," *Guardian*, 11 (1964) in 6 parts; Henry Wellesley, Lord Cowley, to Edward Stanley, private, 16 January 1859, Canning Papers, 6; and *Pegu Administration Report, 1858-9*, p. 168, and *1859-60*, p. 173.

17. Phayre to Canning, 26 April, and Canning to Phayre, 16 July 1856, Canning Papers, 55/28.

18. Spears to Hopkinson, 23 July 1857, Canning Papers, 55/2320.

19. Hopkinson to Talbot, 8 August 1857, Canning Papers, 55/2320; and C. Beadon to Edmonstone, 24 May 1858, ISP/221 (extracted from a letter to superior in Rome).

20. Hopkinson to Talbot, 21 October, and Bigandet to Hopkinson, 5 November 1857, Canning Papers, 55/2663 and 2739; Hopkinson to Talbot, 3 December 1857, ISP/215.

21. Spears to Hopkinson, 16 December, and Spears to Phayre, 24 December 1857, Canning Papers, 55/3074 and 3271.

22. Phayre to Talbot, 18 January 1858; Phayre to Canning, 14 March 1859; and A. Dorin to Canning, 10 April 1858, Canning Papers, 3271, 55/28, and 91/1155.

23. Phayre to Beadon, 1 May 1859, IPF/203/50; Memo by Phayre, 30 May 1859, ISP/225; and Canning to Phayre, 19 August 1859, Canning Papers, 55.

24. *Journal of Events at Capital of Burma*, by A. P. Phayre, 2-24 November 1859, IPF/203/71.

25. Phayre to Grey, 13 December 1859, IPF/203/71.

26. *Journal of Events at Capital of Burma*, by A. P. Phayre, Audience of 19 November 1859, IPF/203/71.

27. Phayre to Grey, 13 December 1959, IPF/203/71; and Beadon to Grey, 12 January 1860, LPF/204/11.

28. A. R. Young to Phayre, 31 October 1860, and Phayre to Ministers of Burma, IPF/204/72.

29. *Parliamentary Papers*, 1865, 29, "Report upon the Income and Expenditure of British Burmah"; and Canning to Wood, 20 July 1860, Canning Papers, 40.

30. Phayre to Beadon, 30 June 1860, IPF/204/23; R. C. Temple to J. Bowring, 20 December 1860, Canning Papers, 8111; Office Memo by Phayre, 17 September 1860; Anthony Camaretta to Edwards, demi-official, 21 July 1860; and Young to Phayre, 19 October 1860, IPF/204/26.

31. Canning to Temple, 16 January 1861, Canning Papers, 63.

32. Memo on Customs Duties at the Northern Frontier of Pegu, 13 July 1861; Phayre to Canning, 14 July 1861; Temple to Bowring, 1 October 1861; and Canning to Temple, 15 October 1861, ibid., 55/28, 9391 and 63.

33. *Pegu Administration Report, 1856-7*, p. 116; Phayre to Beadon, 2 March 1861; Phayre to Bowring, 16 June 1861; and Fytche to Beadon, 10 October 1861, Canning Papers, 8659 and 8932.

34. Canning to Phayre, 14 May, and Williams to Bowring, 1 August 1861, Canning Papers, 55 and 9107.

35. Bowring to Phayre, 13 July 1861, Elgin Papers, F83/113/3; and Phayre to Bowring, 15 August 1861, Canning Papers, 9097.

36. Williams to Phayre, 29 December 1861, Canning Papers, 9973.

37. Phayre to Bowring, 17 February 1862, ibid., 10, 116; and Phayre to Durand, 15 April 1862, demi-official, in *Parliamentary Papers*, 1864, 42, "Papers as to Commercial Treaty of 1862."

38. Durand to Phayre, 12 May 1862, in "Papers as to Commercial Treaty" (1864); and Elgin to Wood, private, 9 December 1862, Elgin Papers, F83/4.

39. Phayre to Magwe Wungyi, 12 May 1862, IPF/205/10; and Magwe Wungyi to Phayre, 26 June 1862, IPF/205/11.

40. Williams to Grote, 4 and 25 July 1862, Elgin Papers, F83/48/665 and F83/49/757; Phayre to Grey, 13 December 1859, IPF/203/71; and Williams to Phayre, 29 December 1861, Canning Papers, 9973.

41. Phayre to Durand, 20 November 1862, IPF/204/63.

42. Ibid.

43. Ibid.

44. Phayre to Durand, 21 November 1862, ibid.

45. Phayre to Durand, 12 December 1862, ibid.; Phayre to Williams, n.d., IPF/204/66; and Elgin to Wood, private, 19 December 1862, Wood Papers, F83/4.

46. Government of India, *Legislative Proceedings,* January 1862-December 1863 and 14 January 1862, p. 214.

47. Phayre to Durand, 21 November 1862, IPF/204/63; and Sladen Diary, 1 April 1865, IPF/204/78.

48. Phayre to Durand, 10 February 1865 and 29 May 1863, IFP/204/66 and IPF/204/67.

49. Phayre to Durand, 9 June 1864, forwarding Williams's Memo, IPF/204/78; and Clement Williams, *Through Burmah to Western China* (London: William Blackwood, 1868).

50. Williams Diary, 10 February 1864, IPF/204/72.

51. Phayre to Durand, 11 May 1864, IPF/204/73; and Lawrence to Fytche, 22 April 1864, Lawrence Papers, F90/41.

52. Williams Diary, 23 May 1864, IPF/204/78 (published in *Gazette of India*, 3 March 1864); Williams Diary, 21 July 1864, IPF/204/75; and 22 April 1864, IPF/204/78.

53. Durand to Thurlow, 30 January 1862, Elgin Papers, F83/59/1717; Lawrence to Wood, 3 May 1864, Wood Papers, F78/113/2; and Wood to Lawrence, 18 July 1864, Lawrence Papers, F90/25.

54. Lawrence to Wood, 14 July 1864, Wood Papers, F78/113/3; and Williams Diary, 16 and 28 June and 1 July 1864, IPF/204/75.

55. Wood to Lawrence, 16 May 1864, IPF/204/73; Williams to Phayre, 12 August 1864, Phayre to Durand, 7 September 1864, IPF/204/75; and Phayre to Lawrence, 12 August 1864, Wood Papers, F78/113/4.

56. Sladen to Thurlow, 25 June 1862, Elgin Papers, F83/48/527.

57. Secretary of the Government of India to Chief Commissioner of British Burma, 19 May 1865, IPF/204/78; and Phayre to Muir, 9 June 1865, IPF/204/76.

58. Sladen Diary, 19 February 1865, IPF/204/78; 30 October 1865, IPF/204/79; and 10 March 1865, IPF/204/78.

59. Sladen Diary, 10 March 1865, IPF/204/78.

60. Phayre to Sladen, 17 June 1865, Sladen Papers, E290/1A.

61. Phayre to Government of India, 22 October 1866, IPP/437/69; Salisbury to Lawrence, 16 October and 10 December 1866, private, Lawrence Papers, F90/27.

62. Phayre to Sladen, 31 March 1866, Sladen Papers, E290/1A.

63. Phayre to Secretary of the Government of India, 1 June 1866, IPP/437/67; and Lawrence to Salisbury, 30 August 1866, Lawrence Papers, F90/31.

64. Secretary of the Government of India to Chief Commissioner of British Burma, 15 August 1866, IPP/437/68.

65. Sladen Diary, 14 March 1865, IPF/204/78; Phayre to Lawrence 16 October 1866, Lawrence to Phayre, 7 November 1866, Lawrence Papers, F90/63; and Lawrence to Salisbury, 8 November 1866, Lawrence, Papers, F90/31. Lawrence displayed a similar aversion to entangling alliances toward Afghanistan. See G. J. Alder, "The Dropped Stitch–The Course of Anglo-Afghan Relations, 1853-63," *Afghanistan Journal* 1-2 (1974-75): 105-13 and 20-7.

66. Phayre to Secretary of the Government of India, 1 June 1866, IPP/437/67; Phayre to Lawrence, 8-13 August 1866, Lawrence Papers, F90/57; and Thayetmyo to Simla (telegram), 27 October 1866, IPP/437/69.

67. Phayre to Secretary of the Government of India, 10 November 1866, IPP/437/69.

68. Phayre to Government of India, 10 December 1866, 218-5000, IPP/437/70; and Phayre to Lawrence, 1 December 1866, Salisbury Papers, Christchurch, Oxford (microfilm copies, India Office Library and Records, reel 806).

69. Lawrence to King of Burma, 31 January 1867, and Phayre to Secretary of the Government of India, 10 December 1866, 219-5001, IPP/437/70; and Sladen Diary, 23 March 1867, IPP/437/71.

70. Phayre to Lawrence, 12 January 1867, Salisbury Papers, reel 806; and Phayre to Sladen, 28 January 1867, Sladen Papers, E290/1A.

71. Albert Fytche, *Burma, Past and Present,* 2 vols. (London: Kegan Paul, 1878), 1: 87 and 114.

72. Ibid., 1: 205 and 218.

73. Ibid., 1: 66 and 116-7.

74. Salisbury to Lawrence, 10 December 1866, summation of conversation with Fytche, Lawrence Papers, F90/27.

75. Salisbury to Lawrence, 4 February 1867, ibid., F90/28.

76. Fytche to Sladen, 8 August 1866, 25 February and 8 March 1867, Sladen Papers, E290/1B; and Lawrence to Salisbury, 19 January 1867, Lawrence Papers, F90/32A.

77. Fytche to Sladen, 25 February 1867, Sladen Papers, E290/1B.

78. Sladen Diary, 24 December 1866; Fytche to Government of India, 27 February 1867; and Rangoon to Calcutta, telegram, 7 March 1867, IPP/437/70.

79. Calcutta to Rangoon, telegram, 12 March 1867, IPP/437/70.

80. Davies to Government of India, 21 February 1867; and Fytche to Government of India, 11 March 1867, IPP/437/70.

81. Sladen Diary, 13 February 1867, IPP/437/70.

82. Fytche to Government of India, 22 March 1867; and Sladen Diary, 1 May 1867, IPP/437/71.

83. Fytche to Sladen, 30 March 1867, Sladen Papers, E290/1B; and Fytche to Sladen, 22 March 1867, in *Parliamentary Papers,* 1868-69, 46, "Papers Relating to British Burmah," presented 8 June 1869 (hereafter cited "Papers Relating to British Burmah"), p. 3.

84. Ibid., p. 18, Fytche to Governor General, 20 May 1867; and Sladen Diary, 27 April 1867, IPP/437/71.

85. Governor General in Council to Secretary of State for India, 23 January 1876; Secretary of State for India to Governor General of India in Council, 23 March 1867, in *Parliamentary Papers,* 1867, 50, "Papers on the Late Rebellion in Upper Burma" (hereafter cited "Papers on the Late Rebellion"), pp. 23 and 36; Secretary to Government of India to Chief Commissioner of British Burma, 23 April 1867; and Governor General of India in Council to Secretary of State for India, 17 May 1867, in "Papers Relating to British Burmah" (1868-69), p. 5; and D. R. Sar Desai, *British Trade and Expansion in Southeast Asia, 1830-1914* (Columbia, Mo.: South Asia Books, 1977), p. 136.

86. Secretary of Government of India to Chief Commissioner of British Burma, 15 May 1867, in "Papers Relating to British Burmah" (1868-69), p. 11.

87. Government of India to Chief Commissioner of British Burma, 11 April 1867, IPP/437/71.

88. Fytche to Governor General, 20 May 1867, in "Papers Relating to British Burmah" (1868 69), p. 18.

89. Lawrence to Fytche, 19 April and Fytche to Sladen, 14 June 1867, Sladen Papers, E290/1B; Fytche to Sladen, 23 April 1867, IPP/437/71; and Fytche to Sladen, 22 May, and 13 August 1867, Sladen Papers, E290/1B.

90. Fytche to Government of India, 14 June 1867, and Secretary of Government of India to Chief Commissioner of British Burma, 22 July 1867, IPP/437/71.

91. Secretary of Government of India to Chief Commissioner of British Burma, 18 July 1867. Later approved by telegram, Simla to Rangoon, 12 September 1867, IPP/437/72; Fytche to Sladen, 15 May and 1 July 1867, Sladen Papers, E290/1B; and Fytche to Sladen, 6 May 1867, in "Papers Relating to British Burma" (1868-69), p. 15.

92. Secretary of the Government of India to Chief Commissioner of British Burma, 12 July 1867, and Simla to Rangoon (telegram), 16 September 1867, IPP/437/72.

93. Fytche to Sladen, 2 and 12 September 1867, Sladen Papers, E290/1B.

94. Fytche to Governor General, 20 May 1867, in "Papers Relating to

British Burmah" (1868-69), p. 18; and Sladen Diary, 7 July 1867, IPP/437/71.
    95. Government of India to Chief Commissioner of British Burma, 5 September 1867, in "Papers Relating to British Burmah" (1868-69), p. 34.
    96. Fytche to Government of India, 28 October 1867, IPP/438/1.
    97. Chief Commissioner to Government of India, 1 February 1868, IPP/438/1; and L. Allen Goss, notes appended to "Papers on the Late Rebellion" (1867).

CONCLUSION

This study has followed two paths accounting for the action and interaction of two culturally disparate nations. Nineteenth-century British relations with Burma were conflict oriented. Clashes stemmed from divergent cultural, political, economic, and military policies that pitted a traditional Southeast Asian polity against the dynamic British Indian hegemony.

Burmese internal history has been examined for the light it sheds on her external posture. Burma's dilemma was geopolitical in origin. At the center the structure of kingship, rather than the individual monarch, served as a self-weakening element. Polygamous monarchy spawned competition for power among numerous sons. The monarch attempted to fulfill the ideal of fusing religion with politics but was beset by destabilizing familial succession strife. Topography, communications, traditional and parochial administrative hierarchies, and widely dispersed ethnic minorities favored a fragile, decentralized system of government on the periphery. The traditional society was elastic and flexible within its own context. Rulers went about the business of maintaining a modicum of central control, suzerainty over local village headmen, and fending off premature claims to the throne. The Burmese empire reached its territorial peak in the second decade of the nineteenth century.

After 1820 Burmese monarchs were called upon to devise policy for dealing with a dramatically different problem. National policy and peripheral control lapped over into the sphere of external relations as the

Rangoon Government House, from William Eleroy Curtis, *Egypt, Burma and British Malaysia* (Chicago: Fleming H. Revell, 1905)

Mandalay

Burmese and British Indian empires violently converged. The British imposed their standards of governmental efficiency, freedom of commerce, and dynamic world view on a traditional society ill prepared to accommodate such novelties. Three wars and the loss of independence clearly reveal Burmese failure.

But the long road from 1824 to 1886 had its successes as well. The Burmese reacted to defeat. The first war was a great setback for Burmese traditional practices and led to a reassertion of traditional modes. The Empire had suffered amputation, but the mentality of the rulers had not contracted. Through a policy of effrontery the Burmese succeeded in effacing some of the reminders of defeat and humiliation. The British Residency was withdrawn, and the Treaty of Yandabo became a dead letter.

Burma's reaction to the Second Anglo-Burmese War was markedly different and serves to divide the period 1837-67. After King Mindon's accession in 1853 Burma consciously shifted from adherence to traditional statecraft to modernization. Mindon ranks with several other non-Western leaders of the 1850s and 1860s in Egypt, Ethiopia, Thailand, Japan, Afghanistan, and Lesotho, to name a few researched cases, who attempted to reform central government, raise revenue more effectively, adopt Western technology, and be considered as equals in diplomatic relations, without losing self-determination or subverting basic cultural patterns.

Mindon set about increasing his regime's administrative efficiency. Kanaung's task was the selective adoption of Western technology. "Reform" and "industrialization" and "modernization" entered the vocabulary in form if not in language. The military was modernized, and local food production increased in direct response to the loss of Pegu. Mindon's domestic success in establishing firm control and loyalty is marked by his survival as monarch following the revolt of 1866. Mindon employed his traditional economic prerogatives not to enhance his own position but for the welfare of the nation. Unfortunately his ideals were at variance with British notions, which hampered or hamstrung economic planning.

The second path has been Britain's attitude toward Burma. Throughout virtually the entire nineteenth century Britain was reluctant to get embroiled in Burmese affairs, though the geopolitical juxtaposition could not be denied. London and Calcutta desired the maintenance of the status quo and placed restraints on local initiative. Central control over policy was weakened by a four-tiered administrative structure in which London, Calcutta, Moulmein, later Rangoon, and the British diplomatic representative in sovereign Burma struggled in a tug of war over policy. The important changes in policy discussed in this study, the withdrawal of the Residency in 1840, war in 1852, and the treaties of 1862 and 1867, were initiated in response to Burmese policy and changing circumstances. In these critical situations the advantage went to the man on the spot who, influenced by local vested interests, tended to pursue an active and expansive policy. In such a manner Burma came increasingly under British sway during the mid-nineteenth century. Thus Mindon's success in escaping from the Second Anglo-Burmese War without concluding a humiliating treaty and avoiding unequal treaties for a decade was transient. Burma was a landlocked nation in the shadow of the British Indian Empire, and this severely inhibited her freedom of action. Treaties nibbled away at sovereignty and self-determination.

Two symbols emerge from the clashes between Burma and Britain: shoes and guns. The former represented Burmese independence and tradition and the gulf between the two nations' cultures. Arms represented Britain's control over imports via the Irrawaddy River, which placed restraints on Burma's offensive capacity as well as her tools to maintain internal order. While still nominally independent Burma had in great part been subordinated to a Calcutta-Rangoon-based sphere of influence. The revolt of 1866 and the treaty of 1867 mark a watershed in kingship, domestic and foreign policy, and Anglo-Burmese relations. Britain did not honor the arms clause, and Mindon reinstated monopolies. Burma tried desperately to formalize relations with France, Italy, and Germany to serve as a counterpoise to British influence. This marked the Indian summer of Burmese independence. The more treaties Burma secured the more the *raj* was likely to make its stranglehold felt on landlocked Burma. Nonetheless, it was almost twenty years after the conclusion of the 1867 treaty that Upper Burma disappeared in a two-week confrontation. Why the delay if so many thought it inevitable? The reasons for British hesitancy after 1867 reflect the shadowy relationship of 1837. 52 and the forbearance of 1853-67. In 1875 Calcutta ordered the Resident not to meet Burmese ministers unless he could wear his shoes. The Burmese never conceded. A suitable pretext for the withdrawal of the Residency was found in 1879, and diplomatic contact was broken. Burma was on the periphery of the British Indian Empire and interests. Burma existed on the sufferance of Britain, and Britain was prepared to tolerate much from her uncongenial neighbor, rather than annexing her. The causes for the change of policy in 1885 may be amenable to an equation similar to that applied to the causes of the second war. It is testimony to Burma's adaptive modernization under Mindon and Britain's reluctance to expand that the Burmese kingdom survived so long.

GLOSSARY

Ahmudan. Classes who are liable to regular service in some public capacity. Royal service status.

Akyidaw. Household official, comptroller.

Atha. Persons who pay taxes but are not liable for regular service, although they might be recruited in emergencies for army service.

Atwinwun. Lit., "interior burden bearer." Minister of second rank concerned with palace administration. Royal household or palace officers.

Byetaik. Lit., "bachelor quarters." Palace office where the *Atwinwuns* preside.

Dhammathats. The corpus of Buddhist law.

Einshemin. Lit., "hand over Eastern Palace." Crown Prince or heir apparent.

Hluttaw. Lit., "place of release." National council where *Wungyis* sit.

Karma. Merit, the law of deed.

Kula. Lit., "to have crossed over, to come from another place." Foreigner.

Min. Prince.

Mingyi. Great Prince, king, or man with power.

Mons. Inhabitants of Lower Burma. Designated "Talaings" or "Taliens" by their northern conquerors.

Myo. Town or domain.

Myosa. Lit., "eater of the town." A town or an area held in fief.

Myothugyi. Local hereditary elite; township headman.

Myowun. Royal Burmese Governor.

Sangha. Buddhist monks.

Sawbwa. Shan Prince.

Saya. Teacher.

Sayadaw. Royal title of abbot of monastery.

Taikthugyi. Circle headman.

Talien. See *Mons.*

Thathameda. Traditional 10 percent tax in Upper Burma.

Thathanabaing. Temporal head of Buddhist hierarchy.

Thudhamma sect. Buddhist sect established by King Bodawpaya.

Tical. Unit of measure equal to about 2s. 6d. (1856) or 1¼ Rs. Also equal to 1 *kyat.*

Tripitika. Buddhist scriptures.

Tsalwe. Honorary chains of rank worn around neck.

Viss. Unit of measure equal to 100 *ticals.*

Wundauk. Lit., "support or prop for the *Wun.*" Assistant to *Wungyi.*

Wungyi. Lit., "Burden or burden bearer." Also referred to as *Mingyi.* Highest officials of the state who sit in *Hluttaw.*

BIBLIOGRAPHY

MANUSCRIPT SOURCES

INDIA OFFICE LIBRARY AND RECORDS, LONDON

Private Papers:

Auckland-Lyall Correspondence, D552
Durand Collection, D727/3
Elgin Papers, F83
Lawrence Papers, F90
Prinsep and Bogle Correspondence, D662
Sladen Collection, E290
Wood Papers, F78

Government Papers:

India Political and Foreign Proceedings, 1843-68 (IPF)
India Political Proceedings, 1840-66 (IPP)
India Secret Proceedings, 1834-69 (ISP)
L/P & S/5, Secret Letters received from Bengal and India,
    1832-59

BRITISH LIBRARY, LONDON

Auckland Papers, Add. Mss. 37689-37718
Broadfoot Papers, Add. Mss. 40127-40131

Broughton Papers, Add. Mss. 36473-36477
Herries Papers, 3-98
Iddesleigh Papers, Add. Mss. 50013-50064
Peel Papers, Add. Mss. 40471-40472
Phayre Collection, Oriental Mss. 3403-3480

PUBLIC RECORD OFFICE, LONDON

Ellenborough Papers, 30/12
Admiralty Papers, Adm. 5608-5616
Ships' Logs, Adm. 4467-9, 4953-7

COLLECTIONS

Burney Papers, Royal Commonwealth Society, London
Salisbury Papers, Christchurch, Oxford. Microfilm copies in
    India Office Library and Records, London.
Canning Papers, Sheepscar Library, Leeds
Dalhousie Muniments, Scottish Record Office, Edinburgh
Kincaid Papers, Baptist Missionary Archives, Valley Forge, Pa. Micro-
    film copies in personal possession.

UNPUBLISHED THESES

Gupta, Shantiswarup. "British Policy on the Northeast Frontier of
    India (1826-86)." Ph.D. dissertation, Oxford, 1948.
Kyin Swi. "The Judicial System of the Kingdom of Burma." Ph.D.
    dissertation, University of London, 1965.
Ma Thaung, "British Interest in Trans-Burma Trade Routes to China,
    1826-1876." Ph.D. dissertation, University of London, 1954.
Nilsson, Janell Ann. "The Administration of British Burma, 1852-1885."
    Ph.D. dissertation, University of London, 1970.
Piness, Edith L. "Moulmein to Mandalay: Sketches of Anglo-Burmese
    Administrators." Ph.D. dissertation, Claremont Graduate School,
    1977.
Snidvongs, Neon. "The Development of Siamese Relations with Britain
    and France in the Reign of Maha Mongkut, 1851-1868." Ph.D. disserta-
    tion, University of London, 1960.
Stewart, Barbara Justine. "Administrative Beginnings in British Burma,
    1826-1843." Ph.D. dissertation, University of London, 1931.
Thet, Maung Kyaw. "Burma's Relations with Her Eastern Neighbors in

the Konbaung Period, 1752-1819." Ph.D. dissertation, University of
London, 1950.

OFFICIAL AND SEMIOFFICIAL PUBLICATIONS

Burma, Archaeological Department of. *Index Inscriptionum Birmani-
caram.* Rangoon: Government Printers, 1900.
———. *Inscriptions Collected in Upper Burma.* Rangoon: Government
Printers, 1900.
India, Government of. *Burma Administration Reports* (1853-70).
———. *Catalogue of the Hluttaw Records.* 2 vols. Rangoon: Government
Printers, 1901, 1909.
———. *Correspondence for the Years 1825-26 to 1842-43 in the Office of
the Commissioner, Tenasserim Division.* Rangoon: Government
Printers, 1929.
———. *Legislative Proceedings.* Calcutta: Government Printers, 1862-63.
———. *Lower Chindwin Gazetteer.* Rangoon: Government Printers, 1912.
———. *Pegu Administration Reports* (1853-70).
———. *Selected Correspondence of Letters Issued from and Received in
the Office of the Commissioner, Tenasserim Division.* Rangoon:
Government Printers, 1929.
Great Britain, Parliament. *Debates.* 1851-54.
———. *Papers Relating to Hostilities with Burmah* 36 (1852).
———. *Further Papers Relating to Hostilities with Burmah* 67 (1852-53).
———. *Copy of Treaty with King of Burmah, 10 November 1862* 40 (1863).
———. *Papers as to Commercial Treaty of 1862* 42 (1864).
———. *Reports on Income and Expenditure of British Burmah, by R.
Temple, Esq., and Lt.-Col. H. Bruce* 39 (1865).
———. *Papers on the Late Rebellion in Upper Burma* 50 (1867).
———. *Correspondence on Treaty with Court of Ava, concluded on 26
Oct. 1867* 46 (1868-69).
Page, A. J. *Pegu Gazetteer.* Rangoon: Government Printers, 1917.
Scott, J. G. and Hardiman, J. P., comps. *Gazetteer of Upper Burma and
the Shan States.* 5 vols. Rangoon: Government Printers, 1900.
Sladen, Edward Bosc. *Narrative of the Expedition to Explore the Trade
Routes to China Via Bhamo.* Rangoon: British Burma Press, 1869.
Spearman, H. R., ed. *British Burma Gazetteer.* 2 vols. Rangoon: Govern-
ment Printers, 1880.
Taw Sein Ko. *Selections from the Records of the Hluttaw.* Rangoon:
Government Printers, 1889.
Yule, Henry. *Reports of the Mission to Ava in 1855.* Calcutta: Govern-
ment Printers, 1856.

BOOKS

Abrol, Mridula. *British Relations with Frontier States, 1863-1875.* New Delhi: S. Chand, 1974.

Adas, Michael. *The Burma Delta: Economic Development and Social Change on an Asia Rice Frontier, 1852-1941.* Madison: University of Wisconsin Press, 1974.

Arnold, Edwin. *The Marquis of Dalhousie's Administration of British India.* 2 vols. London: Saunders, Otley and Co., 1862, 1865.

Baillie, John. *Rivers in the Desert, or Mission Scenes in Burma.* London: Seeley, 1858.

Baird, J. G. A., ed. *Private Letters of the Marquess of Dalhousie.* Edinburgh: William Blackwood and Sons, 1910.

Baker, Thomas Turner. *The Recent Operations of the British Forces at Rangoon and Martaban.* London: Thomas Hatchard, 1852.

Banjeree, Anil Chandra. *The Eastern Frontier of British India, 1784-1826.* 2d ed. Calcutta: Mukherjee, 1964.

———. *Annexation of Burma.* Calcutta: Mukherjee, 1944.

Bartlett, C. J. *Great Britain and Sea Power, 1815-1853.* Oxford: Clarendon Press, 1963.

Barretto, William Louis. *King Mindon.* Rangoon: Burma Union Press, 1935.

Bastian, Adolf. *Die Geschichte der Indochinesen aus einheimischen Quellen: Die Völker des östlichen Asian, Studien Reisen.* Leipzig and London: Truebner, 1866.

Bayfield, George Thomas. *Historical Review of the Political Relations between the British Government in India and the Empire of Ava, from the Earliest Date on Record to the Present Year.* Calcutta: Government Printers, 1835.

Bearce, George D. *British Attitudes Towards India, 1784-1858.* London: Oxford University Press, 1961.

Bennett, Paul J. *Conference under the Tamarind Tree: Three Essays in Burmese History.* New Haven: Yale University Southeast Asia Studies, 1971.

Bigandet, Paul Ambrose. *An Outline of the History of the Catholic Burmese Mission from the year 1720 to 1887.* Rangoon: Hanthawaddy Press, 1887.

Binney, Julliette. *Twenty-six Years in Burmah; Records of the Life and Work of Joseph G. Binney, D. D.* Philadelphia: American Baptist Publishing Society, 1859.

Braibanti, Ralph, ed. *Asian Bureaucratic Systems Emergent from the British Imperial Tradition.* Durham, N.C.: Duke University Press, 1966.

Briggs, John Patrick. *Heathen and Holy Lands: Or, Sunny Days on the Salween, Nile and Jordan.* London: Smith Elder & Co., 1859.

Bright, John, and Rogers, James E. Thorold, eds. *Speeches on Questions of Public Policy by Richard Cobden.* London: Macmillan, 1878.

Broadfoot, William. *The Career of Major George Broadfoot.* London: J. Murray, 1888.

Brown, D. Mackenzie. *The White Umbrella: Indian Political Thought from Manu to Ghandi.* Berkeley and Los Angeles: University of California Press, 1953.

Browne, Horace Albert. *Reminiscences of the Court of Mandalay, Extracts from the Diary of General Horace A. Browne, 1859-1879.* Woking: The Oriental Institute, 1907.

Cady, John F. *The Roots of French Imperialism in Eastern Asia.* Ithaca: Cornell University Press, 1954.

———. *A History of Modern Burma.* Ithaca: Cornell University Press, 1958.

———. *Southeast Asia: Its Historical Development.* New York: McGraw-Hill, 1964.

Cheng Siok-Hwa. *The Rice Industry of Burma, 1852-1940.* Kuala Lumpur: University of Malaya Press, 1968.

Christian, John L. *Modern Burma.* Berkeley and Los Angeles: University of California Press, 1942.

Cobden, Richard. *How Wars are Got up in India: The Origin of the Burma War.* London: W. and F. G. Gash, 1853.

Cochrane, W. W. *The Shans.* Rangoon: Government Printers, 1915.

Colchester, Lord. *History of the Indian Administration of Lord Ellenborough.* London: Bentley, 1874.

Colvin, John Russell. *The Last Lieutenant Governor of the North-West under the Company.* Oxford: Clarendon Press, 1895.

Conacher, James B. *The Aberdeen Coalition, 1852-1855: A Study in Mid-Nineteenth Century Party Politics.* Cambridge: Cambridge University Press, 1968.

———. *The Peelites and the Party System, 1846-52.* Newton Abbot: David and Charles, 1972.

Cowan, C. D., and Wolters, O. W., eds. *Southeast Asian History and Historiography.* Ithaca: Cornell University Press, 1976.

Cox, Hiram. *Journal of a Residence in the Burmhan Empire and more particularly at the Court of Amarapoorah.* London: J. Warren, 1821.

Crawfurd, John. *Journal of an Embassy from Governor General of India to the Court of Ava.* London: Henry Goulburn, 1829.

Davis, John H. *The Forest of Burma.* Gainesville, Fla.: University of Florida, 1960.

Desai, Walter Sadgun. *History of the British Residency in Burma, 1826-1840.* Rangoon: University of Rangoon, 1939.

——. *A Pageant of Burmese History.* Bombay: Orient Longmans, 1961.

Dharm Pal. *Administration of Sir John Lawrence in India (1864-1869).* Simla: Minerva Book Shop, 1952.

Dobbs, Richard Stewart. *Reminiscences of Life in Mysore, South Africa, and Burma.* Dublin: G. Herber, 1882.

Dodwell, H. H., ed. *The Cambridge History of the British Empire.* Vol. 4. Cambridge: Cambridge University Press, 1929.

Dumont, Prosper. *Le Général D'Orgoni, Sa Mission, en France et à Rome et Plan de Campagne pour une Croisade Française en Indo-Chine et en Chine.* Nancy: Vagner, 1858.

Durand, H. M. *The Life of Major-General Sir Henry Marion Durand.* 2 vols. London: W. H. Allen, 1883.

Elias, Ney. *Introductory Sketch of the History of the Shans in Upper Burma and Western Yunnan.* Calcutta: Foreign Department Press, 1876.

Elwin, Verier, ed. *India's North-East Frontier in the Nineteenth Century.* Bombay: Oxford University Press, 1959.

Fielding-Hall, Harold. *The Soul of a People.* London: Bentley, 1899.

Forbes, C. J. F. S. *British Burma and Its Peoples: Being Sketches of Native Manners, Customs and Religion.* London: Murray, 1878.

Foucar, E. C. V. *They Reigned in Mandalay.* London: Dobson, 1946.

Fremantle, Edmund R. *The Navy As I Have Known It, 1849-1899.* London: Cassell, 1904.

Furnivall, John Sydenham. *An Introduction to the Political Economy of Burma.* 2d ed. Rangoon: People's Literature Committee, 1957.

——. *Colonial Policy and Practice: A Comparative Study of Burma and Netherlands India.* New York: New York University Press, 1948.

Fytche, Albert. *Burma, Past and Present, with Personal Reminiscences of the Country.* 2 vols. London: Kegan Paul, 1878.

Ghosh, Suresh Chandra. *Dalhousie in India, 1848-56: A Study of his Social Policy as Governor General.* New Delhi: Munshiram Manoharlal, 1975.

Godwin, Henry T. *Burmah: Letters and Papers Written in 1852-53.* London: N. p., 1854.

Gopal, S. *The Viceroyalty of Lord Ripon, 1880-1884.* Oxford: Oxford University Press, 1953.

——. *British Policy in India, 1858-1905.* Cambridge: Cambridge University Press, 1965.

Gouger, Henry. *Personal Narrative of Two Years' Imprisonment in Burmah, 1824-26.* London: Murray, 1860.

Graham, Gerald S. *The Politics of Naval Supremacy: Studies in British Maritime Ascendancy.* Cambridge: Cambridge University Press, 1965.

——. *Great Britain in the Indian Ocean: A Study of Maritime Enterprise, 1810-1850.* Oxford: Clarendon Press, 1967.

Grampp, William D. *The Manchester School of Economics.* Stanford: Stanford University Press, 1960.

Grant, Colesworthy. *Rough Pencillings of a Rough Trip to Rangoon in 1846.* Calcutta: Thacker, 1853.

Gray, James. *The Alaungpra Dynasty.* Edinburgh and London: Ballentyne Press, 1887.

Hall, Daniel George Edward. *Early English Intercourse with Burma, 1587-1743.* London: Longmans, 1928.

——, ed. *The Dalhousie-Phayre Correspondence, 1852-1856.* London: Oxford University Press, 1932.

——. *Europe and Burma: A Study of European Relations with Burma to the Annexation of Thibaw's Kingdom, 1886.* London: Oxford University Press, 1945.

——. *Burma.* London: Hutchinson University Library, 1950.

——. *Michael Symes, Journal of his Second Mission to the Court of Ava in 1802.* London: Allen and Unwin, 1955.

——, ed. *Historians of South-East Asia.* London: Oxford University Press, 1961.

——. *Henry Burney: A Political Biography.* London: Oxford University Press, 1974.

Hare, E. C. *Memoir of Edward Hare, C. S. I., Late Inspector-General of Hospitals.* London: Grant Richards, 1900.

Harvey, Geoffrey E. *History of Burma: From the Earliest Times to 10 March 1824, the Beginning of the English Conquest.* 2d ed. London: Cass, 1967.

——. *British Rule in Burma, 1824-1942.* London: Faber and Faber, 1946.

Herries, Edward. *Memoir of the Public Life of the Right Hon. John Charles Herries.* 2 vols. London: John Murray, 1880.

Hobson, John Atkinson. *Richard Cobden, The International Man.* London: T. Fisher Unwin, 1919.

Hunter, William Wilson. *The Marquess of Dalhousie and the Final Development of the Company's Rule.* Oxford: Clarendon Press, 1895.

Imlah, Albert Henry. *Lord Ellenborough.* Cambridge: Harvard University Press, 1939.

Jones, William Devereaux, and Erickson, Arvel B. *The Peelites, 1846-1857.* Columbus: Ohio State University Press, 1972.

Keeton, Charles Lee. *King Thebaw and the Ecological Rape of Burma.* Delhi: Manohar Book Service, 1974.

Knaplund, Paul. *The British Empire, 1815-1939.* London: Hamish Hamilton, 1942.

Kunstadter, Peter, ed. *Southeast Asian Tribes, Minorities, and Nations.* Princeton: Princeton University Press, 1967.

Laurie, William F. B. *The Second Burmese War: A Narrative of the Operations at Rangoon, in 1852.* London: Smith, Elder & Co., 1853.

———. *Papers on Burmah.* London: N.p., 1870.

Law, Algernon, ed. *India under Lord Ellenborough: Selections from the Ellenborough Papers.* London: Murray, 1926.

Leach, Edmund R. *Political Systems of Highland Burma: A Study of Kachin Social Structure.* London: Athlone Press, 1954.

Lebar, Frank M.; Hickey, Gerald C.; and Musgrave, John K. *Ethnic Groups of Mainland Southeast Asia.* New Haven: Human Relations Area Files Press, 1964.

Lee-Warner, William. *The Life of the Marquis of Dalhousie, K. T.* 2 vols. London: Macmillan, 1904.

Lehman, F. K. *The Structure of Chin Society.* Urbana: University of Illinois Press, 1963.

Macaulay, R. H. *History of the Bombay Burmah Trading Corporation, Ltd., 1864-1910.* London: N.p., 1934.

MacClagan, Michael. *Clemency Canning: Charles John, 1st Earl Canning, Governor-General and Viceroy, 1856-1862.* London: Macmillan, 1962.

McCord, Norman. *The Anti-Corn Law League.* London: Allen and Unwin, 1958.

Malcom, Howard. *Travels in South-eastern Asia.* 2 vols. Boston: Gould, Kendall, and Lincoln, 1839.

Ma Mya Sein. *Administration of Burma: Sir Charles Crosthwaite and the Consolidation of Burma.* Rangoon: Zabu Meitswe Pitaka Press, 1938.

Marks, John Ebenezer. *Forty Years in Burma.* New York: E. P. Dutton, 1917.

Marshall, Harry Ignatius. *The Karen People of Burma: A Study in Anthropology and Ethnology.* Columbus: Ohio State University Bulletin, 1922.

Marshall, W. H. *Four Years in Burma.* London: Skeet, 1860.

Marshman, John C. *How Wars Arise in India: Observations on Mr. Cobden's Pamphlet entitled "The Origin of the Burmese War."* London: N.p., 1853.

Martin, Briton, Jr. *New India, 1885.* Berkeley and Los Angeles: University of California Press, 1969.

Mason, F. *Burmah, Its People and Natural Productions.* Rangoon: Ranney, 1866.

Mason, Philip [Philip Woodruff]. *The Men Who Ruled India.* 2 vols. London: Jonathan Cape, 1953-54.

Maung Htin Aung. *Burmese Drama.* London: Oxford University Press, 1937.
——. *Burmese Folk-Tales.* Calcutta: Oxford University Press, 1949.
——. *Burmese Law Tales: The Legal Element in Burmese Folk Lore.* London: Oxford University Press, 1962.
——. *Folk Elements in Burmese Buddhism.* London: Oxford University Press, 1962.
——. *The Stricken Peacock: Anglo-Burmese Relations, 1752-1948.* The Hague: M. Nijhoff, 1965.
——. *Burmese Monk's Tales.* New York: Columbia University Press, 1966.
——. *Epistles Written on the Eve of the Anglo-Burmese War, 1824.* The Hague: Martinus Nijhoff, 1967.
——. *A History of Burma.* New York: Columbia University Press, 1967.
——. *Burmese History Before 1287: A Defence of the Chronicles.* Oxford: Asoka Society, 1970.
Maung Maung. *Burma in the Family of Nations.* Amsterdam: Uitgeverij Djambatan, 1956.
——. *Law and Custom in Burma and the Burmese Family.* The Hague: Martinus Nijhoff, 1963.
Mendelson, E. Michael. *Sangha and State in Burma.* Edited by John P. Ferguson. Ithaca: Cornell University Press, 1975.
Mills, Lenox Algernon. *British Malaya, 1824-67.* 2d ed. Kuala Lumpur: Oxford University Press, 1966.
Milne, Leslie. *The Shans at Home.* London: Murray, [1911?].
Mi Mi Khaing. *Burmese Family.* London: Longmans, 1946.
Moore, R. J. *Sir Charles Wood's Indian Policy, 1853-66.* Manchester: Manchester University Press, 1966.
Moulton, E. C. *Lord Northbrook's Indian Administration, 1872-1876.* Bombay: Asia Publishing House, 1968.
Nash, Manning. *The Golden Road to Modernity: Village Life in Contemporary Burma.* London: John Wiley, 1965.
——, ed. *Anthropological Studies in Theravada Buddhism.* New Haven: Yale University Southeast Asia Studies Cultural Report Series, 1966.
Niharranjan Ray. *An Introduction to the Study of Theravada Buddhism in Burma.* Calcutta: Calcutta University Press, 1946.
Nostitz, Pauline. *Travels of Dr. and Mrs. Helfer in Syria, Mesopotamia, Burma and Other Lands.* 2 vols. London: Bentley, 1878.
Panikkar, K. M. *Asia and Western Dominance.* 2d ed. New York: Collier Books, 1969.
Patton, Alfred S. *The Hero Missionary or a History of the Labors of the*

Rev. Eugenio Kincaid. New York: Dayton, 1858.

Pearn, Bertie Reginald. *A History of Rangoon.* Rangoon: American Baptist Mission Press, 1939.

Pe Maung Htin, and Luce, G. H. *The Glass Palace Chronicle of the Kings of Burma.* Rangoon: Rangoon University Press, 1923.

Pemberton, Robert B. *Report on the Eastern Frontier of British India.* Reprint ed. Gauhati, Assam: Department of Historical and Antiquarian Studies, 1966.

Phayre, Arthur P. *History of Burma, including Burma Proper, Pegu, Taungu, Tenasserim and Arakan. From the Earliest Time to the End of the First War with British India.* Reprint ed. London: Susil Gupta, 1967.

Philips, C. H. *The East India Company, 1784-1834.* Manchester: Manchester University Press, 1940.

Pointon, A. C. *The Bombay Burmah Trading Corporation Limited, 1863-1963.* Southampton, England: Millbrook Press, 1964.

Prasad, Bisheshwar. *The Foundations of India's Foreign Policy, 1860-1882.* Calcutta: Ranjit Printers, 1955.

Prasad, Nandan. *Paramountcy under Dalhousie.* Delhi: Ranjit Printers, 1964.

Purser, W. B., and Saunders, K. J. *Modern Buddhism in Burma.* Rangoon: Christian Literature Society, 1914.

Rahim, Muhammad Abdur. *Lord Dalhousie's Administration of the Conquered and Annexed States.* Delhi: S. Chand, 1963.

Read, Donald. *Cobden and Bright: A Victorian Political Partnership.* London: Arnold, 1967.

Redfield, Robert. *The Little Community.* 2d ed. Chicago: University of Chicago Press, 1965.

Richardson, David. *The Damathat or the Laws of Menoo.* Moulmein: American Baptist Mission Press, 1847.

Robertson, Thomas Campbell. *Political Incidents of the First Burmese War.* London: Bentley, 1853.

Saletor, Bhasker Anand. *Ancient Indian Political Thought and Institutions.* London: Asia Publishing House, 1962.

Sangermano, Padre Vincentius. *A Description of the Burmese Empire.* 5th ed. London: Susil Gupta, 1966.

Sao Saimong Mangrai. *The Shan States and the British Annexation.* Ithaca: Cornell University, Department of Asian Studies, 1965.

Sar Desai, D. R. *British Trade and Expansion in Southeast Asia, 1830-1914.* Columbia, Mo.: South Asia Books, 1977.

Sarkisyanz, Emanuel. *Buddhist Backgrounds of the Burmese Revolution.* The Hague: M. Nijhoff, 1965.

——. *Peacocks, Pagodas and Professor Hall: A Critique of the Persisting use of Historiography as an Apology for British Empire-Building in Burma.* Athens, Ohio: Ohio University Center for International Studies, 1972.

Scott, James George. *Burma, From the Earliest Times to the Present Day.* London: T. Fisher Unwin, 1924.

[Shway Yoe]. *The Burman, His Life and Notions.* 2d ed. New York: Norton, 1963.

Scott O'Connor, Vincent C. *Mandalay and other Cities of the Past in Burma.* London: Hutchinson, 1907.

Semmel, Bernard. *The Rise of Free Trade Imperialism.* Cambridge: Cambridge University Press, 1970.

Singhal, D. P. *The Annexation of Upper Burma.* Singapore: Eastern Universities Press, 1960.

Sinha, D. P. *Some Aspects of British Social Policy and Administrative Policy in India during the Administration of Lord Auckland.* Calcutta: Punthi Pustak, 1969.

Six Months at Martaban During the Burmese War. London: Partridge, Oakey and Co. [1854?].

Smith, Donald Eugene. *Religion and Politics in Burma.* Princeton: Princeton University Press, 1965.

Smith, George, ed. *Physician and Friend, Alexander Grant: His Autobiography and His Letters from the Marquis of Dalhousie.* London: Murray, 1902.

Smith, R. Bosworth. *Life of Lord Lawrence.* 2d ed. London: Smith Elder & Co., 1883.

Spiro, Melford E. *Buddhism and Society. A Great Tradition and its Burmese Vicissitudes.* London: George Allen & Unwin, 1971.

Stevenson, H. N. C. *The Economics of the Central Chin Tribes.* 2d ed. London: Gregg, 1969.

Stewart, A. T. Q. *The Pagoda War: Lord Dufferin and the Fall of the Kingdom of Ava, 1885-6.* London: Faber and Faber, 1972.

Symes, Michael. *Account of an Embassy to the Kingdom of Ava in 1795.* London: Bulmer, 1800.

Tarling, Nicholas. *British Policy in the Malay Archipelago, 1824-1874.* 2d ed. Kuala Lumpur: Oxford in Asia, 1969.

Tate, D. J. M. *The Making of Modern South-East Asia.* Kuala Lumpur: Oxford University Press, 1971.

Thayer, P. W. *Nationalism and Progress in Free Asia.* Baltimore: The Johns Hopkins Press, 1956.

U Khin Mg Kyi, and Daw Tin Tin. *Administrative Patterns in Historical*

Burma. Singapore: Institute of Southeast Asian Studies, 1973.

U Tin (of Sagaing). *Kòn-baung-zet Maha-ya-zawin-daw-gyi* [Great royal chronicle of the Kòn-baung dynasty]. 3 vols. Mandalay: Hanthawaddy Pitakat Press, 1922-23.

U Tin (of Pagan). *Myanma Min Okchopon Sadan* [Administration of Burma under the Burmese kings]. 5 vols. Rangoon: Government Printers, 1931-3.

Trager, Helen G. *Burma Through Alien Eyes: Missionary Views of the Burmese in the Nineteenth Century.* New York: Praeger, 1966.

Tun Wai. *Economic Development of Burma from 1800 to 1940.* Rangoon: University of Rangoon, 1961.

Turnbull, Colin M. *Indiàn Presidency to Crown Colony: The Straits Settlements, 1826-1867.* London: Athlone Press, 1972.

Tyson, Geoffrey W. *The Bengal Chamber of Commerce and Industry, 1853-1953. A Centenary Survey.* Calcutta: D. A. Lakin, 1952.

Vincent, Frank. *Land of the White Elephant.* London: Harper, 1873.

Wayland, Francis. *Memoir of the Life and Labors of the Rev. Adonirum Judson, D. D.* 2 vols. Boston: Phillips, Sampson and Co., 1954.

Wheeler, James Talboys. *Journal of a Voyage up the Irrawaddy to Mandalay and Bhamo.* Rangoon: N.p., 1871.

White, Herbert Thirkell. *A Civil Servant in Burma.* London: Arnold, 1913.

Williams, Clement. *Through Burmah to Western China.* London: William Blackwood, 1868.

Wilson, Horace Hayman. *Documents Illustrative of the Burmese War, with an Introductory Sketch of the Events of the War.* Calcutta: Government Gazette Press, 1827.

——. *Narrative of the Burmese War in 1824-26.* London: W. H. Allen, 1852.

Winks, Robin W., ed. *The Historiography of the British Empire-Commonwealth.* Durham, N.C.: Duke University Press, 1966.

Winter, Christopher T. *Six Months in British Burmah: or, India beyond the Ganges in 1857.* London: Bentley, 1858.

Wolesley, Garnet. *The Story of a Soldier.* Westminster: Constable, 1903.

Woodman, Dorothy. *The Making of Burma.* London: Cresset Press, 1962.

Wylie, MacLeod. *The Gospel in Burmah: The Story of its Introduction and Marvellous Progress among the Burmese and Karens.* New York: Sheldon and Co., 1860.

Yule, Henry. *A Narrative of the Mission to the Court of Ava in 1855,* reprint ed. Kuala Lumpur: Oxford University Press, 1968.

ARTICLES

Adas, Michael. "Imperialist Rhetoric and Modern Historiography: The
  Case of Lower Burma Before and After the Conquest." *Journal of
  Southeast Asian Studies* 3 (1972): 175-92.
Alder, G. J. "The Dropped Stitch—The Course of Anglo-Afghan Rela-
  tions, 1853-63." *Afghanistan Journal* 1-2 (1974-5): 105-13 and 20-7.
Anonymous. "The Tenasserim Provinces—Their Statistics and Govern-
  ment." *Calcutta Review* 8 (1847): 72-145.
——. "Commercial Morality and Commercial Prospects in Bengal."
  Calcutta Review 9 (1848): 163-89.
——. "Martin on the Re-occupation of Negrais." *Calcutta Review* 116
  (1849): 257-81.
——. "Tenasserim Teak Timber Traffic." *Calcutta Review* 21 (1853):
  98-169.
——. "Report of a Trial for Rebellion held at Maulmain by the Com-
  missioner of Tenasserim." *Journal of the Royal Asiatic Society,
  Bengal Branch* 14 (1845): 747-54.
Blackmore, Thaung. "The Founding of the City of Mandalay by King
  Mindon." *Journal of Oriental Studies* 5 (1959-60): 82-97.
——. "Dilemma of the British Representative to the Burmese Court
  After the Outbreak of a Palace Revolution in 1866." *Journal of
  Southeast Asian History* 10 (1969): 236-52.
Brailey, Nigel J. "A Re-Investigation of the Gwe of Eighteenth Cen-
  tury Burma." *Journal of Southeast Asian Studies* 1 (1970): 33-47.
Burney, Henry "Memoir of Giuseppe d'Amato." *Journal of the Royal
  Asiatic Society, Bengal Branch* 1 (1832): 349-53.
——. "The Burmese Revolution." *Colonial Magazine and Commercial
  Maritime Journal* 7 (1842): 71-80 and 176-84.
Chew, Ernest. "The Withdrawal of the Last British Residency from
  Upper Burma in 1879." *Journal of Southeast Asian History* 10
  (1969): 253-78.
Christian, John L. "Burma in the American State Papers." *Journal of
  the Burma Research Society* 26 (1936): 110-15.
——. "A Diplomatic Mission from Burma to America." *Journal of
  the Burma Research Society* 29 (1939): 187-92.
Conacher, James B. "Peel and the Peelites, 1846-1850." *English
  Historical Review* 73 (1958): 431-52.
Desai, Walter Sadgun. "The Rebellion of Prince Tharrawaddy and the
  Deposition of Bagyidaw as King of Burma, 1837." *Journal of the*

Burma Research Society 25 (1935): 109-20.

——. "Bagyidaw as Ex-King, 1837-1846." *Journal of the Burma Research Society* 28 (1938): 233-43.

Dharm Pal. "British Relations with Burma (1864-1868)." *Indian Historical Quarterly* 21 (1945): 271-83.

Duroiselle, Charles. "Pageant of King Mindon Leaving his Palace (1865)." *Memoirs of the Archeological Survey of India* 27 (1925).

Enriquez, C. M. "Capitals of the Alaung-paya Dynasty." *Journal of the Burma Research Society* 5 (1915): 117-28.

——. "Bandula – A Burmese Soldier." *Journal of the Burma Research Society* 11 (1921): 158-62.

Ferguson, John P. "The Quest for Legitimation by Burmese Monks and Kings: The Case of the Shwegyin Sect (19th-20th Centuries)." In *Religion and Legitimation of Power in Thailand, Laos, and Burma,* edited by Bardwell L. Smith. Chambersburg, Pa: Anima, 1978.

Furnivall, John S. "The Fashioning of Leviathan: The Beginnings of British Rule in Burma." *Journal of the Burma Research Society* 29 (1939): 1-137.

Galbraith, John S. "The 'Turbulent Frontier' as a Factor in British Expansion." *Comparative Studies in Society and History* 2 (1960): 150-68.

——. "Myths of the 'Little England' Era." *American Historical Review* 67 (1961): 34-48.

Gallagher, John, and Robinson, Ronald. "The Imperialism of Free Trade." *Economic History Review,* 2d ser., 6 (August 1953): 1-15.

Godakumbura, C. E. "Relations between Burma and Ceylon." *Journal of the Burma Research Society* 49 (1966): 145-62.

Hall, D. G. E. "Tragedy of Negrais." *Journal of the Burma Research Society* 21 (1931): 59-133.

——. "Phayre's Private Journal of His Mission to Ava in 1855." *Journal of the Burma Research Society* 22 (1932): 68-89.

——. "Burney's Comments on the Court of Ava, 1832." *Bulletin of the School of Oriental and African Studies* 20 (1957): 305-14.

——. "Henry Burney, Diplomat and Orientalist." *Journal of the Burma Research Society* 41 (1958): 100-10.

——. "British Writers of Burmese History from Dalrymple to Bayfield." In *Historians of South-East Asia,* edited by D. G. E. Hall. London: Oxford University Press, 1961.

——. "Anglo-Burmese Conflicts in the 19th Century: A Reassessment." *Asia* 6 (Autumn 1966): 35-52.

Harvey, Geoffrey E. "French Relations with Mandalay." *Guardian* 5 (June 1958): 31-3.

———. "Burmese and English Despatches of the Eve of the First Anglo-Burmese War, 1824-26." *Journal of the Burma Research Society* 17 (1923): 109-28.

Heine-Geldern, Robert. "Conceptions of State and Kingship in Southeast Asia." *Far Eastern Quarterly* 11 (1942): 15-30.

Hla Thein. "Mindon's Burma as Seen by an Englishman." *Guardian* 15 (December 1968): 29-31.

Khin Maung Nyunt. "The 'Shoe Question' or the Loss and Regaining of Our Independence." *Guardian* 11 (February 1970): 21-8.

Kitzan, Laurence. "Lord Amherst and the Declaration of War on Burma, 1824." *Journal of Asian History* 9 (1975): 101-27.

Kyaw Thet. "Burma: the Political Integration of Linguistic and Religious Minority Groups." In *Nationalism and Progress in Free Asia*, edited by P. W. Thayer. Baltimore: The Johns Hopkins Press, 1956.

Langham Carter, R. R. "Queen Me Nu and Her Family at Palangon." *Journal of the Burma Research Society* 19 (1929): 31-5.

———. "U Htaung Bo's Rebellion." *Journal of the Burma Research Society* 26 (1936): 33-4.

———. "Burmese Rule on the Toungoo Frontier." *Journal of the Burma Research Society* 27 (1937): 15-32.

———. "The Burmese Army." *Journal of the Burma Research Society* 27 (1937): 254-76.

Leach, Edmund R. "The Frontiers of Burma." *Comparative Studies in Society and History* 3 (1960): 49-68.

Lieberman, Victor V. "Ethnic Politics in Eighteenth-Century Burma." *Modern Asian Studies* 12 (1978): 455-82.

Ma Kyan. "King Mindon's Councillors." *Journal of the Burma Research Society* 44 (1961): 43-60.

Ma Thaung. "Burmese Kingship in Theory and Practice During the Reign of Mindon." *Journal of the Burma Research Society* 42 (1959): 171-85.

Maung Maung Tin and Morris, T. O. "Mindon Min's Development Plan for the Mandalay Area." *Journal of the Burma Research Society* 49 (1966): 29-33.

Mendelson, E. Michael. "Religion and Authority in Modern Burma." *World Today* 16 (1960): 110-18.

———. "The King of Weaving Mountain." *Journal of the Royal Central Asian Society* 48 (1961): 229-37.

———. "The Uses of Religious Scepticism in Modern Burma." *Diogenes*

41 (1963): 94-116.

Nash, June C. "Living with Nats: An Analysis of Animism in Burman
  Village Social Relations." *Anthropological Studies in Theravada Buddhism,* edited by M. Nash. London: John Wiley, 1965.

Nash, Manning. "Ritual and Ceremonial Cycle in Upper Burma." In
  Anthropological Studies in Theravada Buddhism, edited by M. Nash.
  London: John Wiley, 1965.

Pearn, Bertie Reginald. "Journey of Lt. Sconce and Captain Watson into
  Shan States in 1863-64." *Journal of the Burma Research Society* 14
  (1924): 207-17.

——. "The Commercial Treaty of 1862." *Journal of the Burma Research
  Society* 27 (1937): 33-52.

Pepys, Walter Courtenay. "A Visit to the King of Burmah." *Colburns New
  Monthly Magazine* 142 (1868): 526-40 and 643-54.

Pfanner, David E. "The Buddhist Monk in Rural Burmese Society." In
  Anthropological Studies in Theravada Buddhism, edited by M. Nash.
  London: John Wiley, 1965.

Philips, Cyril. "Dalhousie and the Burmese War of 1852." In *Southeast
  Asian History and Historiography,* edited by C. D. Cowan and O. W.
  Walters. Ithaca: Cornell University Press, 1976.

Pollak, Oliver B. "Recent Trends in Nineteenth Century Burmese Historiography." *Journal of Oriental Studies* 14 (1976): 86-90.

——. "Candour and Confidentiality: Textual Criticism of Two Greek
  Letters on Anglo-Burmese Relations, 1838." *South East Asian Studies*
  14 (1976): 302-6.

——. "Dynasticism and Revolt: Crisis of Kingship in Burma, 1837-1851."
  Journal of Southeast Asia Studies 7 (1976): 187-96.

——. "The Origins of the Second Anglo-Burmese War (1852-53)." *Modern
  Asian Studies* 12 (1978): 483-502.

Preschez, Philippe. "Les Relations entre la France et la Birmanie au
  XVIIIe et au XIXe Siecles." *France et Asie* (1967).

Sarkisyanz, Emanuel. "On the Changing Anglo-Saxon Image of Burma."
  Asian Studies 4 (1966): 226-35.

——. "Messianic Folk-Buddhism as Ideology of Peasant Revolts in Nineteenth and Early Twentieth Century Burma." *Review of Religious Research* 10 (1968): 32-8.

Spiro, Melford E. "Buddhism and Economic Action in Burma." *American
  Anthropologist* 68 (1968): 1163-73.

Stern, Theodore. "*Ariya* and the Golden Book: A Millenarian Buddhist
  Sect Among the Karen." *Journal of Asian Studies* 27 (1968): 297-328.

Stuart, C. H. "The Formation of the Coalition Cabinet of 1852." *Transactions of the Royal Historical Society,* 5th ser., 4 (1954): 45-68.

Tarling, Nicholas. "British South-East Asian Interests in the 19th Century." *Journal of Southeast Asian History* 7 (1966): 97-110.

Temple, R. C. "The Order of Succession in the Alompra Dynasty of Burma." *Indian Antiquary* 21 (1892): 287-93.

Tinker, Hugh. "Arthur Phayre and Henry Yule: Two Soldier-Administrator Historians." In *Historians of South-East Asia,* edited by D. G. E. Hall. London: Oxford University Press, 1961.

U Tet Htoot. "The Nature of the Burmese Chronicles." In *Historians of South-East Asia,* edited by D. G. E. Hall. London: Oxford University Press, 1961.

Vivian Ba. "The First Burmese Embassy to France in 1856." *Guardian* 9 (April 1962): 20-1.

———. "The Second Burmese Embassy to France." *Guardian* 9 (May 1962): 31-3.

———. "The Early Catholic Missionaries in Burma." *Guardian* 10 (April 1963): 17-23; (May 1963): 21-25; and (June 1963): 11-20.

———. "The Confidential Mission of Count Henri de Sercey." *Guardian* 11 (August-December 1964).

———. "The Beginnings of Western Education in Burma: The Catholic Effort." *Journal of the Burma Research Society* 47 (1964): 287-323.

———. "One Centenary Recalls Another." *Journal of the Burma Research Society* 48 (1965): 65-79.

———. "King Mindon and the World Fair of 1867 held in Paris." *Journal of the Burma Research Society* 48 (1965): 17-25.

———. "Some Papal Correspondence with the Kings of Burma." *Journal of the Burma Research Society* 50 (1967): 11-19.

———. "Court Life and Festival in King Mindon's Palace." *Guardian* 14 (October-November 1967): 20-4 and 16-20.

Walsh, Warren B. "The Yunnan Myth." *Far Eastern Quarterly* 2 (1943): 272-85.

Wheeler, James Talboys. "Reminiscences of Ava." *Calcutta Review* 54 (1872): 118-43.

Williams, Donovan. "The Council of India and the Relationship Between the Home and Supreme Governments, 1858-1870." *English Historical Review* 81 (1966): 56-73.

Yi Yi. "The Thrones of the Burmese Kings." *Journal of the Burma Research Society* 43 (1960): 97-123.

———. "Life at the Burmese Court under the Konbaung Kings." *Journal*

of the Burma Research Society 44 (1962): 85-129.
———. "The Judicial System of King Mindon." *Journal of the Burma Research Society* 45 (1962): 7-27.

PAMPHLETS

Adamson, C. H. E. *Narrative of an Official Visit to the King of Burma, in March, 1875.* Newcastle-on-Tyne: N.p., 1878.

Cady, John F. *Political Institutions of Old Burma.* Ithaca: Southeast Asia Program Data Papers, 1954.

Collis, Maurice. *Courts of the Shan Princes.* London: China Society, 1939.

Crisp, May Flower. *A Treatise on Marine Architecture and the Art of Ship-building.* Calcutta: N.p., 1826.

———. *Manning the Navy.* Calcutta: N.p., 1846.

Duroiselle, Charles. *Guide to the Mandalay Palace.* 2d ed. Calcutta: Government of India Publications, 1931.

Hagen, Everett E. *The Economic Development of Burma.* Washington, D.C.: National Planning Commission, 1956.

Hla Pe. "Burmese Chronicles, A Study in Burmese Historiography." Typescript. London: [1964?].

Marshall, Harry Ignatius. *The Karens of Burma.* London: Longmans, 1945.

Martin, James Ronald. *Memoir on the Political, Naval, Military and Commercial Advantages of the Re-occupation of Negrais Island.* Calcutta: N.p., 1843.

Solomon, Robert. *Saya San and the Burmese Rebellion.* Santa Monica: Rand Corporation, 1969.

Stewart, J. A. *Buddhism in Burma.* [Rangoon?]: N.p., [1939?].

Stuart, J. M. B. *Old Burmese Irrigation Works.* Rangoon: Government Printers, 1913.

Taw Sein Ko. *Archaeological Notes on Mandalay.* Rangoon: Government Printers, 1917.

NEWSPAPERS AND MAGAZINES

Asiatic Journal, 1839-42
Baptist Missionary Magazine (Boston), 1840-55
Calcutta Review, 1845-55
Examiner (London), 1850-53

Guardian (London), 1850-54
Illustrated London News, 1845-67
Journal of the Indian Archipelago, 1857-60
Journal of the Royal Asiatic Society, Bengal Branch, 1832-60
Manchester Guardian, 1850-54
Maulmain Chronicle, 1837-51
Oriental Baptist (Calcutta), 1847-50
Times (London), 1850-54

Index

ABOUT THE AUTHOR

Oliver P. Pollak is Associate Professor of History at the University of
Nebraska at Omaha. Specializing in the history of the British Empire,
he has compiled several bibliographies on southern Africa in addition
to contributing articles to such journals as *Modern Asian Studies, African
Affairs,* and *Albion.*